Bevis Hillier's
pocket guide to
Antiques

Mitchell Beazley

Key to symbols

Retail values

- *A* under £50
- *B* £50–100
- *C* £100–250
- *D* £250–500
- *E* £500–1,000
- *F* £1,000–4,000
- *G* £4,000–7,000
- *H* £7,000–10,000
- *I* over £10,000
- ❐ value of 19th-century copy (made *c.*1860)

Availability

- VR very rare
- R rare
- FC fairly common
- C common

"Forgeability"

- ⚲ Beware of forgeries or copies

Abbreviations

- C century
- NY New York

Note on valuation symbols

Price ranges given are London projections for Spring 1982, with a built-in allowance for inflation. The value of an object will fall *within* the limits indicated, rather than corresponding with the whole of the range. Price is affected by many variables—the state of the economy, the condition and detailed appearance of the piece, whether it is marked or signed, fluctuations in taste, wavering exchange rates, and whether one is buying from a dealer in the capital or in the provinces, or from an auction house. Readers are therefore advised to treat the valuation symbols as no more than an approximate comparative guide.

Numbers in brackets in the text refer to illustrations within the same section.

Acknowledgements

The author and publishers wish to thank the following for advice on text or illustrations. Inclusion in the list does not necessarily imply agreement with the views expressed. All advisers are based in London unless specified. *Furniture:* Zal Davar, Israel-Sack Inc. (NY), Brian Morgan (Bluett & Sons Ltd), David Nickerson (Mallett at Bourdon House Ltd). *Pottery and Porcelain:* R. Allbrook (Theydon Bois), Roger Bluett, Donald Bonny (Sydney L. Moss Ltd), Jack Feingold (Gem Antiques, NY), Anne George (Albert Amor Ltd), M. Gillingham (John Sparks Ltd), Jack Hillier, Jonathan Horne, Robert Jones (R. & J. Jones), the Stradlings (NY), Donald Towner, Rotraut Weinberg (Antique Porcelain Co.). *Glass:* Ward Lloyd, Patricia McCaulay (Spink & Son Ltd), Vincent Rocco (NY). *Firearms and Edged Weapons:* Diana Keith Neal. *Jewellery:* Geoffrey Munn (Wartski). *Enamels:* Susan Benjamin (Halcyon Days). *Ivory:* Gordon Balderston (Christie's). *Netsuke and Inro:* N.K. Davey (Sotheby's). *Jade:* M. Gillingham (John Sparks Ltd). *Papier mâché:* Susan Benjamin (Halcyon Days), Zal Davar, M. Gillingham (John Sparks Ltd). *Wood:* Susan Benjamin (Halcyon Days), Tony Foster (A. & E. Foster, Naphill, Buckinghamshire). *Clocks and Watches:* Charles Lee (R.A. Lee Ltd). *Silver:* Ian Harris (N. Bloom & Son), Francis Norton (S.J. Phillips Ltd), C.J. Shrubsole (S.J. Shrubsole). *Metalwork:* Roger Bluett, Simon Brady (Sotheby's), Raymond Casimir (Jack Casimir Ltd), Peter Hornsby (Robin Bellamy Antiques, Witney, Oxfordshire), Victoria Horswell (Sladmore Gallery), C.J. Shrubsole (S.J. Shrubsole). *Carpets and Rugs:* C.W. and M.C. Heddon (Vigo Carpet Gallery). *Textiles:* M.J. Mayorcas. *Toys and Dolls:* Olivia Bristol (Christie's), Mary Hillier, Susan Mayor (Christie's), Deborah Ohlman (Christie's). *Looking Glasses:* David Nickerson (Mallett at Bourdon House Ltd). *Additional American valuations:* Christie's and Sotheby's in New York.

Edited and designed by
Mitchell Beazley Publishers
87–89 Shaftesbury Avenue, London W1V 7AD

© Mitchell Beazley Publishers 1981
All rights reserved

ISBN 0 85533 317 0

Typeset by Servis Filmsetting Ltd, Manchester
Printed in Hong Kong by Mandarin Offset International Ltd
Colour reproduction by Gilchrist Brothers Ltd, Leeds

Editor Robert Saxton
Designer Jacquie Gulliver
Executive Editor Susannah Read
Art Editor Douglas Wilson
Production Julian Deeming
Colour picture research Brigitte Arora
Illustration B.L. Kearley Ltd

CONTENTS

INTRODUCTION

No-one can hope to be an expert on "antiques". Those who claim to be are human fakes. A lifetime is not enough to master a subject such as Chinese porcelain or Art Nouveau silver. So this book cannot make you a connoisseur: that can only be achieved by reading the grander studies, by visiting museums, by handling pieces in antique shops, by acquiring and living with examples, by making a few ridiculous mistakes and, above all, by *specializing*. What the book *can* do if you are a would-be collector is help you choose your special field. Many (but, of course, not all) of the possibilities are clearly displayed here, like goods in a mail order catalogue. If you specialize already you will find the guide useful for on-the-spot reference and for extradisciplinary forays. Of course, you can admire without acquisitiveness, and another part of my intention is to provide a background for visits to public collections. (This is why some of the illustrations show expensive pieces which few collectors can aspire to own.)

I am a writer who delights in beguiling detail and anecdote. Usually, I can't see a tangent without rushing off along it. But here my natural discursiveness has been held in check by the demands of the miniature format. This may well have been beneficial to my literary style. It will certainly benefit the enquiring reader, who will get straight to the meat without having to wade through fancy pie-crust.

It is by no means all *my* meat. W.H. Auden said, "Copying one book is plagiarism, copying two books is research". I have relied enormously on the books and personal advice of specialist scholars and dealers. I would claim only that I have gone to the very best of them, many of them friends. I would particularly like to thank M.J. Mayorcas, Diana Keith Neal and Geoffrey Munn. Others who have helped are acknowledged (less elaborately than they deserve) on page 2. I am also deeply obliged to the staff of Mitchell Beazley: to James Mitchell for commissioning the book, to Susannah Read for overseeing it with a necessary blend of sternness and sympathy, to Jacquie Gulliver for a splendid design and to Bob Saxton, who has worked harder on the book than I have—a master of encapsulation, he could lever an Ugly Sister's foot into Cinderella's glass slipper, and "slipshod" might describe some of the passages he has excised.

Concentrated vitamin C can be taken over a long period to guard against colds, or gulped down to deal with a cold when it arrives. This book can be used in similar ways: to prepare for the moment when a bargain finally turns up, or as emergency aid when it does. The collecting bug is better than a cold in the head, but it is equally infectious—and there is no known cure.

Bevis Hillier

4

FURNITURE

People do not collect furniture in the way they collect wine glasses or snuff boxes. A collection of 20 Georgian tables is an absurd concept—quite apart from the expense that would be involved. Furniture is collected to furnish a room, so the buyer should have a clear idea of what harmonizes with what. For example, rustic furniture does not go with the metropolitan elegance of Sheraton.

Woods

The furniture collector needs to learn to identify different woods. One good way is to visit museums, where the woods of different pieces are stated on their labels. Note that ash is easily mistaken for oak, but differs from it in being susceptible to woodworm. Mahogany occurs in two varieties: Spanish (from Cuba, San Domingo and Puerto Rico) and the lighter and softer Honduras.

Veneers and inlays

Veneering—the application of thin layers of wood to the carcase—allowed expensive woods to be used economically. It also enabled the cabinet-maker to use a structurally weak but finely figured wood to best advantage. "Oyster shell" veneers came from olive or laburnum branches. "Burr" woods have a knotty figure caused by malformations of the trunk. Marquetry and parquetry are two related ways of making patterns out of veneers, the former in naturalistic designs, the latter in geometrical. Inlaying is the decorative technique by which a hollow is made in the carcase and filled with solid blocks of wood. Intarsia is a variant form, using complex, pictorial motifs.

Lacquer and japanning

Lacquerwork in the strict sense is the creation of a hard decorative surface by applying coats of purified tree-sap. The best work was done in Japan: hence the name "japanning" to describe imitations done in Europe from the 17th C.

Fakes and reproductions

To decide whether a piece is genuine it is useful to study the development of construction techniques.

Nails were hand-cut, and hence irregular, until c.1790. Arc-shaped saw marks (e.g. on a drawer bottom) are evidence of late manufacture, as the circular saw was not introduced until the early 19th C. Dovetail joints on drawers are a good guide to age. They were in use on quality furniture by the 1680s and ran straight through to the drawer front, concealed by an applied moulding. By the end of the century they stopped short of the front and were narrower. The more dovetails, the older the piece. Other factors to consider when dating are patina (mellowing), wear, handle fastenings, key escutcheons, lock types and stylistic consistency.

Hybrids

Some pieces of furniture have been made from parts of others. For example, an occasional table may be the result of adding a tray to the base of a pole screen.

ENGLAND

The Age of Oak. Oak was the staple material of English furniture from the Middle Ages until the reign of Charles II. The main scope for the collector is chairs and stools, chests, cupboards, tables and beds. Early chairs are called back-stools (stools with backs), and many have a box-like construction, based on chests. In the late 16th c the wainscot (planked) chair gave way to an open-framed type with panelled back, sometimes upholstered. (2) By the 17th c the farthingale chair, with back support raised clear of the seat, was popular. The two main types of stool were trestle and legged. The term "joint stool" is used for stools made by joinery. (3)

Chests began as primitive dug-outs, but framed and planked ones were made from the 13th c, panelled ones from the 15th. (4) Cupboards were originally "cup-boards"—sideboards for displaying plate, without enclosed spaces or doors. In the late 16th c the three-tiered open court cupboard developed, often ornately carved. Aumbries and livery cupboards were used for storing food, while tall press cupboards held clothes and valuables. (5) A dole cupboard was hung on a wall for dispensing charity food, but the term is sometimes misapplied to an ordinary food cupboard (properly known as a food hutch).

The trestle table was an early form, easy to clear and store. The frame table, with four legs joined by stretchers, came into regular use during the 16th c.

The bed developed from the simple box to the "wainscot" (with panelled bedsteads at both ends), and then to the "post" (with posts supporting the tester, or canopy). The "stump" bed is low-slung, while the "truckle" (or "trundle") has wooden wheels.

The Age of Walnut. Walnut was used for furniture in Tudor times, especially for beds. But its fashionable days date from c.1670. The taste for the flamboyant, which Charles II and his court had picked up in exile, gave place to the more reticent manner of the William and Mary period, when Dutch styles naturally came in. After 1685 there was also a strong Huguenot influence, at its grandest in the muted Louis XIV baroque of Daniel Marot. (10)

This was the great age of lacquered and marquetry furniture. Marquetry colours toned down by c.1690 and by 1700 naturalistic

---

English oak furniture, 17th C

1 **Gate-leg table**, 17th c FC *E*

2 **Carved armchair**, mid-17th c **◨ ९** *F*

3 **Joint stool**, 17th c FC *D*

4 **Coffer** with carved triple-
panelled front, 17th c **◨ ९** *E*

5 **Aumbry** with carved motifs
VR *F*

6 **Commonwealth press
cupboard ◨** *F*

6

English walnut furniture, 17th–early 18th C

9 **William and Mary card table**
FG ♀ *F*
10 **Dining chair in the style of
Daniel Marot**, *c.*1700 VR *G* (set of
four)
11 **Queen Anne chest on stand,**
*c.*1705 FG ♀ *F*
12 **Chair with cabriole legs and
claw-and-ball feet,** *c.*1720 ◑ ♀ *H*
13 **Queen Anne bureau,** *c.*1710
◑ *F*

7 **Charles II caned armchair on
twist-turned legs,** *c.*1680 FG *E*
8 **William and Mary chest,**
*c.*1690, inlaid in the 19th c ◑ *F*

---

motifs (copied from Flemish work) were being ousted by
arabesques and "seaweed" or "endive" marquetry. The greatest
age of walnut furniture is Anne's reign (1702–14), with its finely
figured veneers.

Gate-leg tables, often with "barley-sugar" twisted legs, were
popular in Charles II's reign (1), and chairs had elaborate carving
and turning. (7) From *c.*1675 s-shaped scroll designs ("Flemish"
scrolls) were used for front legs. William and Mary chairs were
simpler, with a definite backward tilt. Turned legs remained in
vogue, as did woven cane seats and backs. Feet were ball- or bun-
shaped. Many chairs were expensively upholstered, as were the
new day-beds (couches).

A major feature of Queen Anne chairs and cabinets was the
cabriole leg, which in fine-quality work had carvings on the knee.
(12) Chairs often had solid splats and removable stuffed seats. From
1660 small occasional tables were made for tea-drinking, cards and
dressing. (9)

Increased literacy and postal services led to the introduction of
writing bureaux during the Restoration. The earliest had a sloping
fall-front and rested on a stand. Queen Anne examples, which often
stood on a chest of drawers, had elaborate interiors, sometimes
with secret compartments. (13) A bookcase top could be added to
form a bureau-bookcase. China cabinets date from William and
Mary's reign.

The Age of Mahogany. Mahogany, competing strongly with
walnut after *c.*1725, had largely replaced it for the most fashionable
work by *c.*1750.

William Kent (1684–1748), the first architect to use furniture in
his schemes, used mainly gilt softwoods, but also some parcel-gilt
mahogany. His lavish marble-top side-tables have an Italian
baroque flavour; prominent female masks decorate much of his
work. (14) Giles Grendey produced impressive lacquerwork
before 1755. Thomas Chippendale's highly influential *Gentleman
and Cabinet Maker's Director* (1754) popularized furniture in a

English furniture, 18th C

14 15 16 17

14 Giltwood marble-top centre table in the style of William Kent, diam. 105cm v̯R̯ F
15 Chippendale ladder-back chair FC ⚲ E
16 Chippendale chair with pierced and carved splat ® ⚲ F
17 George II mahogany corner cupboard with "broken pediment", c.1750 FC F
18 Chippendale-style mahogany desk ® ⚲ ⊡ H (1900–1920s)

18

restrained rococo style, with touches of the contemporary fashion for neo-Gothic and *chinoiserie*.

Neo-classicism began c.1760 in the furniture of Robert Adam, with fluting, classical motifs (urns, medallions, rams' heads etc.) and fine inlays. Cabriole legs gave way to straight and tapered. In 1788 George Hepplewhite's *Cabinet-makers' and Upholsterers' Guide*, published two years after his death, interpreted the new classical style for craftsmen, frequently recommending mahogany. Thomas Sheraton's *The Cabinet-Makers' and Upholsters' Drawing Book* (1791–4) bridged the gap between neo-classicism and Regency. Sheraton-style furniture was light, delicate and straight-lined. Satinwood was used for the finest pieces, although tropical woods later became popular. Fine craftsmen of the age include William Vile, Pierre Langlois, the Linells and George Seddon.

The desk was a new feature in the rich man's library by 1750, with drawers or cupboards either side of the kneehole. (18) Some were serpentine-fronted. Sheraton preferred the cylinder-front to the fall-front. The bureau-bookcase and other combined pieces came into fashion, sometimes topped with a broken pediment.

Chippendale-style chairs were in rococo, Chinese or Gothick styles, with pierced and carved splatwork, including the famous "ribband back" as well as ladder backs of traditional country design. (15; p 100, nos 1, 2) The Adam brothers introduced a lighter chair, with oval or lyre backs and straight legs. Hepplewhite was best known for his shield backs but also designed hearts, ovals and lyres. (24) For splats he favoured wheat-ear motifs or the Prince of Wales's feathers. Sheraton chairs had rectangular backs with upright splats, and were sometimes in painted beech instead of mahogany or satinwood. (25) Carving was replaced by inlay on the top rail, and striped material was used for upholstery. The country-made Windsor chair, first made in the Queen Anne period, continued to be popular; the comb back style gave way to the hoop back after 1750.

Chests of drawers are another important product of the Age of Mahogany. Up to c.1750 they were still straight-fronted, but then serpentine-shaped commodes based on French designs came in.

Neo-classical commodes often have fine inlay work, with circles or ovals depicting mythological scenes. (22) Sheraton is associated especially with the bow-fronted chest of drawers, but designed in a variety of other shapes.

Small tea tables became increasingly popular before mid-century, as did breakfast tables. In the Adam period there was a fashion for oval, semicircular, kidney-shaped and serpentine tables. The finest were of satinwood with tops painted by artists such as Angelica Kauffmann. When sideboards came in, there was less demand for large tables. Sheraton designed many delicate small ones, as well as ladies' work tables with ingenious drawer arrangements. He also popularized the Pembroke table, with two folding side-flaps hinged on a narrow centre part. (32) Hepplewhite and Sheraton both designed elegant sideboards; Sheraton's have a brass rail at the back to hold plates.

The Regency style. Two new strains are apparent in Regency furniture: French taste (favoured by the Regent himself and his architect Henry Holland, who designed in the Louis XVI style); and a new accuracy in the imitation of the antique, promoted by Thomas Hope, a millionaire who designed his own furniture, adapting ancient models. (27) Hope liked expanses of flat veneer with small gilt-metal (ormolu) ornaments or sparse ebony inlay. He also favoured *torchères* (vase-stands) like Greek or Roman tripods, and severely classical couches with scrolled ends.

English furniture, 18th C

cabinet-on-stand VŘ *F*
21 George III Gothic lacquer cabinet VŘ ᛩ *G*
22 George III bow-fronted satinwood commode ⬤ *F*
23 George III *chinoiserie* mahogany silver table, *c.*1755 ⬤ ᛩ *E*
24 Hepplewhite-style painted shield-back chair ⬤ ᛩ ⬛ *E* (set of five)
25 Sheraton chair FC *E*

19 George III mahogany cylinder bureau with Gothic elements FC *F*
20 George III mahogany

But there was a more "pop" side to Regency, well illustrated in Ackermann's *Repository* (1809-28). Nelson was the pop hero of the age: hence the "Trafalgar" chair (30); hence, too, the Egyptian revival, though this owed as much to Napoleon's Egyptian expedition as to Nelson's victory on the Nile. Sphinxes and crocodiles now entered the repertoire of designers.

Distinctive Regency pieces included the sofa or couch, the drum table with tripod support, and the *chiffonier* (low cupboard with shelves for books). The sideboard took the form of a table between flanking cupboards. Rosewood was preferred, and brass inlay work, lion-mask handles and reeded corner-columns were common. The mahogany and gilt furniture of Thomas Chippendale the Younger was dignified and well proportioned. But from 1811, with the end of wartime austerity, a profound change in taste was evident: everything became grosser. Turned legs replaced the "scimitar" legs of the Trafalgar chair, and Corinthian capitals ousted Doric and Tuscan.

English furniture, early 19th C

26 Regency beechwood chair, painted to simulate bamboo FC *C* (pair)

27 Egyptian armchair by Thomas Hope, 1800–07 VR *H*

28 George IV mahogany breakfast table, c.1820 FC *D*

29 Regency mahogany armchair, c.1815 FC *F* (set of eight)

30 Trafalgar chair, after 1805 FC *E*

31 Rosewood centre table in the style of Thomas Hope, 19th c B *G*

32 Small Pembroke table, c.1805 FC *D*

33 Regency mahogany console table FC *F* (pair)

**34 Ormolu-mounted *lit en bâteau* B *F*

35 Rosewood side cabinet VR *F*

Victorian. Victorian furniture is of two main kinds: progressive and popular. Both relied overwhelmingly on past styles. Renaissance, Gothic and rococo revivals loomed large in the stylistic repertoire. (36, 43, 46)

The first of the great reformers was A.W.N. Pugin, who wanted to revive the "honesty" of Gothic by which joints were shown on the surface. He was supported by John Ruskin. William Morris, who founded his furniture firm in 1861, was a Ruskin disciple, and the furniture made by him and his collaborators (Philip Webb, William Burges, J.P. Seddon), often with Pre-Raphaelite decoration, is obedient to Pugin/Ruskin ideals. (43) Morris & Co. also made simple rush-seated chairs. (45) Bruce Talbert (1838–81)

English furniture, Victorian

36 Neo-rococo mahogany pedestal cabinet, carved and veneered, *c.*1850 VR *F*

37 Walnut oval dining table, *c.*1860 FG *E*

38 Walnut *chaise longue*, *c.*1860 FG *D*

39 Mahogany side chair, *c.*1860 FG *E* (set of four)

40 Rosewood and parcel-gilt side cabinet, *c.*1870 ® *G*

41 Mahogany side chair, *c.*1840 FG *E* (set of four)

42 Whatnot, *c.*1835 ® *D*

43 Painted wardrobe, based on design by Burges, 1870s ® *F*

44 Balloon-back walnut side chair, 1860 G *D*

45 "Sussex" armchair, Morris & Co. FG *B*

46 Neo-Gothic chair, based on design by Pugin, *c.*1840 VR *F*

broke away from the Gothic in sternly rectilinear furniture with geometric decoration. A bigger break with historicism came with the Japanese-inspired furniture of E.W. Godwin in the 1870s and 80s. The next stage of progressivism was the Arts and Crafts Movement, which aimed to offer an alternative to low commercial standards.

Meanwhile, comfort had become the main criterion of popular furniture. Most early Victorian furniture is of plain mahogany, rosewood or oak, but by the mid-Victorian period inlay was popular. Deep all-over upholstery was especially common in the 1840s and 50s. Leading London furniture houses included Gillow, Trollope, Howard, Thomas Fox and Johnstone & Jeanes. In the late Victorian period (1880–1901) a style satirically known as "bracket-and-overmantel" came in, based on architecture: plate-glass mirrors were often incorporated.

FRANCE

The Renaissance to 1715. Very little French furniture of the 16th c has come down to us. The most common surviving piece is the dresser, and walnut was the most frequently used wood. (2, 4) Wars with Italy introduced the French to the Italian Renaissance. Reliefs on chairs, dresser panels and double-decker cupboards (*armoires à deux corps*) show obvious Italian influence. The mannerist idiom was commonest in the south of France, Burgundy and west Switzerland. Hughes Sambin of Dijon made cabinets and dressers with grotesque carved ornament, and in 1572 issued his own set of designs for furniture.

In the mid-17th C France took the lead in the arts. Rich tapestries were in use on furniture as well as on walls. The luxury pieces that survive were almost entirely made by imported foreign craftsmen, especially Italians. But the emphasis changed in 1663 when the Manufacture Royale des Meubles de la Couronne was set up at

French furniture, Renaissance

1 Renaissance *caquetoire* (chair with trapezoidal seat) ⓑ ९ *F*
2 Walnut dresser, 16th c ⓑ ९ *G*
3 Louis XIV walnut and marquetry commode in the manner of Boulle ⓑ *I*
4 Early 16th-c dresser ⓑ ९ ◫ *F*
5 Louis XIV Boulle centre table, late 17th c ⱽⱤ ९ ◫ *F*

Gobelins, by Colbert, chief minister to Louis XIV. Now import of luxury goods was restricted and French makers, under strict state control, took the lead in satisfying the opulent tastes of the aristocracy. The first director of the Manufacture was Charles Le Brun, whose inaugural task was to decorate and furnish the new palace of Versailles.

The most celebrated cabinet-maker of the period was André-Charles Boulle (1642–1732), who, after a phase of producing wood marquetry, turned to intricate inlays of tortoiseshell and brass—a technique (popular until the late 19th C) which still bears his name. Much of Boulle's work was for the Crown. Many pieces attributed to him are in fact by later hands. (3, 5; p 98, no. 2)

In the 17th C veneers on luxury furniture were usually in lightly sculpted ebony (hence the name *ébéniste* to describe a French cabinet-maker). Precious metals and semi-precious stones were incorporated, and turned decoration was popular. The commode was introduced *c.*1700; somewhat earlier, the bureau began life as a table with two sets of drawers beneath the top, flanking the kneehole. Wardrobes appeared in the late 17th C. Armchairs were often throne-like, sometimes with extravagantly arched stretchers.

From 1715 to the Revolution. France led furniture fashion through the 18th C and during the early 19th C. The periods into which collectors divide the furniture are: Régence (*c.*1715–30); Louis XV (*c.*1730–74); Louis XVI (*c.*1774–85); Directoire (*c.*1785–1810); and Empire (ending *c.*1830).

There were interesting provincial centres of furniture-making, for example Grenoble, Lyons and Normandy, but Paris was supreme. Under the Parisian guild system, a division of labour was rigorously enforced, from which only the *Ebéniste du Roi*, employed directly by the Crown, was exempt. The *menuisiers* (joiners) produced everything made of wood. The main job of the *ébénistes* was enriching with veneers and marquetry. From 1743 to 1790 members of the Paris guild had to stamp their names on their furniture.

The death of Louis XIV in 1715 and his succession by a small boy controlled by a pleasure-loving Regent put an end to the formal, pompous court life of the age of the Sun King. Apartments became smaller, which meant smaller furniture, more elegant than monumental. Boulle marquetry passed temporarily out of fashion. The new taste was for elaborate wood marquetry with ormolu mounts. Lines became curvier, and function was often concealed beneath decoration. (p 98, no. 1)

French furniture, 18th C

6 Régence giltwood console table 🅑 ٩ *F*

7 Giltwood *bergère*, mid-18th c 🅑 ٩ *I*

8 Louis XVI walnut armchair 🅑 ٩ *F*

9 Louis XV marble-top commode, attributed to Cressent, *c.*1740 V̄R̄ *I*

10 Louis XV corner cabinet, mid-18th c V̄R̄ ٩ ▢ *I*

11 Louis XV *canapé* 🅑 ٩ ▢ *E*

12 Louis XVI porcelain-mounted console table, stamped M. Carlin 🅑 *I*

13 Louis XV kingwood and marquetry bureau, by G. Feilt V̄R̄ ▢ *I*

14 Transitional marquetry commode V̄R̄ ٩ ▢ *F*

15 Louis XV *bureau plat*, mid-18th c 🅑 ٩ ▢ *I*

16 Louis XVI straw-seated lyre-back chair 🄵🄲 *C*

17 Louis XV parquetry commode, *c.*1740 🅑 ٩ ▢ *I*

In Louis XV's reign the rococo was born, with its shell motifs, calculated asymmetry and writhing interlaced curves. The typical Louis XV commode had two or four drawers in two layers, with longer legs than the Régence type. (9) The *encoignure* was a corner cupboard, usually supplied as a pair. (10) From the middle of the century the *commode à vantaux* was made (with doors enclosing the front). The writing table (*bureau plat*) was given its definitive form in this reign; sometimes a *cartonnier* (cabinet or pigeonholes for papers) was placed on top. (15) The *secrétaire à abattant* (drop-front writing cabinet) became popular from the 1750s. (18) After *c.*1760 there was a vogue for the *bonheur du jour* (ladies' small writing table on tall legs, with drawers in a raised part at the back): this was much imitated in 19th-c England. The *bureau-toilette* was half writing table, half toilet table. Chair types included the *marquise* (double armchair), *bergère* (armchair with closed upholstered sides and back, sometimes winged) and *voyeuse* (with padded rail for spectators at card games to lean on.) (7)

The opening of trade routes with the Far East brought oriental goods to France, introducing a taste for lacquer and oriental woods for inlays. Some of the most attractive pieces of the period were decorated with *Vernis Martin*, a lustrous imitation lacquer, often in bright blues, reds or greens.

Among the leading *ébénistes* of the period were Charles Cressent (1685–1758), already active during the Régence (9), Antoine-Robert Gaudreau (*c.*1680–1751), and one formerly known only for his signature, B.V.R.B., but identified in the 1950s as Bernard II van Risenburgh. The two supreme Louis XV *ébénistes* were Jean-François Oeben (*c.*1720–63), who trained with Boulle, and Oeben's artistic successor Jean-Henri Riesener (1734–1806). Both were German by birth. Oeben's furniture often contains mechanical apparatus. Riesener continued in Oeben's rococo style until *c.*1770, then took to Boulle, and later the Louis XVI style. His marquetry is exquisitely crafted; his bronze mounts are integrated with the wood surface with amazing smoothness.

Furniture motifs

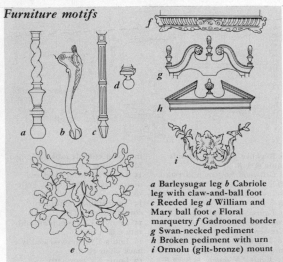

a Barleysugar leg *b* Cabriole leg with claw-and-ball foot *c* Reeded leg *d* William and Mary ball foot *e* Floral marquetry *f* Gadrooned border *g* Swan-necked pediment *h* Broken pediment with urn *i* Ormolu (gilt-bronze) mount

Long before the accession of Louis XVI in 1774, a reaction had begun against the extreme excesses of the rococo. French collectors speak of the "Transitional" period, when some furniture combined rococo and neo-classical features. (14) Riesener was the great *ébéniste* of this reign, Georges Jacob (1739–1814) the greatest *menuisier*. Martin Carlin worked in a delicate feminine style. (12) Furniture-making processes were refined and perfected. As Marie-Antoinette was German, more German *ébénistes* were patronized, including Adam Weisweiler and Jean Guillaume Beneman. Furniture became more straight-lined and delicate. Chair legs lost their scrolls and became straight, tapering and fluted. (8) Porcelain (including Sèvres) was increasingly set into furniture.

The Directoire and Empire styles. The Revolution ended the guild system, but some workshops continued production, including that of Georges Jacob I and his sons. For J.L. David, artist and revolutionary leader, Jacob had made furniture with red and black upholstery from "Etruscan" designs supplied by David himself. "Etruscan" was the keynote of the Directoire period (named after the government of 1795–9), but there was an Egyptian influence as well. (18) Typical pieces included the *méridienne* (day-bed with either one or two curl-over arm ends), the *athénienne* (three-legged wash-stand) and the vase-stand. (25) The first gondola-shaped beds, enveloped in draperies, date from the end of the century.

French furniture, 19th C

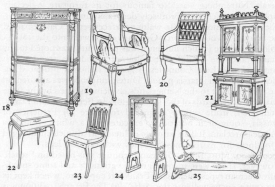

18 Directoire *sécretaire à abattant*, c.1795 FC *I*
19 Mahogany and parcel-gilt armchair, c.1810 ⊕ ♀ *F*
20 Mahogany armchair, stamped by Jacob *frères* ⊕ *F*
21 Gothic cupboard, 19th c FC *F*
22 Louis Phillipe kingwood

poudreuse with brass and pewter inlay ⊕ *F*
23 Charles X chair FC *D*
24 Empire thuyawood secretaire, signed by Jacob, c.1820 V̌R̄ ⊡ *F*
25 Empire mahogany and ormolu *méridienne* V̌R̄ *F*

The industry recovered from the effect of the Revolution under the firm rule of Bonaparte's First Consulate (1799–1804). The Empire style (1804–15), Napoleon's propaganda vehicle, spread through Europe with his conquests, but also through engravings. The finest work was by Jacob Desmalter et Cie. From 1806 the Continental blockade prevented imports of mahogany from the English colonies. This inflated the value of mahogany (in which Napoleon's palaces were therefore furnished) but also increased the use of native woods. Furniture became increasingly heavy, bronze mounts coarser, and draperies were used in abundance. Rectangular-backed chairs superseded scroll-backed. Console tables often had animal supports. Egyptian motifs became more popular after Napoleon's campaigns on the Nile. The Gothic style developed after 1815, and chairs with traceried, crocketed backs were fashionable in Paris c.1830–45.

In the Second Empire (1848–70) a variety of upholstered seats was made including *pouffes, crapauds* (low armchairs) and various types of settee. One of the best furniture-makers of the time was L.E. Lamarchand, who imitated Boulle and 18th-c lacquer pieces.

GERMANY

1500–1700. The Renaissance permeated Germany more slowly than France. The Germans clung to the Gothic, mixing it with the new Italianate motifs to create hybrids. In the early 16th C some cabinet-makers published woodcuts of furniture designs, including Peter Flötner (c.1485–1546), who designed cupboards with Renaissance touches, and another cabinet-maker known only by his initials, H.S. In south Germany the architecturally inspired "façade cupboard" was a popular 16th-C type, often overcrowded with mouldings. North German pieces were severer, and carved oak was predominant, in contrast with the softwoods of the south, which lent themselves more to marquetry and painting. (4) Wardrobes succeeded two-tier cupboards in the 17th C.

Augsburg was an important centre for cabinets, cupboards and desks, many of them lavish showpieces made for export. Its specialities were intarsia work and the use of precious stones and metals. Nuremberg was also famous for its furniture, especially cupboards, which were profusely decorated until the early 18th C when a preference for plain walnut surfaces set in. Oak remained the favoured wood in north Germany until well into the 18th C. Cologne, where French influence was powerful, was noted for its intarsia and use of different coloured woods—a trend which spread to the Low Countries. Eger in Bohemia produced intricately sculpted intarsia panels. Dutch influence was apparent in the states closest to the Netherlands, as demonstrated by the large fruitwood cupboards of the Trier region. In Berlin, Gerard Dagly, after 1687, made superb lacquered furniture for Frederick of Prussia, some of it beautifully executed on a white ground to imitate porcelain. Italian baroque influence in Munich encouraged a fondness for marble-mosaic tables with caryatid legs.

1700–1900. Most 18th-C German furniture was based on French. However, there were many regional variations and some specifically German types, such as the Frankfurt cupboard, which kept its late 17th-C shape well into the 18th C. (6) The French tradition was strong in Munich: pieces by leading French *ébénistes* were imported and copied. Another influence was the decorative designs of the Flemish architect François Cuvilliés (1695–1768), whose furniture amalgamated the delicate French style with the more florid Bavarian rococo. At Würzburg can be seen the magnificent carved console tables made by the court sculptor Wolfgang van der Auvera (1708–56), who was trained in Vienna, where he came

---

German furniture, Renaissance

1 Oak coffer, with inlay decoration, late 17th c **⊕** *F*
2 Imperial chair, 1574 V̄R̄ *I*
3 Marquetry *armoire*, early 17th c **⊕** *H*
4 Oak cupboard, 17th c **⊕** *G*
5 Marquetry cabinet, 17th c **⊕** *G*

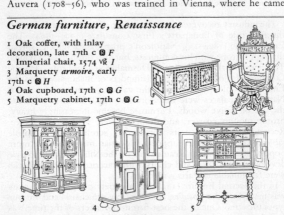

16

under Italian influence. Important cabinet-makers of the mid-century included Johan Georg Nestfell (1694–1762), a master of marquetry, and Carl Maximilian Mattern, who worked at Würzburg from 1733 until his death in 1770, employing ivory and coloured woods. (See p 97, no. 4)

In Dresden and its environs the Electors of Saxony established a furniture centre which had its palmiest days from 1670 to 1763. Typical of Dresden production are the writing cabinets with upper doors fitted with looking-glasses. Among the finest products were the lacquer pieces of Martin Schnell, appointed lacquerer to the court in 1710 and active there until 1740.

German furniture, 18th and 19th C

6 Walnut cabinet, veneered, Frankfurt, c.1700 🄱 ৭ 🄳 F
7 Marquetry chest, 18th c, ht 85cm 🄱 G
8 Biedermeier oak chair 🄵🄲 F (set of six)
9 Biedermeier walnut chair, c.1820–25 🄵🄲 F (pair)
10 Mahogany centre table, c.1820 🄵🄲 F

11 Parquetry commode, perhaps by A. Roentgen, mid-18th c 🄱 🄳 F
12 Biedermeier satinwood chest of drawers, c.1825 🄵🄲 E
13 Viennese mahogany cylinder bureau, c.1825 🄱 H

The best 18th-c furniture in Berlin was made under Frederick the Great (1740–86). Some was designed by the sculptor and interior decorator Johann August Nahl (1710–85), whose exuberant, French-style work can be seen in the palace of Sans Souci, Potsdam. Magnificent ormolu against tortoiseshell veneers was a speciality of Johann Melchior Kambli, who worked at Potsdam and Berlin from 1746.

The Rhenish cabinet-maker Abraham Roentgen (1711–93) and his son David (workshop active 1737–99) were successful in marrying influences from France and England into their own tradition. (11) David Roentgen, the greatest German furniture-maker, favoured *trompe l'œil* intarsia and ingenious mechanical devices.

In the early 19th c Germany adopted a rather pedantic version of the Napoleonic Empire style. After 1815 this then gave way to a more relaxed and intimate middle-class style known as Biedermeier, with plainer surfaces and fewer gilt-bronze mounts. (8, 9, 12) Josef Danhauser of Vienna, who thrived from 1804 to 1830, was the best craftsman.

THE LOW COUNTRIES

In the early 17th c in the northern Protestant states of the Netherlands, which had split with the southern Catholic ones in 1579, furniture began to develop a national style. Cupboards replaced chests. The distinctive two-tier *Beeldenkast* of the province of Holland, decorated with carved caryatids, was superseded after the mid-century by baroquely ornamented two-door cupboards.

Dutch and Flemish furniture, 17th–19th C

1 Flemish ebony and tortoiseshell cabinet, 17th c VℝⒹ *F*

2 *Beeldenkast*, north Netherlands, *c.*1630 VℝⒹ *F*

3 Oak draw-leaf table on cup-and-cover baluster legs, 17th c ⒷG

4 Walnut *bombé* chest, mid-18th c FⒸG

5 Walnut side table, *c.*1670 ⒷG

6 Walnut and marquetry chair in an early 18th-c style, 19th c FⒸC

7 Mahogany clothes press, *c.*1780 FⒸG

8 Marquetry drop-leaf table, *c.*1780 FⒸF

(2) The so-called "Zeeland chests" had two stages but lacked the vertical emphasis of the *Beeldenkast*. Gilded tables, with exuberantly carved supports, were typical of the baroque period. (5) Antwerp specialized in elaborate many-drawered cabinets.

Netherlands chairs in the 17th C became generally rectangular, with vase-shaped legs, the back uprights topped with lion heads or shield-bearing lions. They are usually of walnut and are upholstered in leather, velvet or cloth, attached by large brass studs.

After 1685 Huguenot refugees added their talents, among them the influential Daniel Marot. William of Orange's accession to the English throne brought some English influence, especially in chairs, which acquired pierced splats and cabriole legs. (6) Marquetry panels in the splats were a typically Dutch feature. By the mid-18th C, rococo was coming in. Dutch commodes were on the French model, though more exaggeratedly *bombé* (i.e., swirlingly convex). (4) The best late 18th-c furniture in the neo-classical rectilinear style had accomplished marquetry. (7) In the south Netherlands oak wardrobes were decorated with scrolls and flowers asymmetrically carved.

Carel Breytspraak made Empire furniture for the royal palace of 1808 in Amsterdam. An Empire flavour persisted in the work of G. Nordanus, cabinet-maker from The Hague, but in the mid-19th C a bastard Biedermeier style was predominant.

SCANDINAVIA

Little Scandinavian furniture has survived from before the 17th C, owing to the use of soft deal and pine in the absence of hardwoods. Work produced in Denmark and Sweden in the later 17th C reveals a mix of English, Dutch and German influences. Trade with

England was boosted by the Great Fire of London in 1666, for huge quantities of Scandinavian wood were suddenly needed to rebuild the capital. In return English furniture was imported. The English high-backed chair influenced Danish and Norwegian makers. When the cabriole leg was introduced in the 18th C it was incongruously combined with stretchers in the earlier manner.

Dutch influence was especially strong in the 17th C when Holland was a great maritime power. Dutch floral marquetry and *bombé* shapes were imitated in Stockholm and Copenhagen in the early 18th C. (p 99, no. 5) (In the 1770s French-inspired marquetry came in, depicting musical instruments, books and human figures.)

French rococo became a court style in Scandinavia after the 1730s. (2) Furniture was imported from France and some Swedish cabinet-makers went to Paris to study. Gallic neo-classicism caught on quickly. Georg Haupt worked in Paris and brought a fully developed Louis XVI style back to Sweden in 1769. The Masreliez brothers (Swedish but of French extraction) worked in a neo-classical mode for the Swedish court in the later 18th C.

German influence was particularly strong in Denmark, as many of the Danish aristocracy were of German origin. An important mid-18th-C maker was Mathias Ortmann, whose work progressed from Anglo-Dutch to Germanic rococo. (4) In 1777, when the Danes set up a Royal Furniture Emporium, the German cabinet-maker Georg Roentgen was invited to Copenhagen to take part. But in 1781 Carsten Anker became director of the Emporium and his preference was for English (Hepplewhite/Sheraton) taste. Norwegian furniture, as before, followed Danish example, though with less elegance. On late 18th-C chairs a distinctively Norwegian feature is a band of fluting along the lower edge of the front seat rail. English influence waned in the 19th C, especially in Denmark and Norway after the British attack on Copenhagen in 1807. French Empire was especially prominent in Sweden.

Scandinavian furniture, 18th and 19th C

1 Swedish cane-seated chair in the English style, 18th c **⊙** *G*

2 Norwegian rococo walnut chair *c.*1770 **⊙** ⚲ *F*

3 Norwegian pine cabin bed, 19th c 🅵🅲 *C*

4 Danish cabinet, by Mathias Ortmann, *c.*1751 V̄R̄ *I*

5 Danish Empire commode, *c.*1810–15 **⊙** *F*

6 Scandinavian giltwood console table, *c.*1770 🅵🅲 *E*

7 Swedish giltwood *bergère*, *c.*1800 🅵🅲 *G* (pair)

8 Swedish rococo commode, Stockholm, 1771 **⊙** *H*

ITALY

Italian furniture is often less well-carpentered than the best French and English work. Splendour and vivacity of design meant more to craftsmen than the "finish" prized by Chippendale or Riesener. Some Italians maintained rigorous standards, such as Andrea Brustolon (1602–1732), a maker of fantastic chairs supported by carved blackamoors (8), or Antonio Corradini (1668–1752), a Venetian sculptor who doubled as a carver of chairs swarming with cherubs. For the most part, though, these were artists turning their talents to furniture, not *vice versa*. The first Italian *ébéniste* in the full French sense was Pietro Piffetti (*c.*1700–77), whose inlaid cabinets and tables are of undisputable quality, if over-fussy in detail.

Italian furniture, 17th–19th C

1 Walnut *cassapanca*, Renaissance ⓑ *F*
2 Venetian giltwood baroque side table, 17th c ⓑ ▱ *F*
3 Walnut chair, 17th c ⓑ *E*
4 Walnut writing table ⓑ *F*
5 Venetian walnut folding chair, 16th c ⓑ *F*
6 Bone-inlaid ebony table, north Italy, 19th c ⓑ ▱ *F*
7 Scarlet lacquer commode, north Italy, 18th c ⓑ *F*
8 Venetian sculptured armchair, by Brustolon, 1700 ⓑ ▱ *F*

Naturally, Italian Renaissance furniture, where it can be found, is in high demand—the *cassone* (chest), sometimes richly decorated with painted panels, the *cassapanca* (bench-cum-chest), the *armadio* (large cupboard), the *credenza* (sideboard or buffet) and the X-shaped chair. (1, 5)

Italy was the fountainhead of the baroque style as well as of the Renaissance, and early in the 17th C the overwhelming energy of the baroque erupted in furniture—in triumphant curves, extravagant console tables, and marble inlays.

Italian furniture became less interesting in the 18th C as French influence took over. Italian rococo is often simply an overblown version of the French, though there are charming regional variations. (7) The best early 18th-C work was from Venice, whose output included *bombé* commodes and extended sofas. Lacquerwork was most expert in Rome and Piedmont.

Even in the neo-classical period, when Italians might have been expected to draw directly from ancient sources, it was still French influence which dominated. Napoleon's conquest of Italy led to a heavy dose of Empire style, overtaken from the mid-19th C by the "Dantesque" Renaissance revival.

SPAIN AND PORTUGAL

As in France and Germany, Gothic and Renaissance coalesced in Spain at the beginning of the 16th C. Renaissance styles triumphed eventually, but the Moorish legacy was also potent, encouraging fine leatherwork and intricate geometric patterns. Walnut was the commonest wood, and the most popular furniture type was the chest. Early 16th-C Catalan chests were of late Gothic form, the lids painted inside and a door to one side of the front concealing a set of drawers for trinkets. Renaissance chests, by contrast, often copied the Italian *cassone*.

Chairs replaced benches. The X-frame chair (*sillón de cadera*) came in early in the 16th C. (1) A little later the most characteristic Spanish chair appeared: the *sillón de fraileros*, or monk's chair, with a fretted and carved front stretcher. (2) Many were hinged for folding. The drop-leaf cabinet (*varguéno*), resting on either a panelled chest or a trestle stand, was another Renaissance invention. (4) It was often decorated with *mudéjar* marquetry.

In the 17th C, highly decorated baroque *varguéños* were produced and another type of cabinet developed, without a fall-front and topped by a gilt gallery. In Portugal the recapture of Brazil from the Dutch (1654) led to the use of Brazilian woods such as jacaranda. (8) Chairs with high arched backs, turned legs and tooled leatherwork were made. Inventive turning was characteristic of Portuguese furniture, and was applied to the headpiece of a distinctive type of bed.

Spanish and Portuguese furniture, 16th–19th C

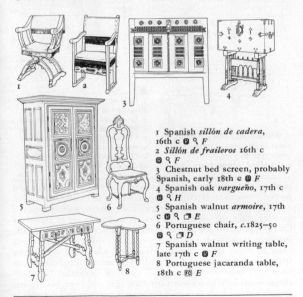

1 Spanish *sillón de cadera*, 16th c **B Q** *F*
2 *Sillón de fraileros* 16th c **B Q** *F*
3 Chestnut bed screen, probably Spanish, early 18th c **B** *F*
4 Spanish oak *varguéño*, 17th c **B Q** *H*
5 Spanish walnut *armoire*, 17th c **B Q ◻** *E*
6 Portuguese chair, c.1825–50 **B Q ◻** *D*
7 Spanish walnut writing table, late 17th c **B** *F*
8 Portuguese jacaranda table, 18th c **FC** *E*

In the 18th C, with the House of Bourbon on the Spanish throne, French influence showed itself in gilding and rococo curves. The ornate *varguéño* gave way to the French-inspired commode. Early examples were of solid carved wood, but more ambitious pieces were made after 1768. Chair forms were often basically English, with gilt decoration.

Spanish Empire furniture is usually of mahogany with bronze mounts, and heavier than the French. Gothic forms were revived in the 19th C, and a popular style was "Isabellino", a Spanish version of Louis Phillipe and Second Empire with an accent on comfortable upholstery and neo-rococo decoration.

THE UNITED STATES

From 1620 until the Revolution of 1775, most of the settlers in America were British. They had to adapt English designs to American conditions: furniture was too bulky to import, and anyway tended to shrink and crack in the drier air and had no resistance to the insects encountered. English pieces were therefore not available as patterns. American furniture is less showy than English, more serviceable and durable. Designs were vital but unabashedly utilitarian. They also had a pronounced vertical emphasis, the extra height giving an impression of narrowness. The earliest surviving pieces, dating from c.1650–70, show Jacobean features. (4) The woods used were American oak, pine and maple, with oak (which was lighter than the English variety)

American furniture, 17th and 18th C
Value symbols refer to New York estimates expressed as pounds

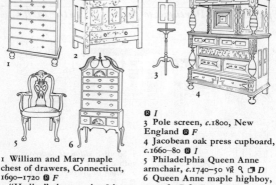

🄱 *I*
3 Pole screen, c.1800, New England 🄱 *F*
4 Jacobean oak press cupboard, c.1660–80 🄱 *I*
5 Philadelphia Queen Anne armchair, c.1740–50 VR 🜊 ▱ *D*
6 Queen Anne maple highboy, 1740–60 🄱 🜊 ▱ *F*

1 William and Mary maple chest of drawers, Connecticut, 1690–1720 🄱 *F*
2 "Hadley" chest, early 18th c

predominant. Among the finest pieces were oak chests, court and press cupboards and trestle dining tables, the most popular table in 17th-C America being the gate-leg. The more legs there are on a gate-leg table, the greater its value. Armchairs were of either the Carver type (with one row of vertical spindles in the back) or the Brewster type (with two rows)—19th-C copies are much more likely to occur than originals. High-back Charles II-style chairs later came into vogue. Chests of drawers acquired the distinctive form of a chest over drawers in the base. So-called "Hadley" chests, made in Massachusetts between 1675 and 1740, have fronts entirely carved with entwined vegetation, often round the initials of the owner. (2) Other chests had sunflower or tulip motifs carved in panels, as well as black-painted applied turning. The Dutch-influenced William and Mary style, most recognizable by its ball feet, spread from England to America about the beginning of the 18th C (though of course there were already Dutch settlers). (1) It was popular until c.1720. Americans liked this style, for it was less bulky than the Jacobean and therefore more suitable for smaller houses. Walnut became the usual wood, carved or in veneers. A group of Bostonians specialized in a rather naïve form of lacquering. In this period the highboy comes in—a tall chest of drawers on a high stand. The lowboy was a truncated version, with a single drawer or shallow layer of drawers. (9) Another innovation was the upholstered armchair.

American furniture, 18th and early 19th C
Value symbols refer to New York estimates expressed as pounds

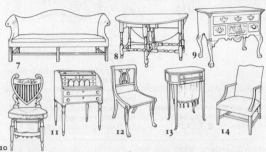

7 **Chippendale sofa**, c.1800–10
🄱 ٩ 🖵 *D*

8 **Pennsylvania walnut gate-leg table**, c.1725–50 🄵🄲 ٩ *G*

9 **Philadelphia lowboy**, c.1760–70 🄱 ٩ 🖵 *E*

10 **Shield-back rush-seated chair**, c.1815 🄱 *F*

11 **Cylinder-top desk, Mass.**, 1800–19 🄵🄲 *F*

12 **Lyre-back chair, New York**, 1810–20 🄱 ٩ *F*

13 **Work table with silk work-bag, Boston**, c.1800 🄵🄲 *F*

14 **"Martha Washington" or lolling chair, Mass.,** c.1795 ٩ *F*

In America furniture produced even as late as 1760 is generally called "Queen Anne" (although she died in 1714). Furniture for the richer homes became more elegant. The cabriole leg was standard, except in the American form of Windsor chair, with its angled legs and round spindled back—the more spindles the older it is. (19) Chairs are generally smaller than in England at this time. The most elegant ones were made in Philadelphia. (5) On highboys and lowboys six turned legs gave way to four cabriole, the missing two surviving vestigially as pendant knobs at the front. (6) Secretaries were given doors with arched panels. Gate-leg tables gave place to drop-leaf.

In America collectors hardly ever use the term "Georgian", and the progression, c.1760, is straight from "Queen Anne" to "Chippendale". The Chippendale manner, in mahogany, was most markedly practised in Philadelphia between 1760 and 1776 by fine cabinet-makers such as Thomas Affleck, John Folwell, Benjamin Randolph and William Savery. (7) Softwood was generally used for the main structure of case furniture (in contrast to the use of hardwoods in England), and dowel-and-tenon construction continued to be employed until the late 18th C. American "Chippendale" is more restrained than English, as rococo frivolity did not sort well with the Puritan tradition. It lasted until about 1785, and introduced chairs with cupid's bow top rails, claw-and-ball feet, Gothic or *chinoiserie* splats. The "Marlborough" leg (straight tapering leg of square section) appeared. John Townsend of Newport, RI, made handsome "block-front" furniture, in which the centre front recedes in a shallow curve flanked by slightly convex ends. (20)

American furniture, 18th and early 19th C

Value symbols refer to New York estimates expressed as pounds

15 **Sheraton table, by D. Phyfe,** *c.*1800–15 FC ९ *G*

16 **Sofa, with carving attributed to Samuel MacIntire, Salem, Mass., 1800–10** ◉ ९ ◻ *D*

17 **Slat-back chair, early 18th c** FC ९ *E*

18 **Hepplewhite tambour-front secretary,** *c.*1790 ◉ ९ ◻ *D*

19 **Rhode Island Windsor chair, early 19th c** FC ९ ◻ *C*

20 **Cherry block-front chest of drawers, 1770–90** ◉ ९ ◻ *D*

21 **Painted chair,** *c.*1815 © ९ *A*

Adam's designs were not published in America, and never caught on. By the time they might have been expected to permeate from England, the Revolution had sundered Anglo-American cultural relations. The "Chippendale" style was followed directly, after the resumption of trade in 1784, by various hybrid Hepplewhite/Sheraton styles, with shield-back and square-backed chairs, much reeding on rails and arms, and serpentine-fronted sideboards. A new type of desk, the tambour, had sliding doors made up of vertical strips. (18) Excellent painted furniture was produced in Baltimore and elsewhere. By the end of the century, lowboys and highboys were being replaced by smaller chests of drawers, and there was an increased production of small occasional tables. Tulip, poplar and white pine, sometimes used instead of mahogany, are signs of American manufacture. Veneers and inlays were common after *c.*1790. (p 99, no. 7)

From *c.*1805 to *c.*1825, American chairs and sofas were influenced by French Directoire styles, with "sabre-shaped" curves. The leading maker in this style was the brilliant Duncan Phyfe (1768–1854) in New York, who made much use of the lyre motif. (12, 15) His earlier work reflects Sheraton's patterns.

Instead of English Regency, America was attracted to the bulky and showy Napoleonic Empire style. Furniture became increasingly gross in the late Empire period: Duncan Phyfe scathingly called it "butcher furniture". In New York Charles-Honoré Lannuier made highly elaborate pieces in a mixture of Directoire and Empire idioms.

By contrast, the furniture made in the 19th C by the Shakers, a celibate sect, was lean and functional, and usually of pine, maple, walnut or fruitwoods. Shaker chairs are distinguished by the slenderness of their posts.

In the later part of the century some exuberant works of great individuality, though often with similarities to revivalist English Victorian designs, were produced. John Belter, who opened a shop in New York in 1844, was an important manufacturer who created an elaborately carved variant of neo-rococo using bentwood (plywood bent into curves by steam). Belter is best known for his "parlour suites". At least two of his competitors, Charles A.

Baudouine and Joseph Meeks, copied his technique and style. Alexandre Roux, in New York, drew upon a vast range of historical themes. From the 1840s cast-iron furniture, now much collected, was made.

CHINA AND JAPAN

China. The flimsy, frivolous pastiche of Chinese taste we call *chinoiserie* bears little relation to the well-made, solid furniture with which the Chinese surrounded themselves.

The best surviving Chinese work dates from the 15th–18th C. Modern taste goes for pieces in plain polished hardwood with very little fancy decoration—mainly in rosewood and a greyish-brown timber which the Chinese delightfully called "chicken-wing-wood". Bamboo furniture and insect-resistant lacquered furniture were popular in south China.

The Chinese were expert joiners. Construction was entirely by mortise-and-tenon joints, dovetailing and a little glue. The joints are usually concealed. (Nails or dowels indicate later repair work.) Veneers are rare, but coloured woods were often used in combination.

Furniture was designed to be set against the walls. The Chinese tucked their possessions away: hence a wide variety of chests and cupboards. (4) Chairs are of three kinds: a box-frame base with a straight back and arms (6); a box frame with swinging curved back (called an "abbot's chair"); and a collapsible type with round or straight back. Although the Chinese taste was generally for plainness, some lavish lacquer furniture was made for palaces in the 17th and 18th C. From the late 17th C the lacquered screens known to us as "Coromandel" screens were made.

Japan. Japanese furniture was moveable—even the fireplace was replaced in Japan by a charcoal burner that could be moved around the room. Walls were also moveable, and consisted of a paper-covered framework. As in China, screens were an important ingredient of interior design. They were made of strong paper, were generally about 1.5m high, and some were exquisitely decorated by painters such as Maruyama Ōkyō. (3) Free-standing furniture was in general small and of lacquered wood. Japanese lacquer is of unrivalled quality, but standards declined sharply after *c*.1870 in the mass of pieces made for export to Europe.

Oriental furniture, 17th–19th C

1 Chinese lacquer table, 18th c
🅑 G
2 Chinese trestle-type side table, 17th-18th c 🅑 I
3 Japanese screen, painted by Maruyama Ōkyō V🅡 G
4 Japanese chest of drawers, late 16th c V🅡 I
5 Marble-top table, south-west

China, *c*.1650 🅕🅒 F
6 Chinese mother-of-pearl inlaid rosewood armchair 🅒 E

POTTERY
= & =
PORCELAIN

The collector must learn at the outset to distinguish between pottery and porcelain. Pottery is opaque when held to the light: porcelain is translucent. The only minor difficulty is that some types of stoneware (a hard non-porous pottery) are also slightly translucent.

Hard-paste and soft-paste porcelain

The ingredients of hard-paste (or true) porcelain, which was first made in China, are kaolin (white china clay) and a feldspathic rock, *petuntse*. Before firing, the paste is usually covered with a feldspathic glaze. Unglazed white porcelain is known as "biscuit". All Chinese and much continental porcelain (after the secret was discovered at Meissen in the early 18th C) are hard-paste. But most 18th-C English porcelain, and early Sèvres, are soft-paste: the various formulae, devised in an attempt to imitate the Chinese, involved a mixture of clay and ground glass.

The ability to differentiate the two porcelain types is crucial. The glaze on soft-paste lies *on* the paste instead of being fused *into* it: it is therefore thicker and inclined to gather in hollows or to crack or craze. Soft-paste often has air mixed up in the body, showing as paler patches ("moons") when held to the light. Unglazed areas of soft-paste are porous: this can be tested using a dot of ink.

Glazes and decoration

Lead glazes were general until the end of the 19th C, except on salt-glazed stoneware and hard-paste porcelain. They can be made opaque by the addition of tin oxide, producing a pottery type that has a variety of names depending on country of origin: delft (Holland and England), faience (France, Germany and Scandinavia) and maiolica (Italy).

The application of relief decoration to the surface of a piece is called "sprigging". Slip (diluted clay) was often trailed freehand on pottery for decorative effect. *Sgraffito* is a technique of cutting through a covering of slip to expose the body underneath. Decoration on both pottery and porcelain frequently took the form of painting in enamels, or transfer printing, before addition of the glaze. Embellishment could also be "overglaze".

Copies and forgeries

The commonest deception in ceramics concerns marks (see pp 180–81 for a selection of these). A notorious bogey is Samson of Paris, a skilled 19th-C copyist. Today his pieces have a *cachet* of their own, but the Samson mark has often been removed by another hand, and a forged 18th-C mark substituted.

Commonly copied types of European ceramics include Sèvres, Chelsea and tin-glazed earthenware.

BRITISH POTTERY

Slipwares. The earliest commonly surviving English slipware (red earthenware decorated with a diluted clay) dates from the 17th C. Most surviving examples are from Staffordshire, some from London and from Wrotham, Kent. A few large dishes decorated in trailed slip bear the name of Thomas Toft and a date in the 1670s. Designs on dishes include lions, mermaids and Adam and Eve. The ornamental use of freely trailed slip (2) gave way in the 1720s to a method by which wares were press-moulded and coloured slip received into a recessed design. "Marbled" and "feathered" slipwares also became common. (1)

Stonewares. At a time when true porcelain was being made only in China, John Dwight experimented with porcellaneous stoneware at his factory at Fulham, London (founded c.1672), although his main output was red unglazed and grey salt-glazed stoneware. He made wine bottles, "Bellarmines" (pear-shaped wine jugs with a moulded mask on the neck) and some excellent figures.

Staffordshire produced brown salt-glazed stoneware from the end of the 17th C, and white salt-glazed stoneware mainly in the period 1740–60. (5) Early wares are often enlivened with stamped reliefs. A simple incised decoration was sometimes used, the incisions filled in with blue pigment to create a type known as "scratch blue". (7) Some relief-decorated stoneware in eccentric shapes (e.g. camel teapots) was produced by slip casting in plaster moulds. A brilliant palette of enamel colours was available.

Elers, Astbury and Whieldon wares. John Philip and David Elers came to England from Holland in 1686. They made a fine red stoneware at Bradwell Wood, Staffordshire (c.1694–1700). The legend that John Astbury (1686–1743) feigned idiocy to learn the Elers' secrets is myth, but he certainly made similar wares. Teapots and jugs of the Astbury type, in red, buff or black clay ornamented with applied white sprigs and then lead-glazed, survive in considerable quantity (3), but figures (from c.1730) are rare and commonly forged.

English pottery, 17th and 18th C

1 Marbled slipware honey pot, c.1690–1700, ht 15.2cm ◨ *E*
2 Slipware tyg (multiple-handled beaker), Wrotham, 1711, ht 17.1cm ◨ *F*
3 Astbury-type jug, c.1745, ht 11.4cm ◨ *E*
4 Wedgwood-Whieldon pineapple teapot, c.1760–65 ◨ ९ *E*

5 Staffordshire salt-glazed teapot, c.1730 ▣ *E*
6 Whieldon cow creamer, c.1750–60 ◨ ९ ▭ *B*
7 Salt-glazed puzzle jug with "scratch-blue" decoration, c.1750–60 ◨ *E*

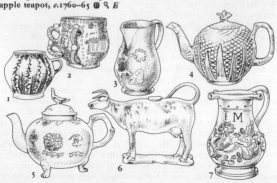

The variegated wares usually called "Whieldon" were made by Thomas Whieldon of Fenton (active 1740–80) and by numerous imitators. His products included marbled "agateware" teapots, milk jugs and cow creamers (6), and "tortoiseshell" plates and dishes, as well as the now rare groups and figures. Josiah Wedgwood partnered Whieldon from 1754 to 1759 and revived the use of a brilliant green glaze, employed on "pineapple" and "cauliflower" pieces. (4)

Josiah Wedgwood. Josiah Wedgwood (1730–95) revolutionized English ceramics manufacture—by whole-hogging neo-classicism and by manufacturing improvements. He is best known for the rather insipid blue and white "jasper" stoneware, but also made "black basaltes" (unglazed black stoneware), "Etruscan" wares painted with red figures on a black ground, creamware (creamy white earthenware with a transparent glaze) and jaspers in lilac, yellow, sage-green and black. (14) Creamware (Queen's ware) was decorated with transfer printing by Sadler & Green, and later with enamelling; it sounded the death-knell of the tin-enamel industry. (8; p 109, no. 2) Wedgwood employed some fine neo-classical artists (e.g. Flaxman) to design the reliefs for his wares. He also made portrait cameos. Most Wedgwood pieces are plainly marked. "Wedgwood & Bentley" was used on many ornamental wares from 1769 to 1780, while other pieces were marked simply "Wedgwood". "England" or "Made in England" appears on pieces after 1891.

The Wood family and Prattware. The Wood family of Burslem, Staffordshire, are famous for their figures. Most sought are those of Ralph Wood (1715–72), covered with coloured lead glazes in a way that resembles enamelling. His son, also Ralph (1748–95), actually used enamels instead of glazes. (12) Enoch Wood (1759–1840) produced portrait busts of the famous, basaltes, blue-printed earthenware for America, and enamel-decorated figures.

The name of Felix Pratt of Fenton is associated, often inaccurately, with many attractive figures, jugs, Toby jugs and other wares decorated in high-temperature underglaze enamels and produced from c.1780 to 1820.

Leeds, Liverpool and Bristol. The Leeds Pottery, from c.1770, is best known for its creamware. Enamelling was practised by decorators such as David Rhodes. Many figures were produced from 1790 to 1800, mostly in pearlware—a form of creamware with bluish glaze. (9) Transfer printing was in use by 1780. The factory also made elaborately pierced wares, including epergnes.

Creamware was also manufactured at Liverpool, where the Herculaneum factory was set up in 1796. Bristol produced creamware from c.1785.

English delft. English delft—earthenware with a white opaque tin glaze—was produced in England long before similar wares were made in the Dutch town of Delft. The earliest English use of tin-enamel is a group of jugs ("Malling jugs") of the mid-16th C. Some, in a Rhenish style, have a blue ground flecked with orange and are referred to as "Tygerware".

The delft industry proper seems to have been started at Norwich in 1567 by two Flemish potters, Jacob Jansen and Jasper Andries. The Norwich pottery continued until 1696 or later. About 1571 Jansen moved to Aldgate, London. By c.1620 there is evidence of other Flemish potters active in this area. The earliest specimen of this group of wares is a dish dated 1600 which has blue dashes round the rim—the first of the so-called "blue-dash chargers".

About 1620–25 a different kind of delftware began to be made at Southwark, London. Small barrel-shaped jugs, posset pots, wine bottles and dishes were decorated in blue and manganese in

English pottery, 18th and 19th C

10 **Bristol delft flower brick,** *c.*1740 ® ♀ *D*

11 **Bristol delft plate,** *c.*1750–70 ® ♀ *C*

12 **Figure of Neptune by Ralph Wood,** *c.*1770–80, ht 27.3cm ® *E*

13 **Japanese-inspired stoneware jug,** Staffordshire, 1877, ht 20.3cm FC *C*

14 **Wedgwood jasper "Pegasus" vase,** *c.*1787, ht 61cm FC *E*

15 **Minton majolica asparagus dish,** 1871 FC *B*

8 **Wedgwood transfer-printed creamware tea caddy,** *c.*1780–85, ht 11.4cm FC *C*

9 **Pearlware bust of "Air",** Leeds, 1790, ht 16.5cm ® *C*

imitation of Ming porcelain (p 109, no. 3). The Southwark potteries, and that at Aldgate, were the origin of later factories at Lambeth, Bristol and Liverpool. Common London products of the 17th C are white-glazed wine bottles inscribed with their contents in blue. Puzzle jugs with perforated necks were made, as were mugs, wine cups, bleeding bowls, apothecaries' jars and barbers' bowls.

As cultural links between England and Holland increased in the late 17th C, Dutch delft influenced English. A strong source of inspiration now, as on Dutch wares, was Chinese porcelain. (11) The early 18th-C tea-drinking vogue spawned teapots, cups and saucers, caddies and sugar bowls, sometimes following silver forms. A popular form of English delftware is the flower brick, a rectangular vase. (10)

Painting on Bristol wares is sometimes complemented by *bianco sopra bianco* borders, decorated in white on a pale grey or lavender glaze. Transfer printing on delftware was a Liverpool development. Production of delftware ceased by *c.*1790.

Nineteenth-century pottery. The early 19th C was the great period of blue and white transfer-printed earthenware from Staffordshire, depicting topographical views or architectural fantasies. Josiah Spode's factory at Stoke was notable for this type of ware. During the partnership there of Copeland and Garrett (1833–47) many pieces were decorated with Italian scenes. Multicolour transfer printing was introduced by F. & R. Pratt of Fenton.

A popular 19th-C medium was white stoneware protected with a smear of lead-glaze. Another much-used technique was slip casting. From the early years of the century, lustre wares, using gold and platinum to create a metallic lustrous effect, were

29

produced at a number of factories in England and Wales. In Sunderland, County Durham, which is especially associated with pink lustre, pieces were transfer-printed with views of the famous iron bridge over the River Wear.

The "Rockingham" glaze, a deep brown containing manganese, probably originated at the Rockingham factory, Swinton, but was extensively used elsewhere. In the 1840s F. & R. Pratt, and Dillwyn & Co. of Swansea, made wares in imitation of red-figure Greek (which they called "Etruscan"). Wedgwood continued to make neo-classical jasper with white decoration, of slightly cruder workmanship than the 18th-C examples. From 1858 to 1875 they employed the Frenchman Emile Lessore as decorator; his work, invariably signed, is highly desirable.

The 1860s' vogue for neo-Renaissance motifs was particularly in evidence at Minton's, where an "Henri II" ware of inlaid coloured clays was made. Maiolica was also imitated, notably by Minton under the direction of Léon Arnoux. The Victorians used the word "majolica", confusingly, to refer to earthenware decorated with coloured glazes. Vegetable dishes, fruit stands, umbrella stands and countless other objects fall under this heading. (15) Like Victorian tiles (p 112, no. 3), these wares still can be collected fairly cheaply.

Doulton & Watts at Lambeth, London (founded 1815), concentrated in their early years on modest salt-glazed stoneware and terracotta pieces. Salt-glazed stoneware was revived in the early 1870s under Henry Doulton.

A popular area for today's collectors is the naïve Staffordshire flat-back figures made from c.1837. Subjects include Garibaldi, Dick Turpin, Prince Albert and countless soppy dogs.

Art pottery. An artist potter was one who followed his own bent, free of the dictates of the factory system. The first English art pottery was salt-glazed stoneware decorated in the Doulton factory, Lambeth, from 1871 by students of the Lambeth School of Art. From about the same time the Martin brothers made their extraordinary wares, including weird "face jugs" and bird jugs. William Morris's disciple, William De Morgan, made highly inventive lustre wares, usually in red. The Della Robbia pottery at Birkenhead, Cheshire (1894–1906), specialized in painted and *sgraffito* decoration. Arty experiments were made with glazes, especially by W. Howson Taylor, whose "Ruskin" pottery, made near Birmingham (1898–1935), was often very beautiful. James Macintyre & Co. of Burslem made art pottery known as "Florian ware" under the direction of William Moorcroft.

BRITISH PORCELAIN

Chelsea. The Chelsea Works, probably the first English porcelain factory, was set up c.1745 by Nicholas Sprimont, a silversmith from Flanders. A fine soft-paste body was used, at first very glassy. Most Chelsea fetches extremely high prices.

During the Triangle Period (c.1745–49) an incised triangle was the mark. (1) Modelling was rather coarse. Occasionally, decoration in the Meissen style was crudely applied. The translucent body shows "pin-hole" imperfections when held to a strong light.

In the Raised Anchor Period (1749–53) the glaze was cloudier, and "pin-holes" gave way to "moons" (translucent patches), common until c.1755. Wares were mostly simple in form, the decoration often based on Japanese Kakiemon designs. (2) Joseph Willems modelled Chelsea figures from c.1749, many copied from Meissen.

In the Red Anchor Period (1753–8) the anchor was painted in red instead of being embossed. The glaze was now whiter. Flower

English porcelain, 18th C

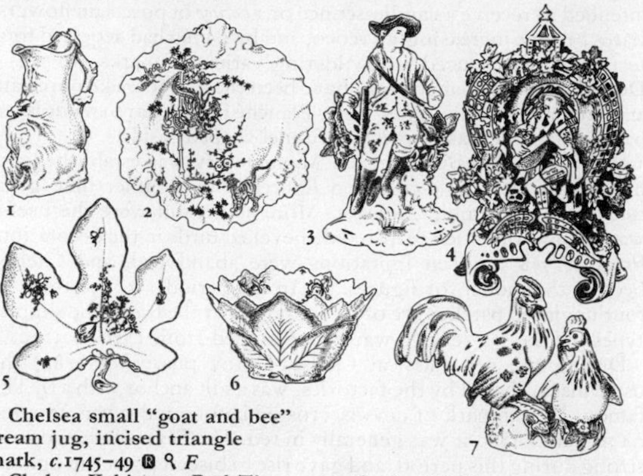

1 Chelsea small "goat and bee" cream jug, incised triangle mark, *c*.1745–49 B *F*
2 Chelsea Kakiemon Red Tiger pattern plate, raised anchor period, 1752 B *F*
3 Derby sportsman, *c*.1765–70, ht 15.2cm FC *D*
4 Chelsea arbour candlestick figure, gold anchor mark, *c*.1760–65 B *F*
5 Bow "fig leaf" dish, *c*.1760, lgth 24.8cm B *E*
6 Longton Hall bowl, *c*.1755 FC *E*
7 Bow cock and hen, *c*.1755–60, ht 8.9cm VR *F*

painting based on Meissen was practised, but also some original botanical designs. The influence of Vincennes/Sèvres began to make itself felt in 1755–6, for example in crimson monochrome landscapes. Tureens were realistically modelled as vegetables, animals, fish and birds. (p 108, no. 2)

French styles predominated in the Gold Anchor Period (1758–70). Bone-ash was added to the paste, reducing its translucency. The glaze was thick but clear, giving a "wet look", and had a tendency to craze. The period was one of rococo excess, with elaborate gilding. New colours included a rich underglaze blue and the "claret" ground imitating the *rose Pompadour* of Sèvres. Figures, surrounded by a mass of leaves and flowers (*bocage*), stood on scrolled rococo bases. (4) (Numerous copies were issued by Samson of Paris, though always of *hard*-paste porcelain.) Many delightful miniatures were produced, e.g. scent bottles.

The factory changed hands in 1769 and again in 1770, when it passed to William Duesbury of Derby. From this time until closure in 1784 is the Chelsea-Derby period, when Derby styles were followed.

Bow. Bow was the first "bone china", containing the ash of burnt bones. The factory was founded *c*.1746. Some of the earliest wares are inscribed "Made at New Canton" and dated 1750 or 1751.

Oriental-style tableware in underglaze blue was made in quantity, but brilliant enamels were also used. A popular enamel pattern was the "Quail" or "Partridge" based on the Japanese Kakiemon manner. From the earliest years the *blanc de Chine* style was practised, with applied prunus blossoms on a white ground. Other *chinoiserie* designs include the peony and fence, and the cross-legged Chinaman. From *c*.1759 some wares had a powder-blue ground decorated with scenes or motifs in a round or fan-shaped panel. Transfer printing was done by Robert Hancock.

Early Bow figures, generally left white, include Muses and popular actors and actresses. In the greatest period (1755–60) figures displayed lively modelling and colouring, but often imitated Meissen. Some figures have a square hole at the back, intended to receive a candle-sconce or a *bocage* of porcelain flowers. Bases became increasingly rococo, and by *c.*1760 had acquired four feet. The factory used a bewildering variety of marks. (6, 7)

Derby. Andrew Planché may have been the first to make porcelain at Derby in the early 1750s. Early Planché figures have an unglazed band round the base, which is funnel-shaped inside.

In 1756 the Derby Porcelain Manufactory was established. Its first wares were pale-coloured figures with a rather blue glaze intended to resemble Meissen. More successful were the useful wares, some of which featured dishevelled birds in the decoration. From *c.*1758 Meissen imitations were abandoned, and Chelsea became the model for figures. (3) In the period 1755–70 three or four unglazed patches are often found under the base. The simpler types of Chelsea service-ware were copied from 1756 to 1760.

During the neo-classical Chelsea-Derby phase (1770–84) the usual mark, shared by the factories, was a gilt anchor with a D. The famous Derby mark of crown, crossed batons and D was adopted *c.*1782; after 1800 it was generally in red. The Sèvres influence was strong during this period, and gave rise to biscuit porcelain figures, and to tableware decorated with swags and festoons. (p 108, no. 4)

The main modellers were Pierre Stéphan and J.-J. Spängler. The most important flower-painter was William Billingsley.

In 1815 the factory was leased to Robert Bloor, who went in for showy "Japan" patterns. The term "Bloor Derby" is used for wares up to 1848, though Bloor went mad in 1826.

Longton Hall. Longton Hall (*c.*1749–60) brought porcelain making into Staffordshire. Much of its porcelain is heavy but surprisingly translucent. Wares include leaf dishes, tureens, sauceboats and teapots imitating fruits or vegetables. (5) Decoration was often in bright colours, and handles were generally inelegant. Some finer porcelain was also made in the Meissen style. A few wares were transfer-printed at Liverpool. Underglaze blue was sometimes used.

Lumpy figures ("Snowmen") were made in the early period. Later figures had scrolled bases picked out in red. The mark of a crossed L was sometimes applied, usually in blue. Longton Hall is eagerly sought and highly priced.

Lund's Bristol and Worcester. A soft-paste porcelain using soapstone was made after 1748 by Benjamin Lund's Bristol factory. (The few pieces that survive are Chinese-style figures and a handful of sauceboats and creamboats.) The enterprise was absorbed in 1752 by the Worcester Porcelain Co., which took over the Bristol moulds.

The early phase (1751–76) at Worcester is referred to as the Dr Wall Period. Most pieces of this time were based on silver or on Chinese porcelain. Enamelling was practised, but the most popular decoration for Chinese-style wares was underglaze blue. (15) Pseudo-Chinese marks were sometimes used. A Worcester version of *famille rose* was adopted by 1760. Transfer-printed wares, dating from 1757, became very popular. (8)

Rococo whimsicality expressed itself in leaf-form dishes, cabbage-leaf jugs and the rare cauliflower tureens. In the early 1760s some elaborate painting was done in London in the atelier of James Giles, where fruit, ruffled birds and dishevelled tulips were painted on. (14) Such decoration was applied to blank panels on wares already partly decorated in underglaze blue. These pre-decorated areas were commonly given an effect of overlapping scales (much reproduced by Samson of Paris). The Sèvres influence, potent from 1770 to 1784, led to rich and various ground colours and elaborate gilding. Topographical representations are characteristic of the late 18th C. Worcester figures are extremely rare.

Until 1783 Worcester was thinly potted, with a glaze that suffered from crazing. By transmitted light the body colour is often greenish, sometimes orange, and later sometimes grey.

The period 1776–93 is the Davis & Flight Period, succeeded by the Flight & Barr phase when an incised B mark was sometimes used. The impressed mark of B.F.B. (Barr, Flight & Barr) under a crown was in use from 1807 to 1813. The final period of these bewildering partnerships was Flight, Barr & Barr, continuing until 1840, when Robert Chamberlain (who had set up a rival establishment c.1786) took over. (13) In 1801 a third Worcester factory was established by Thomas Grainger. From 1852 to 1862 the original works was run by Kerr & Binns. Fine decoration was carried out at this time by Thomas Bott, who imitated Limoges enamels.

English porcelain, 18th and 19th C

8 Worcester mug, transfer-printed by Robert Hancock, c.1763 FC D
9 Lowestoft blue and white printed "sparrow-beak" creamjug, c.1778 FC C
10 Liverpool blue and white coffee cup and saucer, Chaffers' factory, c.1758 B E
11 Caughley blue and white transfer-printed dish, c.1785–90, lgth 26cm FC C
12 Plymouth *famille verte* coffee cup, c.1770 B B
13 Chamberlain's Worcester scent bottle, decorated with shells and seaweed on a gilt seaweed ground, c.1835 FC D
14 Large Worcester blue-scale "cabbage leaf" jug, painted in the atelier of James Giles, c.1765–70 ʔ F

Liverpool. Useful blue and white porcelain was a main product of Liverpool. The characteristic bluish glaze commonly formed a pool on the underside of the base—the "thundercloud" effect. Richard Chaffers, by 1756, was producing Worcester-like porcelain. His most common type was a bulbous mug enamelled with a Chinese scene. The factory passed to Philip Christian & Son in 1769.

James, John and Seth Pennington made bowls and other wares painted in a "sticky" blue. Transfer printing is often found in a dark shade of red. (10)

Caughley and Coalport. The Caughley Works, Shropshire, was run from 1772 by Thomas Turner. Most of the soft-paste wares made from this date were blue and white in poorish imitation of Worcester. Two shades of blue are typical, one greyish, the other raucously violet. Under Turner's proprietorship the Willow Pattern and the Broseley Blue Dragon were introduced, based on Chinese models. The commonest Caughley mark was a C, often drawn to look like a Worcester crescent. The impressed word "Salopian" was also used. (11)

John Rose bought the factory in 1799 and used it to supply his

Coalport factory (founded *c.*1796) with biscuit porcelain for glazing and decorating. Coalport wares were based on Sèvres, Dresden and Chelsea. Highly modelled painted flowers were a theme until 1850.

Lowestoft. Porcelain containing bone-ash was made at Lowestoft, East Anglia, from 1757 until 1799. The paste was similar to that of Bow, though the glaze was thinner. Until *c.*1770, when enamel colours became common, wares were decorated only in underglaze blue. Many pieces bear initials and dates, and sometimes the words "A Trifle from Lowestoft". Oriental designs and marine views were frequent. The range included tea caddies, openwork baskets, cabbage-leaf jugs, mugs with double-twisted handles, globular teapots, toy tea services, and commemorative jugs, punch bowls and plaques. Cream jugs with "sparrow-beak" spouts have a curved "tail" at the base of the handle and a mound in the centre of the inside base. (9) A few figures were made.

Plymouth and Bristol. Plymouth and Bristol were the first two of the three English hard-paste factories. William Cookworthy discovered the raw materials of real porcelain in the late 1740s. He took out a patent for his Coxside factory, near Plymouth, in 1768. The undertaking was transferred to Bristol in 1770.

Mugs are among the best-known Plymouth products. Moulded sauceboats were made, many based on rococo silverware. Other types include vases (some hexagonal), shell-form pieces, tea and coffee pots, leaf-shaped pickle trays and a few figures, most imitating Bow and Longton Hall. Plates and saucers are rare. Oriental decoration in a greyish underglaze blue is quite frequent. Handles on Bristol and Plymouth porcelain are often slightly awry. (12)

Bristol made mainly domestic wares, the most frequently surviving being cups and saucers. A spiralled effect in the paste ("wreathing") is common. Enamelled decoration includes the distinctive "Bristol green". The gilding was outstanding. Flowers were the favourite ornamental motif. Teapots commonly took the form of an inverted pear. Bristol biscuitware is rare and much prized.

New Hall. In 1781 Richard Champion sold his patent to make hard-paste to a group of Staffordshire potters. Some of these seceded and, after a false start, operations were moved to Shelton in the Potteries. Hard-paste porcelain was manufactured here, at the New Hall factory, until *c.*1810, when manufacture of bone china was substituted (until 1835). (17)

The New Hall paste is similar to Bristol's and also subject to "wreathing"; but the glaze is quite different—soft, oily, gathering in hollows. Output was largely of useful wares. Flowers were the commonest form of decoration, but pseudo-oriental patterns were also used. Pattern numbers occur on hard-paste porcelain, while on bone china the mark of "New Hall" in a double circle is commonly found.

Nantgarw and Swansea. The Nantgarw factory, Cardiff, was founded by William Billingsley in 1813. The business was later transferred to Swansea, but Billingsley returned to Nantgarw in 1816 and kept the place going until 1820. The paste, white and translucent, was comparable to that of Sèvres, which was a major influence. Most pieces were sent to London for decoration. Nantgarw products are now scarce. (16)

Porcelain was made at Swansea for a few years only at the beginning of the 19th C, some exquisitely painted with flowers by Billingsley. After 1817 Swansea produced an inferior porcelain with tiny depressions in the glaze. Pieces made to this formula were often marked with crossed tridents. (15)

Rockingham. The Bramelds' factory at Swinton, Yorkshire, was subsidized from 1826 by Earl Fitzwilliam, whose crest, a griffin

English and Welsh porcelain, 19th C

15 Swansea cabinet cup and saucer, 1814–22 [FC] D
16 Nantgarw spill vase, perhaps painted by William Billingsley, c.1813–20 [FC] D
17 New Hall bone-china cup and saucer with pink lustre, c.1815 [FC] C
18 Minton pâte sur pâte vase and cover, by A. Morgan, ht 41cm [FC] F

19 Coalport potpourri vase, ht 46.5cm [FC] E
20 Rockingham cinquefoil dish, c.1826–30, width 25cm [R] E

passant, was used as a mark. The name "Rockingham" henceforth adopted referred to the late Marquis from whom the Earl had inherited his estate. From 1820 to 1842 excellent china was made, using bone-ash paste. The decoration, often highly ambitious, was asymmetrically rococo, with copious gilding. A great dessert service made for William IV bears views of castles and country seats—a favourite Rockingham theme. Tablewares were often decorated with flowers on a pale green ground. Figures (made 1826–30) are very rare. (20)

Other nineteenth-century porcelain. The main 19th-C developments in porcelain were the pâte sur pâte (decoration built up by the application of layers of white slip on a dark ground) introduced by M.-L. Solon at Minton's (18); the neo-rococo style, especially favoured at Coalport (19); and "Parian" ware, a white biscuit resembling marble and much used for small-scale statuary at Copeland's, Minton's and elsewhere. Belleek (County Fermanagh, Northern Ireland) produced a horrible (but collected) version of Parian ware with a slimy iridescent glaze.

The biggest stylistic innovation of the second half of the century came with the Japanese exhibits at the 1862 Exhibition in London. This, at the Royal Worcester factory, inspired pieces made in an ivory-tinted body to resemble "Satsuma" ware. (See also p 51.)

FRENCH FAIENCE

Nevers and Rouen. Early decorative French pottery was mostly tin-glazed earthenware (faience). The best-known faïencier of the early period, working in the Italianate style, was Masseot Abaquesne of Rouen, who from c.1530 made tile pavements for château-owners. He also made drug jars in cool blues and yellows. (4) At Lyons, in the late 16th C, wares were produced that bore a confusing similarity to Urbino maiolica.

Only at Nevers was the Italian tradition translated into something distinctively French. (3) The pictorial style of Urbino was continued there until *c.*1650, but thereafter a joint influence came from baroque silverware and Chinese porcelain. Decoration was applied in colours that included pale blue, orange and yellow, but never red. One well-known style was *bleu persan*—a cobalt-blue ground decorated in white, or sometimes white, orange and yellow, with orientalized birds, flowers or figures. Faience at Nevers reached its height in the early 18th C. By the late 18th C only cheap, popular wares were produced, some decorated with Revolutionary slogans.

In 1647 Edmé Poterat's factory at Rouen was granted a 50-year monopoly in Normandy. When the period expired the number of factories increased to 18. Few of these Rouen wares were pictorial in the Nevers manner. Poterat's famous contribution was blue and white ware in the *style rayonnant*, with rich borders.

Polychrome faience was popular from *c.*1720 to 1750, and featured naïve *chinoiseries* and flower painting. A yellow ochre ground was developed by 1725. Imitations of Rouen faience were made at factories such as Sinceny, Quimper, St Cloud and Lille.

French faience, 17th and 18th C

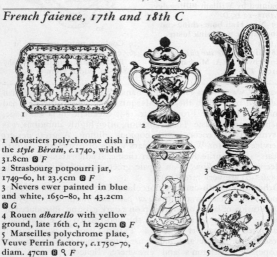

1 **Moustiers polychrome dish in the *style Bérain*, *c.*1740, width 31.8cm ⊗ F**
2 **Strasbourg potpourri jar, 1749–60, ht 23.5cm ⊗ F**
3 **Nevers ewer painted in blue and white, 1650–80, ht 43.2cm ⊗ G**
4 **Rouen *albarello* with yellow ground, late 16th c, ht 29cm ⊗ F**
5 **Marseilles polychrome plate, Veuve Perrin factory, *c.*1750–70, diam. 47cm ⊗ ९ F**

Moustiers and Marseilles. In the south the big factories were at Moustiers and Marseilles. The first factory at Moustiers was started by Pierre Clérissy *c.*1679. Early products include some decorated in high-temperature blue. Hunting-scene borders featured in the decorative repertoire. Later blue and white pieces (*c.*1710–40) are often based on the delicately fantastical designs of Jean Bérain.

Polychrome was practised from 1739 in another Moustiers factory set up by Jean-Baptiste Laugier and Joseph Olerys. Designs were Bérainesque at first, but later progressed to a style in which human or animal figures are loosely disposed among flowers and foliage. (1)

The first Marseilles factory was established in 1679 at St-Jean-du-Désert by Joseph Clérissy. Wares were often very similar to the products of Moustiers or Nevers. At another factory Joseph Fauchier II introduced the idea of painting sparse flowers in high-temperature colours on a soft yellow ground. But the most famous Marseilles product was the beautiful work in low-temperature enamels done after *c.*1750, most strikingly by the Veuve (Widow) Perrin, who represented flowers, fish and seaweed in a free, unacademic style. (5; p 110, no. 3) Marseilles faience, especially with the mark "VP", has often been forged.

Strasbourg, Niderviller and Sceaux. The factories at Strasbourg (founded 1721) and other places near the German frontier were more strongly affected by the rococo than were Moustiers and Marseilles. In the early Strasbourg period the *style rayonnant* was imitated, with some polychrome and gilding. But in 1748 decorators from Meissen joined the factory, bringing with them the techniques of painting in overglaze enamels and a range of muscular rococo shapes. (2) A common form of flower painting was *fleurs des Indes*, based on the Chinese *famille rose*.

At Niderviller in Lorraine, where faience was produced as well as porcelain, the rococo took a less extreme form than at Strasbourg. An important Parisian manufacture of the late 18th C was Sceaux, which veered from a civilized rococo to neo-classicism. The flower painting here was excellent. Inevitably the decoration shows some cribbing from nearby Sèvres.

FRENCH PORCELAIN

St Cloud. The St Cloud soft-paste factory was begun by *c.*1700. Its heyday was *c.*1725–50. Early wares have a greenish glaze. Decoration was often blue, in the *style rayonnant*. (1) Other decorative forms were applied prunus blossom (as on Chinese *blanc de Chine*) and a scaled pattern suggestive of the artichoke. Cups were made with saucers which had a raised ring to stop the cup from wobbling—*trembleuses*. Teapot spouts and handles had amusing animal and bird heads. Many shapes were based on silver originals. Spice boxes and unpainted "Chinese" figures were

---

French porcelain, 18th and 19th C

1 St Cloud spice box decorated in underglaze blue, *c.*1710 Ⓡ *F*
2 Chantilly teapot in the Kakiemon style, *c.*1735 Ⓡ *F*
3 Chantilly figure of a lady, *c.*1760, ht 23.5 cm Ⓡ *E*
4 Mennecy polychrome custard cup, *c.*1755 Ⓡ *E*
5 Vincennes or Sèvres group of "Grape-eaters" in soft-paste

biscuit, after 1752, ht 24 cm
ⒻⒸ ♀ *E*
6 Sèvres *trembleuse* with *bleu de roi* ground, *c.*1776 Ⓡ *E*
7 Sèvres vase in the Boucher style, 19th c ⒻⒸ *D*

---

among the St Cloud wares. Figures are rare. (p 111, no. 2)

Chantilly. Louis-Henri de Bourbon, Prince de Condé, had a large collection of Japanese porcelain in his château at Chantilly, and wanted a porcelain factory of his own. He got it in 1725 when a man named Ciquaire Cirou brought him the St Cloud secret. Not surprisingly, Japanese porcelain exercised a strong influence over Chantilly. Many motifs were taken from the Kakiemon style, including the "Partridge", "Banded Hedge" and "Squirrel". (2)

The Japanese phase ended *c.*1740, after which Meissen was the main inspiration. It was a blow to Chantilly when the royal Vincennes factory was given a monopoly in porcelain production. Chantilly did not fully obey the edict but reverted to monochrome so as not to attract the royal wrath. Underglaze decoration of small blue flower sprays (the "Chantilly sprig") became popular, especially on plates with moulded basketwork borders. (3)

Mennecy. The Mennecy soft-paste factory was founded in 1734. Early wares resemble St Cloud, though the glaze is smoother and wet-looking and the body a darker ivory. The mature style was chiefly inspired by Vincennes.

The commonest surviving of the Mennecy types are small custard cups and covers painted with flower sprays. (4) Small boxes were made, sometimes in animal shapes. Figures were both glazed and in biscuit, some of the finest made by Nicolas-François Gauron.

Vincennes-Sèvres. In 1738 the Dubois brothers, Gilles and Robert, arrived in Vincennes from Chantilly. They set up a factory in the old royal château. This was unsuccessful, but in 1745 a new company was established which was granted a 20-year monopoly to produce porcelain. In 1753 the enterprise was renamed "Manufacture Royale" (and five years later became sole property of Louis XV). A factory mark of two interlaced Ls was introduced, supplemented by a date letter (A for 1753, B for 1754 etc.; AA for 1778, BB for 1779 etc.). In 1756 the site was moved to Sèvres.

The early speciality was exquisitely moulded porcelain flowers. Jardinières, jugs, ice pails and trays were also made. The first of the many famous ground colours was a slightly uneven *bleu lapis* (sometimes known as *gros bleu*). After 1752 production changed towards silver-pattern wares, with a continuing influence from Chantilly. *Bleu celeste* (turquoise) was used as a ground from 1752, yellow from 1753, violet and green from 1756, *rose Pompadour* from 1757 and an even *bleu de roi* from 1763. Gilt patterns were used to break up these grounds. (6; p 110, no. 4)

The Sèvres style was the antithesis of Louis XIV baroque. Making love, not war, was now the theme. J.-J. Bachelier, art director from 1751 to 1793, enlisted the services of Boucher, who painted putti in monochrome. Pretty flowers and birds were favoured. More elaborate painting of the later period included Meissen-inspired shipping and harbour scenes. The Sèvres range included complete services (from 1753), tea sets, potpourri vases, toilet ware and clock cases. (7)

The earliest Vincennes figures were glazed: they are now very rare. Most figures after 1751 were left in biscuit. (5) The influence of Boucher on early biscuit groups of children and pastorals was felt until the arrival, in 1757, of the modeller E. M. Falconet, who looked back to the masters of the baroque.

From the early 1770s Sèvres introduced a hard-paste porcelain. New ground colours were devised: brown, black and a dark blue. An innovation of the 80s was the fusing of translucent enamels over silver or gilt foil. Decoration by this time was purely neo-classical. Biscuit reliefs in the Wedgwood style were moulded from *c.*1785. During the First Republic a popular form of ornament was

Revolutionary emblems. (p 110, no. 1)

Sèvres forgeries are usually well marked, especially with an early date letter, which may not tie in with the style of decoration. There are more copied pieces than genuine pieces, so the collector must be especially wary.

Nineteenth-century porcelain. A hard-paste factory was set up at Fontainebleau in 1795. Jacob and Mardochée Petit operated here from 1830, producing vulgarized neo-rococo wares, usually with poor-quality gilding.

GERMAN POTTERY

Hafner ware. From the 16th C to the early 17th, *Hafner* ware was produced in Germany. The word means stove-maker but refers to a class of lead-glazed pottery embracing not only stove tiles but vessels made in a similar way, such as round-bellied jugs on which an ornamental pattern of raised lines kept the coloured glazes from merging.

Stoneware. An early Germanic contribution to ceramics was salt-glazed stoneware. At the Rhineland town of Sieburg, tall, slender jugs (*Jakobakannen*) were made as early as 1400. (1) Other distinctive types were the *Schellen* (tall, cone-like tankards) and the *Schnabelkannen* (long-spouted jugs), both with elaborate relief decoration. Underglaze blue was especially common in the Westerwald potteries. (2)

At Kreussen in Franconia the Vest family made stonewares from the early 16th C. Whereas Kreussen stoneware had a brown or black slip beneath the glaze, in Freiburg and other centres in Saxony this was absent. In the earliest period at Meissen (see below) a fine red stoneware was made.

German faience. Hamburg became a well-known faience centre in the mid-17th C. A factory at Frankfurt had its heyday from *c.*1667 to 1723, producing Chinese-style pieces in the manner of Delft. (4) Faience was also produced at Stockelsdorff, near Lübeck, and at Kellinghusen in Holstein.

German pottery, 15th–19th C

1 *Jakobakanne* stoneware jug, Sieburg, 15th c, ht 26.5cm [FC] *E*

2 Westerwald stoneware jug, *c.*1700, 31cm [FC] *D*
3 Mettlach stoneware stein, *c.*1900, ht 19.5cm [FC] *D*
4 Enamelled faience teapot, Frankfurt-am-Main, *c.*1700 [B] *E*

GERMAN PORCELAIN

Meissen. In 1708 an alchemist named J.F. Böttger achieved a superb white porcelain like the Chinese. Augustus the Strong, his patron, was delighted, and in 1710 founded the Meissen factory, near Dresden, which produced the first hard-paste porcelain in Europe. Its earliest work was based on silver forms. Decoration, often floral, was in primitive enamel colours, gilding or a purplish

39

lustre. At the end of the Böttger period (before 1719) the first *chinoiseries* in gilt silhouette were applied.

From 1720 to *c*.1735 the factory had the services of a brilliant *chinoiserie* artist, J.G. Höroldt. (6; p 110, no. 2) A whiter body was introduced, and a more colourful palette. The Japanese Kakiemon style was an important influence, and the well-known *indianische Blumen* ("Indian flowers") were based on Japanese flower painting. Topographical painting was introduced in the early 1720s. Harbour scenes enjoyed a vogue in the 30s, battles and *commedia dell' arte* scenes in the 40s, pastoral subjects in the 50s. *Deutsche Blumen*, a type of floral decoration based on botanical illustration, were popular after *c*.1735. (1)

In 1727 Meissen hired its first great modeller, J.G. Kirchner, but he was sacked in 1733 and replaced by an even finer modeller, J.J. Kändler, whose work has a marvellous lightness and vivacity. (7) The earliest figures were in strong colour, often with *indianische Blumen* on a gold or black ground. By 1750 the palette was becoming paler, and rococo scrollwork on the bases was soon introduced. The so-called "Academic Period", beginning in 1763, was a neo-classical phase, owing a debt to Sèvres. (8)

The earliest Meissen marks include a pseudo-Chinese square character and "KPM". In 1724 crossed swords became standard. The debased versions of earlier wares made in the 19th C are commonly referred to as "Dresden". (2, 4)

Other porcelain factories. C.K. Hunger from Meissen took the porcelain secret in 1719 to Vienna, where Claudius Du Paquier had

German and Austrian porcelain, 18th and 19th C

1 **Meissen potpourri vase** decorated with *deutsche Blumen*, blue crossed swords mark, mid-19th c ht 35cm FC *E*

2 **Dresden coffee pot**, factory reject, late 19th c, ht 22.4cm FC *C*

3 **Franz Dorfl Vienna plate**, painted by F. Tenner, late 19th c, diam. 25.8cm C *D*

4 **Dresden jay**, mid-19th c C *E*

5 **Nymphenburg mastiff**, perhaps by Bustelli, *c*.1760 B *F*

6 **Meissen** *chinoiserie* **teapot**, painted by J.G. Höroldt, *c*.1723 B *G*

7 **Meissen "crinoline" group**, by J.J. Kändler, B *H*

8 **Meissen oval** *verrière*, *c*.1785 FC *D*

9 **Vienna cup and saucer**, *c*.1785 FC ? *D*

set up a factory. After the concern was sold to the State in 1744, L. Dannhauser and J.J. Niedermeyer modelled some delightful figures. In the late 18th C Sèvres was copied. (3, 9)

Hard-paste was made at Höchst from 1750 to 1796. Tablewares made here were usually accompanied by fanciful scrollwork. Other centres were Frankenthal (1755–1800). Nymphenburg (from 1753), Ludwigsburg (1759–1824), Fürstenberg (from 1753) and Berlin (from 1761). It is the figure modellers who give this group of factories their main distinction. The greatest was Franz Anton Bustelli of Nymphenburg, famous above all for his 16 *commedia dell'arte* figures. His models usually suggest carved wooden prototypes, and have swivelled hips and thin, flat bases. (5)

J.P. Melchior of Höchst, Frankenthal and Nymphenburg—he was engaged at Höchst in 1767 and made its reputation—is best known for his figures of children.

THE NETHERLANDS

Dutch delft. Tin-glazed pottery came to the Netherlands from either Spain or Italy. In 1512 Guido di Savino, from Castel Durante, set up a pottery in Antwerp. By the third quarter of the 16th C tin-glaze potteries were established at Middelburg, Rotterdam, Haarlem, Amsterdam, Dordrecht and Friesland. Large quantities of tiles were made in these places. By the early years of the 17th C there was also some modest production at Delft, which became crucially important by mid-century and gave its name to this type of ware.

Dutch delft, 17th and 18th C

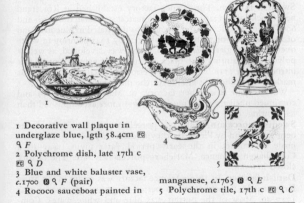

1 Decorative wall plaque in underglaze blue, lgth 58.4cm 🄵🄲 ⚈ *F*
2 Polychrome dish, late 17th c 🄵🄲 ⚈ *D*
3 Blue and white baluster vase, *c.*1700 ⚈ ⚈ *F* (pair)
4 Rococo sauceboat painted in manganese, *c.*1765 ⚈ ⚈ *E*
5 Polychrome tile, 17th c ⚈ *C*

Early among delft wares were "blue-dash" chargers—big dishes with a border of short blue strokes. At this stage only the fronts of dishes were covered in tin glaze; the backs had a thin lead glaze.

At the beginning of the 17th C two shiploads of Chinese porcelain arrived in Amsterdam, and soon the Dutch were trying to copy blue and white wares. Potting became finer, designs more sophisticated. Backs as well as fronts of dishes were now tin-glazed.

During the ascendancy of Delft, outlines in manganese purple (the technique was called *trek*) were added to blue and white wares. A coat of clear lead glaze (*kwaart*) was sometimes superimposed over the tin glaze to give a high gloss resembling porcelain. The finest late 17th-C wares made at Delft were by Samuel van Eenhoorn, most of them fairly accurate copies of the Chinese. The "Greek A" factory run by van Eenhoorn was taken over by Adrianus Kocks, whose "AK" monogram is the most famous—and faked—of all Delft marks. Alongside the Chinese influence, a nationalistic strain also began to appear, in landscape painting and contemporary scenes. By the 1690s European baroque shapes were popular. (p 111, no. 4)

Among the rarest Delft wares are the beautiful pieces made by Rochus Hoppesteyn of the "Young Moor's Head" factory. The products of the De Roos factory (1662–1775) are also among the Delft classics: best known are a series of blue and white plates with New Testament scenes.

Tiles remained the staple product of Delft. (5) They were used not on floors, but for walls and skirting. Biblical scenes were common, executed in manganese purple as well as blue.

Dutch delft was still much in demand in the first half of the 18th C when rococo was assimilated. (4) Polychrome decoration was an 18th-C feature, progressing from high- to low-temperature enamels.

By the 1770s, when loyal tributes to the House of Orange were frequent on delftware, the rivalry of Wedgwood's creamware was making itself felt.

Forged Dutch delft is common. Forgeries made in northern France are convincing, but sometimes the glaze is crazed, as it would not be on the genuine article. Many reproductions sold to tourists are lead-glazed, not tin-glazed.

SCANDINAVIA

Swedish faience. The faience factory established at Rörstrand near Stockholm (1729) enjoyed its greatest success in the 1750s and 60s. The earliest Rörstrand faience was decorated in blue in a kind of *style rayonnant* or with figure subjects. By 1745 painting in white over off-white glaze (*bianco sopra bianco*) was developed, as well as polychrome painting with black outlines. (1) Enamel painting was introduced in 1758. In the early period the factory's output was marked "Stockholm"; after 1758 the mark was "Rörstrand".

Work began at another factory, in Marieberg, in 1759 and continued until 1788. Its modelling was more accomplished than its painting. (4)

Swedish porcelain. Soft-paste porcelain manufacture at Marieberg was begun by Pierre Berthevin (director 1766–69). Mennecy made an impact in the early period, later giving way to a Copenhagen influence. Marieberg porcelain is rare. The factory closed in 1788.

Danish faience. In 1722 a faience factory was set up in the Store Kogensgade, Copenhagen. Its period of greatest prosperity was 1727–49. Most of the output was blue and white wares. Competition, especially from creamware, caused closure in 1769.

Danish porcelain. In 1771 a factory at Copenhagen was established by F.H. Müller. In the early years Germany was the source of both workers and styles. In 1780 the factory became the Royal Danish Porcelain Factory. (2, 5)

Well-modelled figures were a large part of the 18th-C output. After 1867 some fine biscuit figures after the neo-classical sculptor Thorwaldsen were made.

Schleswig-Holstein faience. The factory at Schleswig was begun in 1755. Decoration was characteristically in manganese purple, sometimes with greyish-green. Output included floral-decorated relief-moulded plates and apple tureens.

Scandinavian pottery and porcelain, 18th C

1 Rörstrand faience jar painted in blue and *bianco sopra bianco*, c.1760, ht 40cm ⓑ *F*
2 Copenhagen porcelain teapot with acorn finial, c.1795, Ⓕ ⓒ ♀ *D*
3 Kiel faience cachepôt ⓑ *F*

4 Marieberg white faience sauceboat, 1766 Ⓕ ⓒ *D*
5 Copenhagen porcelain tureen painted in underglaze blue, c.1780–90 Ⓕ ⓒ ♀ *E*
6 Herrebøe faience dish painted in high-temperature blue, c.1765, lgth 55.3cm Ⓕ ⓒ *E*

At Kiel, the best of the Holstein factories, the repertoire of the flower-painters was wider than anywhere in northern Europe. (3) **Norwegian faience.** Peter Hoffnagel found a clay suitable for faience at Herrebøe; production began c.1760 and stopped in 1772. The only colours used were high-temperature blue and manganese, and they were never combined. Various boldly decorated interpretations of the rococo were produced. (6)

ITALY

Italian maiolica. The word maiolica, referring to painted tin-glazed earthenware, is derived from Majorca, whose traders first brought the technique from Spain to Italy. Early maiolica was divided into families. The "green family" has green and purple as the dominant colours, with touches of ochre; while the "relief blue" family is based on cobalt blue, usually with some purple. The typical product of this latter group is the "oak leaf" drug jars of Tuscany. Yellow (from antimony) was discovered by the mid-15th C and was used on some large dishes with borders of Gothicized leaves. From c.1475 Faenza was becoming the major centre of the industry. (1) Early Faenza plaques, dishes and jugs often bore the sacred initials "IHS". The peacock's feather motif was especially popular. The *alla porcellana* design, with blue trailing stems on a white ground, reflected the revelation of Chinese porcelain.

The della Robbia family brought ceramics into the realm of great Renaissance art. Luca (1400–89) decorated large architectural reliefs, to begin with using white over a blue ground, but later more colourfully. Andrea, his nephew, and Andrea's son Giovanni, are also well known.

At the beginning of the 16th C another style enters maiolica: *istoriato*, or narrative painting, first introduced at Faenza. Typical subjects were the scriptures and mythology. (3; p 111, no. 3)

By the mid-16th C the *istoriato* fashion had begun to decline. The reaction was towards a freer manner using sketchy designs with a limited palette of cobalt, yellow and orange. White wares known as *bianchi di Faenza*, often moulded with filigree patterns, developed in the late 16th C. (7)

Italian maiolica and porcelain, 16th–19th C

1 Faenza polychrome *albarello*, early 16th c ® F
2 Doccia coffee cup and saucer, *c.*1760 ® D
3 Urbino *istoriato* plate; first half of 16th c ℻ ⚲ E
4 Doccia hard-paste porcelain bowl, with inner wall painted in underglaze blue, *c.*1740–45, ht 14cm ® E
5 Naples covered tankard, late 19th c ℻ D
6 Capodimonte china-seller,

1753–59, ht 20.3cm ℣ℝ ⚲ H
7 *Bianco di Faenza* latticed bowl, late 16th c, diam. 25.5cm ℣ℝ F
8 Terracotta relief, workshop of Andrea della Robbia, *c.*1500, diam. 99cm ℣ℝ ⚲ H

Italian porcelain. When Marco Polo came home to Venice in 1295 he may have brought back some Chinese porcelain with him. Oriental wares became greatly prized by Italian noblemen, though maiolica was more commonly used at their tables.

In 1575 Francesco I de' Medici of Florence financed the first successful attempt to make soft-paste porcelain in Europe. The first Venetian factory, founded *c.*1720 by Francesco Vezzi, produced during its short career some hard-paste pieces that rival Meissen.

The best Italian porcelain factories were Doccia (founded 1735) and Capodimonte. Doccia's earliest hard-paste ware is easy to identify by its roughness, fire-cracks and dull, sticky-looking glaze. Pieces included coffee and tea wares and brightly enamelled figures with clumsy hands and red-stippled flesh. The factory stuck to the baroque and made little concession to the rococo. (2, 4)

The Capodimonte manufacture was established in 1743 by Charles of Bourbon in the grounds of the palace near Naples. When Charles became King of Spain in 1759 he moved the establishment to Buen Retiro, Madrid. Both figures and service-ware are very rare. (6) The peasant pieces of the chief modeller Giuseppe Gricci have small heads. He also made *commedia dell' arte* subjects.

Hard-paste porcelain wares decorated with figure subjects in relief and enamelled in polychrome have been wrongly attributed to Capodimonte. In fact, they were made by Doccia in the 18th c and, in the 19th, at Naples or in Germany. Other factories include Le Nove (from 1762) and Cozzi's factory at Venice (1765–1812).

SPAIN

Spanish pottery of the Hispano-Moresque type (i.e. tin-glazed earthenware made by the Moors or under Moorish influence) was produced at Valencia from the early 15th C. Decoration often employed lustre pigment combined with blue and was based on bryony and vine leaves, together with Kufic inscriptions. The lustre on the best pieces is generally of a straw colour. The Moorish influence was gradually diluted by Gothic styles. Quality declined after the mid-17th C.

An important faience factory was founded at Alcora in 1726–27, producing imitations of Moustiers wares and some finely painted panels and oval plaques. Many tiles were also made.

The Buen Retiro porcelain factory near Madrid (1760–1808) was a continuation of Capodimonte. The greatest period was before 1788. Specimens are very rare.

THE UNITED STATES

Pottery. The first pottery made in the American Colonies was coarse redware, produced from the late 1600s until well into the 19th C. (6) Irregularities of the manufacturing process often gave rise to attractive mottling, but for more controlled effects coloured glazes or slip were used. The German Mennonites in Pennsylvania produced lively pie dishes, butter pots, money boxes and puzzle jugs that contrasted with the more sober output of New England. *Sgraffito* ornament was a Pennsylvania speciality.

The Shenandoah Valley in Maryland and Virginia was notable for its potters in the 19th C. Foremost among them were the Bell family, whose flowing designs in slip suggest oriental characters.

American pottery and porcelain, 18th and 19th C

Value symbols refer to New York estimates expressed as pounds

1

2

3

4
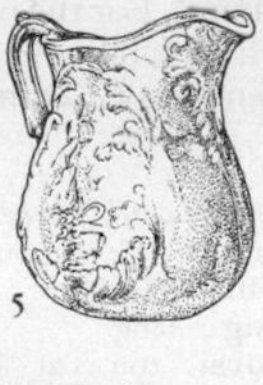
5

6

7

1 White porcelain salt, by Bonnin & Morris, Philadelphia, 1771–72 VR *G*
2 Pottery platter, blue-printed with a Civil War scene, Edwin Bennett Pottery Co., Baltimore, Maryland, *c.*1901 [FC] *A*
3 Mocha-ware pottery pitcher, made in England for the USA. *c.*1800, ht 11.43cm (R) *C*
4 Porcelain vase with painted and gilt decoration, Tucker factory, *c.*1830 VR ⁋ *F* (pair)
5 Bennington brown-glazed pitcher, 19th c [FC] ⁋ *C*
6 Brown-glazed redware mug, 19th c (C) *A*
7 Salt-glazed stoneware crock with cobalt blue decoration, ht 33cm [FC] *B*

Stoneware was developed in the 18th C owing to fears that lead-glazed pottery could be poisonous. (7) Mostly it was grey, and after c.1800 vessels were generally coated inside with brown slip. Decoration was often in cobalt blue, or very occasionally brown. Important centres of production were northern New Jersey (the "Staffordshire of America") and East Liverpool, Ohio. Cream-ware, invented in England by Josiah Wedgwood, inspired many imitators, most importantly at Philadelphia from c.1790. Manufacture dwindled to almost nothing after c.1838.

English imports for the American market included wares blue-printed with eagles and other symbols. American-made printed pottery was not properly launched until 1839, with the work of the American Pottery Manufacturing Co. of Jersey City.

Wares with the lustrous brown "Rockingham" glaze (often known as "Bennington" wares) were widely made from the 1840s until 1900. (5) Majolica, of the kind exhibited by Minton in London in 1851, was adopted as early as 1853 by Edwin Bennett at Baltimore. The best-known producer, in the 1880s, was Griffen, Smith & Hill at Phoenixville, Pennsylvania.

The Rookwood Pottery, founded in Cincinnati in 1880, concentrated on vases and ornamental jugs with simple shapes, a rich green or brown glaze and painted, sometimes Japanese-inspired, decorations. (p 112, no. 1)

Porcelain. The earliest surviving American porcelain was made by Bonnin & Morris at Southwark, Philadelphia, between 1770 and 1772—a group of soft-paste tablewares decorated in the Bow manner, with underglaze blue. (1)

William Ellis Tucker made hard-paste porcelain in Philadelphia from 1826, mainly copying French Empire wares. Effective landscapes were painted in sepia monochrome, combined with simple gilding. The factory closed in 1838. (4)

One of the seminal US ceramic factories of the mid-19th C was at Bennington, Vermont, where John Harrison, formerly of Copeland's in England, introduced a formula for biscuit porcelain, used for figures and relief-decorated jugs. True Parian was not made until after 1875, by Ott & Brewer of Trenton, New Jersey. This firm is most famous, though, for its repellent version (from 1872) of the pearly glazed Irish Belleek wares also imitated by Knowles, Taylor & Knowles of East Liverpool (under the name of "Lotus ware") and by the Lenox Co. at Trenton.

Spellings of Chinese words

The Pinyin system of romanization is followed in this book (except for familiar geographical names). For the benefit of readers who wish to cross-refer to books which follow the old Wade-Giles system, a few conversions are given below. Terms romanized in Pinyin are given first.

Dynasties

Jin	Chin
Qin	Ch'in
Qing	Ch'ing
Song	Sung
Xin	Hsin
Zhou	Chou

Reigns

Chenghua	Ch'êng Hua
Jiajing	Chia Ching
Kangxi	K'ang Hsi
Qianlong	Ch'ien Lung
Xuande	Hsüan Tê
Yongzheng	Yung Chêng
Zhengde	Chêng Tê

Terms and places

Cizhou	Tz'ǔ chou
Dehua	Tê Hua
Ding	Ting
doucai	tou ts'ai
gu	ku
Guan	Kuan
gui	kuei
Jian	Chien
Jingdezhen	Ching-tê Chên
jue	chüeh
Jun	Chun
Longquan	Lung-ch'üan
Ru	Ju
Yixing	I Hsing

CHINA

The Han dynasty. The Han dynasty (206BC–AD220) is mainly associated with red earthenwares. An important innovation was the use of lead glazes to which the red body gave a green colour reminiscent of well-patinated bronze. (1) In pottery that accompanied the dead, the contemporary social scene was re-created in miniature—watch-towers, farmhouses, cooking-pots and figures. (7)

Early stonewares. In the politically disunified Six Dynasties period (AD220–589) great technical advances were made in ceramics. Lead glazes were superseded by a kind probably made from finely crushed feldspar, and high temperatures were attained to produce a dense heavy stoneware sometimes called "proto-porcelain". Bronze prototypes continued to be influential, but heavy wheel-thrown stoneware jars with glazed upperparts were a more typical form.

Yue wares. The Yue wares are an important group of glazed stonewares made in Chekiang province in south-east China. Manufacture flourished by early Tang times (618–906). Though the body was grey, it often oxidized red, and the glaze varied from brownish yellow to grey green. Ewers, jars, dishes and bowls were produced with sparse decoration of birds or flora. (6)

The Tang dynasty. The Tang dynasty (618–906) saw a remarkable flowering of lead-glazed earthenware. Copper, cobalt and iron pigments were added to the glaze to colour it green, blue and amber. Colours were sometimes prevented from running by use of a deep, engraved line, but were mostly applied freehand. (4) The glaze on vases usually stops short of the base. Figures made for tombs included horses, camels, musicians and bulging-eyed monsters. (2; p 101, no. 4) Tang tomb figures have been commonly faked. Fakes are harder and less absorbent than genuine pieces, so a useful (but not infallible) test is to lick one's finger and dab saliva

Chinese pottery and porcelain

1 Han green-glazed granary jar, ht 25.4cm **B** *F*

2 Tang unglazed horse, ht 23cm **FC** **Q** *I*

3 Northern celadon conical bowl, moulded with leaves, diam. 17cm **B** *I*

4 Tang lead-glazed jar, ht 16.5cm **B** **Q** *H*

5 Ding dish with carved lotus design, Song dynasty, diam. 20cm **B** *I*

6 Yue-type vase 9th–10th c, ht 33cm **VR** *I*

7 Han grey pottery figure, ht 54cm **B** **Q** *I*

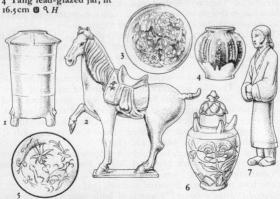

on an unglazed area: if the moisture is absorbed quickly the piece will probably be authentic.

The Song dynasty. The Song dynasty (960–1279) is a period of fine stonewares. Some of the products of kilns in the north are regarded as "classic". These include the beautiful Ding wares made (until *c.*1300) at Ding Zhou in Hopei province. (5) The porcellaneous body was decorated with either incised or moulded designs brought out by the application of an ivory-white glaze. Rims were often protected by a copper band.

Another important group of Song pottery was the celadons— stonewares with a feldspathic, usually green-coloured glaze. Celadons were especially prized in the Near East because they were thought to change colour or break on contact with poison. The Northern type, made in Henan province, was olive-coloured. The type made at Longquan in southern Chekiang had a glaze which varied from leaf green to cold blue green, and the greyish body fired where unglazed to a reddish brown, sometimes used decoratively. (3, 10)

Jun ware was made at Jun Zhou in Henan. The glaze, thick and opalescent, is most commonly a lavender blue, and contains a mass of air bubbles, and sometimes irregular grooves known as "earthworm" marks. Splashes of red and purple often occur. (9)

Other classic Song wares include the rare Ru and Guan types, manufactured to serve the Imperial households in Kaifeng and Hangchow respectively in the early 12th C. (12)

A wide variety of stonewares with black (or deep brown) glazes was also produced in this period. Best known is the grey-bodied Jian ware made in Fukien. High iron content yielded the streaked "hare's fur" effect especially admired by the Japanese. (11)

Cizhou wares. Cizhou is the name for a diversity of stonewares for domestic use made in north China from late Tang times until the 14th C. The glaze, usually transparent, sometimes blue or turquoise, was applied over a covering of slip. Decoration was amazingly varied—carved, incised, *sgraffito* with one or two slips, slip-painted, etc.—and often featured leaf and flower patterns. (13)

Qingpai wares. Qingpai is a thin, translucent porcelain which fires to a reddish colour when unglazed. An alternative name is Yingqing, meaning literally "shadowy blue" and referring to the tinge of the glaze. This type was made from Tang times onwards.

The Yuan dynasty. In the Yuan dynasty (1279–1367) the technique of using cobalt as an underglaze decoration was introduced. Taste now shifted from stoneware to blue and white. Porcelain in this style dating from the 14th C includes some pieces decorated with ducks amid water and vegetation.

The Ming dynasty. Ming porcelain (1367–1644) is white and translucent and is generally tinged buff on the underside of the footring. Most glazes of the early period are thick and uneven, with a bluish tinge.

Superb blue and white wares were made in the reign of Xuande (1426–35). The blue was blackish, with points of especially dense colouring. Motifs included lotus flowers amid scrollwork, and aquatic birds. The reign also saw the perfection of underglaze red, seen at its best on delicate cups ornamented with three red fishes. The Xuande reign-mark was often "borrowed" in the 18th C, when admirable copies were made. (14)

In the reign of Chenghua (1465–87) coloured enamels were introduced, often with blue and white. The *wucai* technique ("contrasting colours") was a combination of enamels and underglaze blue particularly favoured at court. (16)

Sancai ("three coloured") wares, of both stoneware and porcelain, date from the late 15th to 16th C. Turquoise, purple and blue enamels were separated, in the *fahua* technique, by lines of clay in a way that suggests cloisonné work. (18)

An innovation of the Zhengde period (1506–21) was a decoration of incised dragons coloured green on a yellow ground. Blue and white was also revived, and reached heights of excellence in the reign of Jiajing (1522–66), when overglaze iron red was introduced. Fine monochrome porcelain was also popular.

Chinese pottery and porcelain

8 Fukien *blanc de Chine* tripod censer, 17th c, diam. 9cm [FC] *E*

9 Jun tripod censer, painted with red splashes on a lavender ground, Song dynasty, diam. 6cm [R] *F*

10 Longquan celadon bowl with moulded chrysanthemum petals, diam. 12cm [FC] *E*

11 Jian-ware "hare's fur" bowl, 12th–13th c, diam. 12.2cm [FC] *E*

12 Guan-ware bowl with close crackle, 13th c, diam. 19.5cm

13 Cizhou vase with black peony design, Song dynasty, ht 33cm VR ⚲ ⚲ *I*

The Qing dynasty.

During the early years of the Qing dynasty (1644–1912), Jingdezhen, centre of the Chinese porcelain industry, was destroyed by rebels. After its reconstruction, exquisite porcelain was made in the reigns of Emperors Kangxi (1662–1722), Yongzheng (1723–35) and Qianlong (1736–95).

The Kangxi period is one of fine underglaze blue painting, often on pieces made for export. The best-known motif is the early flowering plum (prunus) on a blue ground intended to suggest cracked ice.

Enamelled wares of the Qing dynasty fall largely into two categories, the *famille verte* and the *famille rose*. In the *famille verte* a brilliant green predominates. The *famille rose*, which reached China *c.*1720, was Europe's one contribution to Chinese ceramics technique; its palette includes a rose pink derived from colloidal gold. The finest *famille rose* pieces belong to the reign of Yongzheng. (15)

Enamelled pieces included figures, made from the late 18th c until modern times. In order to retain the fine detail of the modelling, enamels were applied directly on the biscuit porcelain.

An important achievement of the reign of Qianlong was in glazing. Potters now reintroduced copper red, often in combination with cobalt blue. (17) The resultant glazes, characterized by turquoise splashes, are known as *flambés*. One variant is known as *sang de boeuf*, from its similarity to ox-blood. (25) A delicate "peachbloom" (pink mottled with red) was used on small pieces. (19) Glazes often took the form of soft, low-temperature enamels applied in monochrome. (p 101, no. 1)

By the early 18th c the large quantities of porcelain made for export to the West included not only pieces with European-style decoration (e.g. biblical scenes) but also European shapes ornamented in blue and white, *famille verte* or *famille rose*, sometimes in conjunction with European armorial bearings. (21, 24) Among

Chinese pottery and porcelain

14 Ming blue and white bowl, with Xuande reign-mark, diam. 20.8cm ꝟ ♀ ▢ *D*

15 Bowl painted in *famille rose* enamels, with Yongzheng mark, late 19th c ◐ *E*

16 Ming *wucai* jar, *c.*1600, ht 18.5cm ◐ *I*

17 Copper-red bottle, with Qianlong mark, ht 23.5cm ꜰꞓ ♀ *E*

18 Ming *fahua* baluster jar, 15th c ◐ *F*

19 "Peachbloom" beehive-shaped water pot, with Kangxi mark, diam. 12.5cm ꜰꞓ ♀ *G*

20 *Blanc de Chine* figure, 17th–18th c, width 19cm ꜰꞓ ♀ *F*

21 Cup with *famille rose* European armorial decoration, reign of Qianlong ꜰꞓ *B*

22 Yixing teapot, ht 16cm, 19th c ꜰꞓ *C*

23 Blue and white sleeve vase, *c.*1650, ht 20.5cm ꜰꞓ *E*

24 Teapot, with Qianlong mark, mid-18th c ꝟ ♀ *I*

25 Qing stem-bowl with *sang de boeuf* glaze, the interior painted in iron red, Yongzheng reign, diam. 18cm ꜰꞓ *E*

the most sought examples of porcelain decorated for the American market are those depicting ships flying the American flag.

Dehua porcelain. At Dehua in Fukien a fine porcelain was made which became popular from the 17th C. The glaze produced a milkier look than on Jingdezhen wares and the potting tended to be heavy. In Europe the term *blanc de Chine* was applied to this type of porcelain, and it was much copied there, especially the kind decorated in relief with prunus blossom. (8, 20)

Yixing ware. Brown or red stoneware was made at Yixing in Kiangsi province from the mid-17th C. The well-known Yixing teapots, a favourite export, are decorated with low-relief designs or incised inscriptions. Some 19th-C examples were covered with overdone enamel decoration. (22)

KOREA

The best Korean ceramics have a reputation not far short of the best Chinese. Wares fall into three groups, named after dynasties: the Silla (57 BC–AD 936), the Koryo (936–1392) and the Yi (1392–1910). The golden age was the Koryo period, when celadons of the highest quality were made. Inlaying with black or white slip was a characteristic technique used for such wares. Typical forms were ribbed boxes, spouted gourd-like vessels, pierced perfume pots, miniature vases and cups on stands. Lobing, reeding and waved edges were common. Some shapes had a "growing", flower-like character.

JAPAN

Before the 13th C Japan relied largely on imported Chinese pottery, especially for the paraphernalia of tea-drinking. The earliest native wares of interest were stoneware teabowls made at Seto in the province of Owari. A low-fired, lead-glazed earthenware known as *raku* became immensely popular, progressing in colour from black or dark brown to light red, in the 17th C to straw-coloured, and finally to a limited polychrome range. Forms were thick and irregularly shaped. (7)

An artist potter called Kenzan (1660–1743) made beautiful *raku* wares as well as finely painted cream stoneware with a finely crackled glaze. Bizen province is associated with a red or bluish-brown stoneware used for vases, animal figures, etc.

The first porcelain kilns in Japan were set up in the early decades of the 17th C at Arita, Hizen province. Underglaze blue was the first decorative technique (6), but enamelling in colour was introduced *c.*1644. Decoration was simple and asymmetrical, balancing off white areas against painted areas. (1, 2) The generic term for this style is "Kakiemon". Typical patterns include the "Quail", still used today in European factories.

From the end of the 17th C Arita also produced dishes and vases for export in the "Imari" style. (3, 5) Decoration was mainly in a blackish underglaze blue and a dark red, and often featured native brocades as a motif. Imari wares were made well into the 19th C. (See also p 101, no. 3)

Porcelain made in the 19th C at Seto (Owari), Kyoto, Mikawachi and Shiba is still fairly readily obtainable. Kyoto copied Chinese Song celadons and Ming pieces. Late 19th-C "Satsuma" pottery, horrifically overdecorated for the Western market, is infinitely less desirable than late 18th-C work. (4; p 112, no. 2)

Japanese pottery and porcelain

1 **Kakiemon porcelain plate in enamel colours**, 18th c 🖸 ♀ *F*
2 **Kakiemon porcelain teapot** 🖸 ♀ *F*
3 **Imari bowl**, 19th c 🖸 *C*

4 **Gilt Satsuma vase**, 19th c, ht 74cm 🖸 *F*
5 **Imari jar and cover**, late 17th c 🖸 *F*
6 **Arita baluster vase, painted in underglaze blue**, 17th c, ht 27cm 🖸 ♀ *E*
7 **Black *raku* tea bowl, Momoyama period**, diam. 11cm 🖸 ♀ *F*
8 **Small blue and white hexagonal wine cup, Nabeshima**, early 18th c ∇ℝ ♀ *F*

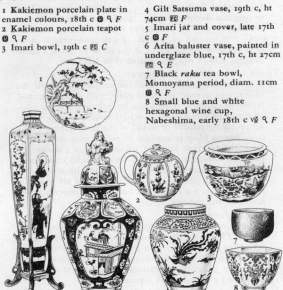

GLASS

Glass is the most magical of all man-made materials. It rings like a bell when tapped ("metal" is the term for its substance, as "paste" is for that of porcelain); yet it can be as transparent as spring water. In keeping with its aristocratic superiority, glass is virtually unrepairable. Damage reduces its value mightily.

The chemistry of glass

Glass is made of silica and alkali. The source of silica is sand (or more rarely, crushed rock). The alkali in old glass came from either wood ash (producing *potash glass*) or burnt seaweed (producing *soda glass*). Potash glass quickly hardens as it cools, leaving little time for manipulation. It is therefore often cut or engraved. Soda glass remains malleable longer, a property that has encouraged the fanciful shapes of Venetian wares. Lead was introduced into glass from the 17th C to create an imitation of rock crystal (which is almost pure silica); it is at its best when multi-faceted.

The impurities in sand included iron, which gave a bluish or yellowish tinge. The Egyptians overcame this by adding manganese—a technique rediscovered in Venice in the 15th C and used in *cristallo* glass. Fine-quality clear glass has been called "crystal" ever since.

Engraving

Engraving on glass was done with a diamond-point or a rotating wheel in conjunction with an abrasive. Diamond-point was used in the 16th C by the Venetians and their imitators. It was also practised in England and in the Netherlands. The technique was superseded in the 18th C by wheel engraving and by enamelled decoration, but continued to be employed for stippling. The use of the wheel to incise a sunken design is known as *intaglio*. By the converse technique of relief engraving, glass is cut away to leave a raised design, which may be polished or left mat.

Three 19th-century techniques

A favourite technique from the second quarter of the 19th C was *overlay* or *cased glass*, with superimposed layers of colours. (Glass can be coloured by the addition of metallic oxides.) Decorative effects were achieved by partial removal of the outer layer. The term *cameo glass* is applied to reliefs that are carved through a surface layer of white fused to a darker ground. *Cameo incrustations* (or sulphides) have a white porcelain relief—often a portrait head—embedded in clear glass. A thin layer of air round the relief gives it a silver appearance. This process was favoured for paperweights.

Detecting forgeries

Forgers find it difficult to reproduce the colour of early metal. They also have trouble simulating wear. Tiny scratches on the base of a piece should be in a multitude of random directions. Unscrupulous use of abrasives generally produces scratches that are too deep, or in too obvious a pattern.

Mould-blown and pressed glass

Moulds were used in the early 19th C for shaping

inexpensive hollow wares. Pieces produced by this process have a somewhat pebbly appearance, and the inside has a pattern corresponding with the outside. Pressed glass differs from mould-blown glass in eliminating the blowing process and using a plunger, which gives a smooth inner surface. Press-moulded imitations of cut glass are easy to spot: their facets lack the sharp edges of cut glass.

Common types of forgery

English wine glasses are among the most forged items, especially twist-stemmed ones. In these the twist is generally deeper inside the stem than in genuine pieces. In evaluating wine glasses it is sometimes useful to remember that on antique examples the foot is almost always wider than the bowl. Special caution should be exercised when buying glasses with Jacobite emblems: some are complete forgeries, others are genuine 18th-c glasses with modern engraving.

Other common forgeries are: German enamelled wares, much copied in the early 19th C; *Zwischengoldgläser*; Irish cut glass, forgeries of which tend to be rather too blue; Nailsea; Bristol blue glass; French paperweights.

ENGLAND

The 16th–17th centuries. Venetians made glass in England from 1549, but the first considerable figure in English glassmaking was the Venetian Jacopo Verzelini (1523–1606), who from c.1577 made wide goblets with hollow knopped stems. (1)

English glass, 16th and 17th C

1 Anglo-Venetian engraved soda-glass goblet, 1586 VR *I*
2 Roemer, by George Ravenscroft, with raven's head in relief, ht 16.5cm VR *I*
3 Tankard, by George Ravenscroft, 1676–8 VR *I*
4 Bowl, by Hawley Bishop, c.1681, diam. 22.2cm VR *G*

5 Typical wine glass of early baluster style, with knop at base, c.1695 ⊗ ⊖ *E*
6 Jug, c.1685, ht 29.8cm VR *G*

For most of the 17th C the industry was dominated by monopolists who imported Venetian glass, or Italian craftsmen who could make a fair imitation of it. In the last quarter of the century a movement to become independent of the Italians reflected the new spirit of scientific enquiry and commercial self-sufficiency. In 1673 the London Glass Sellers' Company engaged George Ravenscroft (1618–81) to undertake glass researches for them. The company had two glasshouses, one at the Savoy, London, the other (mainly experimental) at Henley-on-Thames.

The next year Ravenscroft was granted a patent for a "sort of crystalline glass resembling rock crystal", using flints and potash. The potash produced a defect known as "crisselling"—a network of fine interior cracks. In 1676 he solved this problem by a formula which incorporated lead oxide, and from 1677 his wares, which include baroque helmet-shaped or bell-shaped ewers, bore a punning seal of a raven's head. (2,3) There were other important manufacturers at Southwark, Stourbridge, Newcastle-upon-Tyne, South Shields and Bristol.

In the late 17th C short-stemmed glasses with "wrought buttons" or moulded knops (5) began to give place to simpler shapes with longer stems, at first hollow but soon made solid.

English glass, 17th and 18th C

7 **Decanter,** c.1760 Ⓑ D
8 **Decanter cut in flat diamonds,** c.1760 Ⓑ D
9 **Ewer,** c.1685, ht 12.7cm V̄R̄ G
10 **Posset cup,** c.1685 V̄R̄ I
11 **Dark-green wine bottle, with seal,** 1704 Ⓑ E
12 **Drawn-stem glass with** elongated tear, flared bowl and folded foot, c.1720 Ⓕ Ⓒ B
13 **Drawn-stem glass with waisted bowl and folded foot,** c.1710 Ⓕ Ⓒ B
14 **Newcastle baluster glass, with angular knop,** c.1745 Ⓕ Ⓒ D
15 **Goblet with serpentine stem,** c.1685 V̄R̄ I

The 18th century. In the early 18th C, glassmakers were influenced by the simpler shapes of Queen Anne silver. Solid baluster stems of glasses were formed of discs and knops, and sometimes included an air bubble. After the Treaty of Utrecht (1713) permitted the import of German glass, a Teutonic influence became apparent in the shouldered stem often called "Silesian" but in fact west German. (16) Until now, bowls had been straight-sided funnels, but in George I's reign they developed a waist and flared outwards. (12) As the height of the stems increased, bases became thick and solid, their edges often folded over underneath. Jelly, syllabub and custard glasses were characteristic of these years. From the mid-century glasses became lighter. This was in keeping with the rococo style, but the Excise Duty levied on glass from 1745 to finance the wars with France also encouraged the trend. Interest shifted from shape to decoration: wheel and diamond engraving, painting in enamels, and, until c.1765, the popular air-twist (or "wormed") stems. (17, 18) Spirals of white enamel were used in stems from c.1750, and of coloured glass from c.1755 (most commonly blue, green or ruby) (p 106, no. 3). Combinations of air-twist and opaque white or colour-twist are particularly elusive.

English glasses, 18th C

16 Sweetmeat glass with
Silesian stem, c.1750 ⒻⒸ B
17 Wine glass with air-twist
stem, c.1750 ⒻⒸ C
18 Ale glass with air-twist stem,
c.1750 ⒻⒸ C

19 Jacobite wine glass, with
engraved ogee bowl and
opaque-twist stem, c.1760 ⒻⒸ C
20 Flute decorated in white
enamel by William and Mary
Beilby, c.1770 ⅤⓇ F

The commonest late 18th-C engraved glasses depict hops and
barley or vines. (18) Decanters were now often made in clear glass.
Early ones are globular with a rim for tying down the cork; later
examples, from c.1750, have glass stoppers. From 1760 decanters
became more tapered, the earlier "spire" stoppers giving way to
flat vertical ones, sometimes disc-shaped. (7)

Painting in enamels on glass was not attempted in England until
the 18th C. The Beilby family of Newcastle-upon-Tyne—in
particular William and his sister Mary—were the best-known
practitioners (1762–78). Their main colours are bluish-white and
turquoise. (20; p 106, no. 3)

Enamel painting on opaque white glass (which was exempt from
the Excise Act) was popular in the later 18th C. It is often called
"Bristol" but was not all made there. Many forms follow Chinese
porcelain models. Cornucopia-shaped flower-holders were made
in imitation of Worcester china, as well as finely reeded candlesticks and four-sided tea caddies. "Bristol" painting was often of
pseudo-Chinese figures. White glass was also used for vinaigrettes
and snuff bottles, blue glass for scent bottles. (22, 25; p 108, no. 1)

Increased duties on glass between 1777 and 1787 caused a mass
exodus of English glassmakers to Ireland. Cut glass was popular by
this time and in the Regency period became so much the rage that
Venice was eclipsed as the glassmaking centre of Europe. Regency
cut glass is doggedly referred to as "Waterford", but the output of

Wine glass bowl and stem types

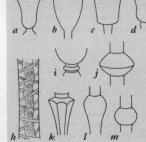

a Bell-shaped bowl b Funnel
bowl c Bucket bowl d Thistle
bowl e Trumpet bowl f
Conical bowl g Ovoid bowl
(For ogee bowl see above, no.
19) h Compound opaque
white twist stem i Collar (or
Merese) j Angular knop (i.e.,
bulge on stem) k Silesian
stem l Inverted baluster
stem m Ball knop

lead glass was probably about ten times greater in England and Scotland together than in Ireland.

The 19th century. Despite the Glass Excise laws the early 19th C produced the weightiest glasses ever made in Britain. The decoration of diamonds, "strawberry diamonds" and stars tended to be more horizontally placed than in the 18th C. This was the period of barrel-shaped decanters with rings round the neck and mushroom stoppers. Towards the mid-century decoration became more vertical again, often with fluting, and cylindrical and globular decanters replaced barrel-shaped in the 1830s and 40s. (24)

The repeal of the Glass Excise Act in 1845 led to a new freedom, exemplified by the cut-glass extravaganzas shown by W.H., B. and J. Richardson and others at the 1851 Great Exhibition. After that, partly because of debased imitations in pressed glass and the criticisms of High Art theorists like John Ruskin, cut glass declined in popularity (until the 80s and 90s) and engraved work superseded it, mainly on globular forms.

English glass, 18th and 19th C

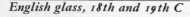

21 Copy (19th c) of late 18th-c cut-glass goblet Ⓕ Ⓒ *A*
22 Tea canister of Bristol type, *c.*1760, ht 14cm Ⓥ Ⓡ *F*
23 Green bottle-glass cream jug, *c.*1800 Ⓑ *D*
24 Heavily cut decanter, early 19th c Ⓕ Ⓒ *B*
25 Opaque white vase, Bristol, *c.*1760, ht 21.6cm Ⓑ *F*
26 Engraved goblet of Sunderland Bridge and Exchange, *c.*1825 Ⓥ Ⓡ *E*
27 Engraved coaching rummer, 1825 Ⓑ *E*

Coloured glass was in demand in the early 19th C. Green bottle glass had been made in England since the time of the Venetian supremacy. At Nailsea, near Bristol, founded in 1788 by John Robert Lucas, bottle glass (which was exempt from the Excise Act) was made in greenish-brown with white spotting and splashing. (28) The second phase of Nailsea production dates from the management of Robert Lucas Chance. From this period (1810–15) come jugs, bowls, pocket flasks and Siamese-twin "gimmel flasks" decorated with pink and blue loops, as well as *jeux d'esprit* (or "friggers") such as pipes, walking sticks and rolling pins. (29, 32)

Coloured glass in imitation of the 1820s Bohemian wares and Biedermeier pieces was made before 1845 (e.g. by Stevens & William of Brierley Hill, near Stroud, and Thomas Hawkes of Dudley). Other makers of coloured glass were Benjamin Richardson of Stourbridge, and George Bacchus & Sons, Rice Harris & Son and Lloyd & Summerfield, all of Birmingham. The 1851 Exhibition was the culmination of the fashion for colour, and included layered (or "cased") glass with cut decoration, often of Gothic form. (31) Opaline glass was made by the Richardsons and

English glass, 19th C

28 Nailsea-type bottle-glass jug, c.1800 **B** D
29 Nailsea-type jug of clear green glass with white waves, early 19th c **B** D
30 Compote of white opaline glass, with green edging and gilding, by W.H., B. & J.

Richardson, Stourbridge, c. early 1850s **FC** B
31 Layered-glass toilet bottle, blue over crystal, by Apsley Pellatt, 1851, ht 18.4cm **FC** B
32 Rolling pin of clear glass with white and ruby waves, c.1825–50 **G** A

J.F. Christy, sometimes in leaf shapes outlined in green. (30) Bulbous jugs with three-lipped mouths in imitation of the Greek were also produced in this material, and Christy did some transfer printing on it. Painted clear glass was made by Henry Cole for Summerly's Art Manufactures, c.1847, and by Richardson and Christy. The designs of historic Venetian glass were copied. (40) Apsley Pellatt (who in 1819 had invented a way of embedding white paste figures, usually busts, into clear glass) made "Anglo-Venetian" frosted glass. (37) Silvered glass was made by James Powell & Sons in Whitefriars. *Millefiori* paperweights—a fashion

English glass, 19th C

33 Engraved champagne glass, with Venetian-style stem, by George Bacchus & Sons, Birmingham, c.1850 **B** B
34 Miniature *millefiori* inkwell, Stourbridge, dated 1848 **FC** D
35 Cameo scent bottle, Birmingham, 1884, ht 10.5cm **B** D

36 Four-colour cameo vase, probably by Thomas Webb & Sons, c.1870–90 **B** H
37 Candlestick with cameo incrustation of classical figure, by Apsley Pellatt, c.1820 **VR** C
38 Enamelled opaline vase on pink ground, c.1850, ht 36cm **FC** C (pair)
39 Green vase, Victorian **G** A
40 Venetian-style bowl, by James Powell & Sons, 1876 **FC** B
41 "Burmese" opaline glass vase, by Thomas Webb & Sons, Stourbridge, c.1890, ht 15.9cm **B** D

from France—were sold in stationers' shops. Paperweight manufacturers included Bacchus in the late 1840s and Rice Harris at the Islington Glass Works.

In the mid-century there was an influx of engravers from central Europe: J.H.B. Millar in Edinburgh; Paul Oppitz at Copeland's in London; Frederick E. Kny and William Fritsche at Stourbridge, working for Thomas Webb; Joseph Keller with Stevens & Williams. Millar introduced the popular engraved fern pattern.

The last decades of the century saw a new interest in intaglio engraving, with its deep cutting and polished edges. The firm of Thomas Webb had the highest reputation for this work; their "cameo" glass is also much collected. (35, 36; p 107, no. 3) Decoration in the 1880s often featured small birds in foliage. In the 90s John Northwood (1836–1902) did intaglio work for Stevens & Williams, while Thomas Hawkes of Dudley was the main exponent of acid etching.

In the 1870s and 80s Webb's introduced exotic new colours of glass, of which the best-known is "Burmese"—an opaque greenish-yellow shading to a deep pink. (41) To this period too belong the often Japanese-inspired designs in pressed glass by Sowerby's Ellison Glass Works, Gateshead. Sowerby's also made an opaque marbled glass known as "slag glass", which is easy to date from the registration marks.

IRELAND

Before 1780 Irish glass was virtually indistinguishable from English. After that date manufacturers responded to changing conditions and a unique style developed that was vital and exuberant.

The large force of Irish Volunteers which had been raised originally against the possibility of a French invasion of Ireland was now used to blackmail England into relaxing its restrictive Acts against the export of Irish glass. (Several pieces of Irish glass carry inscriptions relating to the militia, such as "Success to the Waterford Volunteers".) There followed a period of Free Trade for Ireland which lasted until 1825.

The only Irish city that produced a significant amount of luxury lead glass before 1780 was Dublin. After that date Cork, Waterford and Belfast joined in. The best-known manufacturers were:

Irish glass, 18th and 19th C

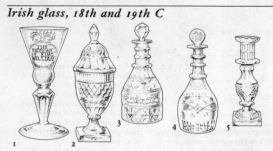

1 Early Williamite glass with Silesian stem, c.1715 🔞 F
2 Covered urn, c.1800, ht 31.7cm 🔞 D (pair)
3 Decanter engraved with racehorses, c.1780 VR E

4 Decanter with engraved "vesica" motif, Cork Glass Co., c.1783–1818 🔞 D
5 Vase-shaped candlestick, with diamond band, c.1800–20, ht 21cm 🔞 D (pair)

Irish glass, 18th and 19th C

6 Cut-glass bowl on separate base, late 18th c VR *F*
7 Cut-glass ice pail on stand, Waterford, *c.*1800 FG *C*
8 Cut-glass hookah base, Waterford, early 19th c ⊗ *C*
9 Moulded bowl with turned-over rim, *c.*1800 ⊗ *C*
10 Scent bottle, Waterford, 1794, lgth 15.2cm ⊗ *C*

Richard Williams & Co., Charles Mulvaney and Jeudwin, Lunn & Co., of Dublin; Benjamin Edwards, the Belfast Glass Works and Smylie & Co., of Belfast; the Waterford Glass House in Waterford (1784–1851)—the only glass factory there, but one which made "Waterford" synonymous with fine cut glass; the Cork Glass Co., the Waterloo Glass House Co. (not surprisingly, founded in 1815) and the Terrace Glass Works, in Cork. A few of these manufacturers used a mark under the base, especially on decanters and finger bowls. Most Irish glass of the 1780s and 90s has a slight dusky tint.

These factories exported on a vast scale. A great deal went to America but the bulk was destined for England. In the neo-classical period covered urns were a common form, often cut with shallow diamond or lozenge patterns. (2) Irish candlesticks tend to have a deeply cut trefoil rim on the sleeve to hold the candle, which in turn slips into a standing socket. Drip-pans have cut vertical edging. (5) A characteristic detail of Irish vases and bowls is a turned-over rim. (9) Decanters, bowls and jugs tend to have moulded shallow flutes on the lower part of the body.

Bowls were made in profusion, for rinsing the mouth as well as the fingers. Decanters (especially dated ones) are perhaps the most desirable pieces. (3, 4) Those produced by the Cork Glass Co. often bear a so-called "vesica" pattern, which resembles cartoon fishes placed end to end. (4)

Ewers and jugs were used by the hard-drinking lower classes in Ireland, and are sometimes engraved with barley heads, hops and vine leaves. On glasses, cut stars and diamonds, with the rarer addition of cut shamrock, are typical decoration. The real rarities, which turn up only once in an Irish moon, are linen smoothers, toddy-lifters (bulb-shaped with a long neck) and hanging lamps. Hookah-bases are often bought to be turned into decanters. (8)

Waterford glass was often faked abroad in the 1920s. A new company, started at Waterford in 1948, made copies of some of its forerunner's pieces. Be especially cautious when buying marked decanters with unusually clear wording on them.

Blown-moulded table glass was cheaply produced in large amounts in the 19th C. It is distinguishable from pressed glass by the appearance of its mould marks, which show as slight convex swellings on the surface.

FRANCE

The French made wonderful stained glass but their glass vessels did not show the same skill and originality. In the Renaissance the Venetian influence took hold as it had in the Netherlands, and French glasshouses were run by Italian immigrants. (1, 2, 3) Only one of these concerns continued to make quality glass for any length of time: that established at Nevers, where the Saroldi family made Italian-style glass for almost 200 years until the 18th C. Their wares included small figures and "toys" of a fusible glass which was sometimes mistaken for enamel, although in fact they were made of glass rods and tubes worked with pincers. Similar figures were later made in Rouen, Bordeaux and Marseilles, and in Paris by Jacques Roux and Charles-François Hazard.

The 18th and 19th centuries. In 1760 the Académie des Sciences offered a prize for a report on how to improve the glass industry, for France still lagged behind most of the rest of Europe. In the subsequent flurry of activity the Verreries de Ste Anne was founded near Lunéville, later to become the famous Baccarat factory. In 1767 the Cristallerie de St Louis was established in the Münzthal in Lorraine and soon earned the Académie's praise for its success in imitating English glass. Mayor Oppenheim from Birmingham started another French factory in 1784, and at Petit Quevilly and later at Rouen made "cristaux blancs, façon et qualité d'Angleterre".

French glass, 16th and 19th C

1 **Venetian-style "marbled" pilgrim bottle,** *c.*1550–1600
VR ꝗ *G*
2 *Latticino* **and gilt wine glass,** *c.*1550–1600 VR *G*
3 **Venetian-style enamelled glass, with gilt work, mid-16th c** VR *I*
4 **Opal-glass vase, St Louis,** *c.*1850 FG *B*

5 **White opaline ewer and basin with gilt-bronze mounts,** *c.*1830, ht 30.5cm VR *F*
6 *Millefiori* **vase, Clichy,** *c.*1848 VR *F*

At the end of the century the French invented, quite independently of the Englishman Apsley Pellatt, the method of enclosing white porcellaneous cameos in cut crystal glass. Desprez of Paris was one of the early craftsmen. His or his sons' names and their Paris address, rue des Récollets du Temple, are sometimes impressed as a mark on the reliefs.

Most of the decorative glass of 19th-C France came from the factories of Baccarat and St Louis, which were amalgamated from *c.*1835. (4) Fine lead-crystal vessels were made at Choisy-le-Roi, in subtle colours and decorated with cutting and engraving. Cut crystal pieces with a neo-classical flavour, often incorporating cameo portraits, were made from the 1820s. Classically simple pieces were produced for the luxury market in opaline glass, in which the fashion changed from white (up to *c.*1830) to rose-pink, apple-green or turquoise. (5)

Paperweights. Today the most sought-after of all French glass, with the possible exception of the wares of Emile Gallé and René Lalique, are the 19th-C paperweights made at Baccarat, St Louis and Clichy.

There are two main kinds of Baccarat paperweights: about two thirds are *millefiori* (meaning literally "a thousand flowers"), and almost one third are flowers. Butterflies and incrustations (cameos) make up the balance. About half the *millefiori* are dated between 1846 and 1849; 1848 is the most common and 1849 the rarest. Sections of multicoloured rods in star shapes and arrow patterns are characteristic *millefiori* forms. Flower weights represent primroses, pansies and clematis. Incrustations include Queen Victoria, Joan of Arc and mythological figures. (10, 12; p 107, no. 1)

French paperweights

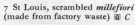

8 St Louis, fruit in a white lattice basket FC *E*
9 Clichy, overlay with *millefiori* tuft B *F*
10 Baccarat, cluster of *millefiori* and animal canes, 1848 FC *E*
11 Clichy, swirl weight in red and white FC *D*
12 Baccarat, butterfly on clear glass ground FC *F*

7 St Louis, scrambled *millefiori* (made from factory waste) G *C*

St Louis produced fewer *millefiori* weights than Baccarat, and about half are known as "*millefiori* mushrooms", as the rods spread out from the base in a mushroom shape. Others combine green foliage to form "bouquets". Most St Louis weights are of flowers, fruit, vegetables and reptiles and are more delicately coloured than those of Baccarat or Clichy. Some were signed and dated; the usual dates are 1847 and 1848, 1847 being much the rarer. (7, 8)

There are no dated Clichy weights and few are signed but it is known that weights were made there from about 1849. Eighty per cent are *millefiori*, the most characteristic of these being the "Clichy rose" with its tightly-packed pink and white petals, and sometimes with green and white leaves. Clichy incrustations were similar to those of Baccarat: Queen Victoria and Napoleon are the most valuable. (9, 11)

French 19th-C paperweights are much heavier than modern reproductions (of which there are many). They vary greatly in value, according to rarity of date and pattern.

GERMANY

It is often hard to identify the precise origin of German glass, and much of it has been indiscriminately labelled Bohemian. From the 14th C, glasshouses were situated in forests, close to the fuel sources, and produced green-, yellow- or brown-tinged domestic wares in *Waldglas* (forest glass), which continued to be made for some centuries. One of the most popular early types of glassware (it stayed in favour 1675–1825) was the *Römer*, a drinking vessel with near-spherical bowl, cylindrical stem studded with prunts, and hollow conical foot. (9) The *Humpen* was a cylindrical glass, commonly enamelled, with a slightly flared foot. (2) It is distinguishable from the *Wilkommen* (greeting glass) only by its lack of an inscription. The *Passglas* was a tall, narrow beaker graduated with horizontal glass or enamel lines which indicated how much to drink before passing the glass on to the rest of the company. (1) Venetian-style *cristallo* was imitated by imported artisans for the royal courts.

Enamelled glass was introduced *c.*1575, at first following Venetian styles. The most sophisticated motif of the period was that used on the *Reichsadlerhumpen* (Imperial eagle beakers)—the double-headed eagle of the Holy Roman Empire with shields hanging from its outspread wings. Commoner themes on enamelled pieces included hunting and riding scenes, allegories, inscriptions and coats of arms, generally of a robust peasant naïveté. Bohemian enamelled glasses often have borders of dots or dashes round the base. Because of stylistic conservatism, late pieces can look deceptively early.

German glass, 16th–18th C

3 Small *Schwarzlot* beaker in the manner of Johann Schaper, Nuremberg, *c.*1760–70 VR *H*
4 Enamelled flask, *c.*1750, ht 14cm FC *D*
5 Scrolled, shell-shaped cup, Silesia, *c.*1745 ⓑ *F*
6 Bohemian goblet, with faceted and engraved bowl, 18th c FC *D*
7 Flask engraved with pseudo-Chinese figures, signed by Anton Wilhelm Mäuerl, Nuremberg, 1719 VR *I*

1 Rhenish *Passglas*, 16th c ⓑ *F*
2 *Familienhumpen* with enamel figures, 1671, ht 23.5cm VR *I*

Decoration became more sophisticated with the *Hausmaler* (painters working at home), who obtained undecorated glass and enamelled it. Johann Schaper of Nuremberg (1621–70), the first to become well-known, worked mainly in *Schwarzlot* (black enamel) and *en grisaille* (grey), with red and gold touches. (3) *Commedia dell'Arte* figures were among his favourite themes. His most favoured vessel was a cylindrical beaker on three bun feet. His followers in Bohemia and Silesia included Daniel Preussler (1636–1733), his son Ignaz, and Johann Ludwig Faber. *Chinoiserie* was popular, often in combination with baroque scrolls and shells.

The many forgeries of enamelled glass often give themselves away by too perfect a metal or over-vivid colour. *Schwarzlot* glasses are very rare. Forged *Humpen* are often perfectly straight-sided (whereas the originals bulge slightly) and invariably have a cover, which is seldom found on the genuine article.

Engraved glass and Zwischengoldgläser. Caspar Lehmann of Prague, at the end of the 16th c, was the first European since the

Middle Ages to engrave glass on the lapidary's wheel. He trained Georg Schwanhardt, who returned to his native Nuremberg in 1622. Schwanhardt's masterly wheel engraving was sometimes supplemented by diamond-point. He was the founder of a Nuremberg school which included Hermann Schwinger and Georg Friedrich Killinger. Nuremberg-type goblets had bowls cut with scrollwork, medallions and classical or historical scenes, and stems ornamented with a variety of knops and collars. (8) Intaglio work was common.

About 1680 a new kind of crystal glass was introduced after experiments like Ravenscroft's in England (see pp 53–4). Early pieces made in Kassel, Potsdam and elsewhere suffered from crisselling. The technique was suited to wheel engraving, which could now be deeper, creating dramatic contrasts of light and shade.

The best period of engraving was 1685–1775. Magnificent work was done in court studios by Friedrich Winter of Petersdorf, who specialized in cameo relief; his brother Martin Winter, who worked at Berlin with Gottfried Spiller; and Franz Gondelach, the genius

German coloured glass

8 Nuremberg amethyst-tinted goblet, late 17th c Vℝ H
9 Green-tinted *Römer*, 17th–18th c, ht 15.5cm Ⓑ C
10 Blue overlay goblet, unsigned, c.1850 FⒸ E

11 Engraved spa decanter, stained in red, c.1850 FⒸ C
12 *Hyalith* mug, Egermann factory, c.1830 Ⓑ F
13 *Lithyalin* beaker, Bohemia, c.1830–40, ht 11.4cm Vℝ F
14 Cameo goblet, by F. Zach, 19th c Ⓑ F

of baroque glass engraving. Gondelach often engraved an eight-point rosette beneath the base of a glass.

The Bohemian workshops were dominant until c.1725, when Silesia took over. Bohemian decoration progressed from small formal flowers and foliage over the entire surface (1700–10) to baroque strapwork and foliage interlacing, sometimes with pseudo-Chinese figures (from c.1720). (6) The latter fashion was also followed notably by Anton Wilhelm Mäuerl in Nuremberg. (7) In the 1730s, when Bohemian work began to have a mass-produced feeling, Silesia was producing lobed goblets with petalled bases, many with engraved views. (5) Some of the best engraving was by Christian Gottfried Schneider (1710–73) at Warmbrunn. Some fine glasses known as *Zwischengoldgläser*, made in Bohemia from c.1730, were decorated with gold leaf sandwiched inside a double wall of glass, the two layers being fused together and the edge gilded. The most common shape was the straight-sided beaker, decorated with a hunting, commemorative or household scene. In the late 18th c the vogue for baroque-rococo engraving gave place to facet or brilliant cutting.

Coloured glass. At Potsdam in the last quarter of the 17th C, Johann Kunckel introduced his famous ruby glass, made from a formula which included gold chloride. This soon became fashionable and was frequently mounted with finely chased metal and sometimes deeply engraved by masters such as Gottfried Spiller. Pieces rarely come within the collector's reach. Blue, purple and green glass was also made in this period, as was *Milchglas*, an opaque white glass introduced to compete with Meissen porcelain.

A wide range of colourings was evolved in the 18th and 19th C. The fashion for imitating Wedgwood pottery or semi-precious stones led to *Hyalith* (black or red) and *Lithyalin* (produced by Friedrich Egermann from 1777 to 1864). (12, 13; p 106, no. 2) Cased or overlay glass was made in large quantities from *c.*1815. (10) Souvenir glassware was aimed at the tourist market, some decorated with paintings in transparent colours depicting romantic ruins and mountain scenes. (11) The best painted work was by the Mohn family in Dresden and Vienna; signed pieces by either Samuel the father or Gottlob the son are rare and costly.

THE LOW COUNTRIES

Dutch and Flemish glass was noted more for decoration than form. Shapes were derivative—in fact for more than a century most of the glass made by the immigrant Italian craftsmen who had settled in Antwerp as early as 1541, and in Liège by 1569, was indistinguishable from Venetian wares. (4)

At the beginning of the 1600s many more glasshouses were established: at Middleburg, The Hague, Rotterdam and Amsterdam. The Bonhomme family from Liège, for example, built up a flourishing glassmaking business, with branches in Huy and Maastricht. Certain serpent-stemmed and winged glasses were becoming identifiably Netherlandish.

Most well-to-do Dutch families possessed one or two *latticino* glass and silver windmill-shaped fantasies as ornaments. (6) Possibly in reaction against this Venetian frivolity, Netherlandish glass manufacturers were soon searching for a new glass in the style of Ravenscroft's in England. By the 1670s English craftsmen were working in Haarlem and in 1680 the Bonhommes were making flint glass *à l'anglaise*. Although the distinctive English ingredient, lead, was missing from this, it did have the crisselled appearance of Ravenscroft glass.

In the 18th C English designs, as well as wares, were widely imported into Holland, which largely contributed to a decline in the Dutch glass industry. By 1771 only a factory at s'Hertogenbosch continued to make good drinking glasses, all other factories having changed over to the production of window and mirror glass, and bottles.

Engraving. There were three main kinds of decoration: diamond-point engraving (*c.*1575–1690), wheel engraving (*c.*1690–1750) and stippling with a diamond-point (*c.*1750–1800). The Netherlands was justly famous for diamond-point, which became a popular pastime—much of the best work was, in fact, done by talented amateurs. Collectors particularly prize the green glass roemers of Anna Roemers Visscher (1583–1651), who combined calligraphy with flowers, fruit and insects. Her work, rarely signed, was never surpassed. Her sister Maria Tesselschade van Schurman (1607–78) did similarly enchanting traceries on fine glass. Other notable engravers include: William Jacobz van Heemskerk (1613–92), an expert calligraphic engraver—many bottles bear his signature and a date between 1648 and 1690 (7); a mid-17th C artist signing himself C.J.M. or C.F.M. (possibly Christoffel Jansz Meyer of The

Hague); and towards the end of the century G.V. Nes and W.M. (for Willem Mooleyser).

In the 18th C the cruder technique of wheel engraving, applied to thicker glass, superseded diamond-point engraving. (1) Prominent in this type of work was Jacob Sang of Amsterdam, to whom some Dutch marine subjects, foliage and scrollwork and finely engraved heraldic glasses have been attributed. Signed work has survived from 1752–62. In the second half of the century portraits on flat glass panels were done by C.C. Schröder, copying 17th-C prints.

Dutch glass, 16th–18th C

1 Wheel-engraved friendship goblet, c.1765 FG E
2 Wine glass with flared bowl and hollow-knop stem, c.1700 B D
3 Stipple-engraved Newcastle goblet, attributed to David Wolff, c.1770 B G
4 Venetian-style wine flute, 17th c VR F
5 Roemer, 17th c VR H
6 Windmill glass in *latticino* and silver, 17th c VR H
7 Diamond-engraved bottle, 1684 VR H
8 Small green roemer, 17th c VR I

Stipple engraving, using a diamond set in a handle and gently tapped with a hammer, was probably a technique first refined by Frans Greenwood from Rotterdam, whose work dates from 1722–55. Contemporaries of Greenwood's who worked in stipple were Aert Schouman in the 1750s and G.H. Hoolart, who flourished c.1775–80. Glasses with stippling are known as "Wolff glasses" after the engraver David Wolff, whose own signed work (dated 1784–95) appears rather laboured by comparison with some of his imitators' examples. (3) Known artists of the Wolff school include Willem Fortuyn, C. Adams and an artist who signed himself V.H. Important 19th-C engravers such as Andries Melort (1779–1849) of Dordrecht and The Hague decorated flat sheets of glass in the style of Dutch Old Masters.

SCANDINAVIA

Sweden. The oldest surviving Scandinavian glass is Swedish of the late 17th C, and Sweden has been a great glassmaking country ever since. Norway began production in 1741 and supplied Denmark during the later 18th C.

The first surviving Swedish pieces were made at Kungsholm Glasbruck in Stockholm (1676–1815), a factory founded by an Italian, G.B. Scapitta, and administered after 1678 by Swedes. The early glass is similar to Venetian, and is often of poor technical quality. Some goblets had stems formed into royal initials, and royal crowns were sometimes used as handles on goblet covers. In the early 18th C Bohemian influence became dominant, with shorter goblet stems and thicker metal, though some Venetian features survive, such as a fold-over foot and a "squashed tomato" swelling in the stem. Wheel engraving was introduced by the German Kristoffer Elstermann, who arrived in 1698 and died 1721. Coats of arms were the main type of engraved decoration.

Kungsholm had royal patronage, but the other 17th-C Swedish glass factory, Skånska Glasbruket (1691–1762) was a more proletarian outfit. Its glass was mainly functional, though late pieces imitated Kungsholm decoration. Glass from this factory has a certain "folk" character. (2) The third of Sweden's historic glassworks was Kosta, founded in 1742 and still in operation. Among their works were small chandeliers.

Norway. The Norwegian glass industry was founded by royal decree at Nöstetangen in 1741. The style in the early years was Germanic. In 1853 the Norwegian glass industry was overhauled, with new factories to supply Denmark as well as Norway. At Nöstetangen, excellent German craftsmen were employed, and one from Newcastle. A cutters' and engravers' workshop was set up, with the German H.G. Köhler in charge, a brilliant artist in the Silesian style, who had previously worked at Copenhagen. (1) The collector should note that on Norwegian engraved glass, a crown or set of royal initials does not necessarily indicate status, but merely reflects a well distributed patriotism.

Scandinavian glass, 18th and 19th C

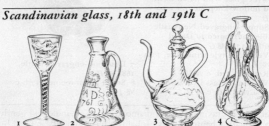

1 **Norwegian engraved glass, by H.G. Köhler, 1771** ⊞ *D*
2 **Swedish decanter, Skånska Glasbruket, 1761** V͞R *D*

3 **Norwegian ewer, Nöstetangen, 1760–70** ⊞ ٩ *D*
4 **Swedish waisted decanter, early 19th c** ⸬ ٩ *D*

In the best Nöstetangen period (1760–70), two kinds of glass were made—a clear, bubbly, pinkish soda-lime, and a more expensive crystal like English lead glass. In the latter, baluster stems of Newcastle type were common for expensive drinking glasses. Larger items were often embellished with trailed threads and moulded surface effects. (3) Nöstetangen closed in 1777, and crystal production moved to Hurdals Verk, where the prevailing style turned from rococo to neo-classical, and coloured glass was frequently used. Hurdals Verk closed in 1809 and production was transferred to a less ambitious factory, Gjövik Verk (1809–47).

VENICE

There were already glassmakers at Venice in the 11th C. It is likely that the Venetians, perhaps before the 15th C, discovered how to decolorize glass using manganese. The resulting clear *cristallo* was made mainly on the island of Murano. (6) The next biggest glassmaking centre was at L'Altare near Genoa.

Venetian glass, 16th–18th C

1 Enamelled *Stangenglas*, second half of 16th c V̄Ṟ *I*
2 Serpent goblet in clear and blue glass, 17th c V̄Ṟ ዒ *F*
3 Covered jug of blue and white "combed" glass, early 18th c V̄Ṟ ዒ *F*
4 *Lattimo* tea bowl and saucer, with gilding, *c.*1720–30 V̄Ṟ *E*
5 *Latticino* covered goblet, late 16th c ⊕ ዒ *F*
6 *Cristallo tazza*, 16th c ⊕ ዒ *F*
7 *Latticino* bowl, late 16th or early 17th c ⊕ ዒ *F*
8 "Ice-glass" beaker, second half of 16th c V̄Ṟ *F*

The Venetian product, though clearer than most Renaissance glass, is rarely without a smoky brown tinge. Intentionally coloured glass was made in green, blue and purple. Semi-precious stones, especially onyx, agate and chalcedony, were imitated. At the end of the 15th C, shapes tended to be based on those of silver.

Venetian soda glass lent itself to being worked with pincers and tongs. The most fanciful wares, extravagantly baroque, date from the 17th C—wine glasses with convoluted winged stems or motifs based on sea-horses. (2) Bodies of vessels were dynamically waved or crumpled, or made to resemble flames. Simpler wares were made to foreign order.

Decoration characteristically took the form of threads of opaque white glass (*latticino*) embedded in the body of a wine glass, ewer or *tazza* (ornamental cup)—either *vetro a reticello* (with criss-crossing threads forming an overall diamond lattice) or *vetro a retorti* (with threads in intricately twisted parallel "canes"). (5; p 166, no. 1) Occasionally, coloured threads were used instead of white. A rarer technique was "crackle-" or "ice-glass", with a pattern of tiny cracks caused by plunging the hot glass in water for a moment and then reheating. (8)

Enamel decoration was common, notably for armorials. (1) Opaque white glass (*lattimo*) was sometimes used in the 17th and 18th C as a substitute for expensive porcelain, and was painted in porcelain style, sometimes with views of Venice after Canaletto. (4) Engraving was rare, although it was popular in Venetian-type glass made in the Netherlands and at Hall (the Tyrol). Quality declined in the 18th C. Bohemian glass was now a formidable rival, and in 1736 Giuseppe Briati obtained a patent to make glass in the Bohemian manner. The Venetian industry was finally eclipsed by the rise of English and Irish cut glass, though Antonio Salviati revived Renaissance styles from the mid-19th C in somewhat sentimental wares.

It is often difficult to distinguish Venetian craftsmanship from imitations *à la façon de Venise* made principally at Liège, Antwerp, Hall, Nuremberg and London. But *façon de Venise* glasses are often in a rather darker or straw-coloured metal.

SPAIN

Catalonia. The principal glassmaking centre, from an early date, was Catalonia. Catalan blown glass, Venetian in style though less dainty and diaphanous, was much prized between 1500 and 1650. (1, 2, 3, 5) Venetian decorative techniques, such as crackling and *latticino*, were also used elsewhere in Spain, but certain Catalan shapes were unique: the covered jar in the shape of an inverted bell; the aspersory (holy water bucket: a bowl-like vessel with bail handle); and the *almorratxa* (rose-water sprinkler with four spouts). The Catalan glass industry declined after *c.*1650 and Venetian styles gave place to the traditional Spanish *cántir* and *porrón* (spouted drinking vessels). (6) The 18th-c *almorratxa* has a narrow bottle neck and shorter spouts than the earlier type.

Spanish glass, 16th–18th C

1 Wine glass with white cords, gilt prunts and pincered decoration, Catalonia, 16th c V&R F
2 *Façon de Venise* small jug of yellowish tint with opaque white strands and looped blue handle and rim, 17th c FC Q B
3 Enamelled vase, Barcelona, late 15th c V&R Q F
4 Bowl, engraved with a château and trees, San Ildefonso,

18th c B E
5 Cock with opaque white stripes and cobalt-blue crestings, probably Barcelona, 16th c, ht 28.5 cm V&R F
6 *Porrón* with rings and stripes of opaque white in a twisted braid, Catalonia, 18th c V&R E
7 Vase of yellowish glass with blue handles and threading, probably 18th c B D

Southern Spain. While Catalonia looked to Venice for inspiration, the southern glassworks of Almeria, Castril and Cartagena looked to Muslim culture. They did not make crystal glass, most of their work being green, full of tiny air bubbles and Arabic in manner, with attenuated necks and bulbous bodies constricted in the middle. Rims tended to be cut off and melted smooth, sometimes with a thick thread round bottle necks. At Seville some Venetian-style wares were made. As in Venice, Bohemian glass won supremacy in southern Spain in the early 18th C. By the mid-18th C the influence of Catalonia was evident.

Castile. Another important centre by the early 16th C was Cadalso in the province of Madrid (Castile). During the 17th C Italian and Flemish glassworkers flocked to Spain, many to Castile. In 1608 a furnace was built at the Escorial under the Venetian glassblower

Domingo Barovier. A factory was opened by the Italo-Fleming Guglielmo Toreata in 1689, in Castilla la Nueva. Most of the Madrid-based factories made coarse versions of Venetian-type wares. The Madrid glass industry went into decline *c.*1700 with the fashion for wheel-engraved glass introduced by Philip V, though from 1720 until *c.*1728 Juan de Goyeneche made wheel-engraved glass in the French style at Nuevo Baztán.

San Ildefonso. In 1728 a Catalan glassworker, Ventura Sit, set up a furnace at San Ildefonso, near the palace of La Granja. Queen Isabella built him a factory on the royal estate, and Philip V encouraged him to make large plates of glass for palace mirrors. Other workmen came to San Ildefonso from Germany and Sweden, including Sigismund Brun from Hanover, who made fine crystal glasses in the late 18th C. Gilt flower decoration was common. Coloured and opaque white glass was also made. Enamel decoration was applied to the typical "San Ildefonso jar", with its Arab shape and cone-like cover topped by a knop or mushroom. The royal factory was closed down in 1829 in the face of Anglo-Irish competition. (4)

THE UNITED STATES

There were four pioneer glass factories in America: at Jamestown, Va. (1608), Salem, Mass. (1639), New York (when it was still New Amsterdam, before 1664) and Shackmaxson, now in the environs of Philadelphia (1683). In 1620 the Jamestown factory began making glass beads for trade with the Indians, and the plant survived the massacre of 1622. Window glass was an urgent 17th-C need, and factories were set up to produce it in Virginia, making bottles as a sideline.

In 1739 Caspar Wistar (1696–1752), a brass-button maker from Philadelphia, turned to glassmaking and started a factory in Salem

American glass, 18th and 19th C
Value symbols refer to New York estimates expressed as pounds

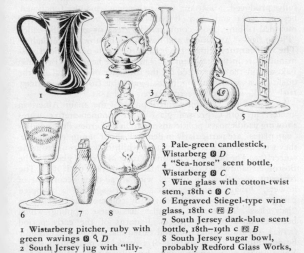

1 Wistarberg pitcher, ruby with green wavings ⓑ ⚲ D
2 South Jersey jug with "lily-pad" decoration ⓑ ⚲ D
3 Pale-green candlestick, Wistarberg ⓑ D
4 "Sea-horse" scent bottle, Wistarberg ⓑ C
5 Wine glass with cotton-twist stem, 18th c ⓑ C
6 Engraved Stiegel-type wine glass, 18th c ⒻⒸ B
7 South Jersey dark-blue scent bottle, 18th–19th c ⒻⒸ B
8 South Jersey sugar bowl, probably Redford Glass Works, New York, 1835–50 ⅤⓇ F

County, N.J., later known as Wistarberg or Allowaystown. It was the first really successful glassworks in America. Wistar imported Dutch glassmakers and the Dutch influence is evident even in the later period. He made window glass in five sizes, bottles, lamp chimneys, snuff and mustard bottles, "electrofying globes and tubes", drinking glasses and other table glass. The earliest wares were of plain glass, but colour was introduced with success. Two-colour work included ruby jugs with dark green wavings. (1) Plain glass and coloured glass were sometimes used in conjunction. Small quantities of a rich dark-blue glass were made, as well as turquoise, opalescent, clear green and the rarer amber and brown. Some coloured glass was whirled with white in the manner of Nailsea (see p 56). Balls of glass (often mistakenly called "witch-balls" today) were blown in various sizes as covers for bowls and jugs. (14) The raised "lily-pad" design uncannily anticipates Art Nouveau in its serpentine swirls. (2) Wistar died in 1752 but his son Richard continued the factory until 1780. Glassware made in the Wistar style, but not assignable to any particular factory or region, is described as being of the "South Jersey" type. A characteristic feature, apart from lily-pad decoration, is the "swan finial", which often in fact looks more like a duck or chicken. South Jersey glass continued to be made until the mid-19th C.

Henry William Stiegel (1729–85) built two glasshouses at Manheim, Pennsylvania, which operated between 1765 and 1774. The wares were comparatively small and fragile, of flint glass. Some were engraved: in contrast to foreign engraving, the designs—tulips, baskets of flowers, sunbursts with birds, borders of intersecting arcs filled with latticework—were executed on thin blown glass and left unpolished, with a "folk art" finish. (6) Typical of Stiegel's wares are pocket flasks, made 1769–74, patterned with a daisy motif within a diamond or hexagon. Except in the case of these items, attributions can only be tentative.

John Frederick Amelung, who founded a factory in Maryland in 1784, was the only American glassmaker of the time to inscribe and date some of his work. Amelung glass, which includes tableware and decanters, is now extremely rare. The Pitkin family success-fully produced glassware in Connecticut, mainly functional, between 1783 and 1830. It tends to have vertical or swirled moulded ribbing, most commonly in green or amber. So-called "Pitkin flasks" are ribbed and have a double-thick lower half.

The 19th century. Pittsburgh became the centre of American glass manufacture in the early 19th C. The factory begun by Benjamin Bakewell in 1808 was noted for the brilliance of its metal and the quality of its wheel cutting, indistinguishable from contemporary Irish work. Bakewell's factory lasted until 1882.

As with blue transfer-printed pottery, the main American interest in 19th-C pressed glass is in commemorative wares showing paddleboats, politicians and military heroes. Pressed glass "cup plates" are particularly in demand: about 76mm in diameter, they were used as a rest for the teacup while tea was drunk from the saucer! (10) The best-known manufacturer of pressed glass was the Boston & Sandwich Glass Co., Mass., from 1826 until 1888. The company specialized in objects with an all-over decoration of flowers, foliage, rosettes etc., raised against a stippled background—a type much sought by collectors and known as "lacy glass". The earliest lacy glass has coarse stippling, which becomes finer in later pieces. Patterns of the early period (c.1825–50) are so numerous and varied that provenance can only be determined, in the absence of a mark, by meticulous study. Valuation, as with paperweights, depends on rarity of design and colour. An especially sought-after pattern is that made for only

American glass, 18th and 19th C
Value symbols refer to New York estimates expressed as pounds

9 Stiegel sugar bowl v℞ ♀ *F*
10 Benjamin Franklin cup plate, Boston & Sandwich Glass Co., Mass., 19th c 🅵🅲 *B*
11 Clear glass jug, 18th c 🅱 *C*
12 "Lacy glass" cake tray, Boston & Sandwich Glass Co., Mass., *c.*1835 🅵🅲 *B*
13 "Liberty" flask, West Willington, 19th c 🅵🅾 *B*
14 Pink and white glass ball, New Jersey, 19th c 🅵🅾 *C*
15 "Satin glass" vase in pewter holder, 19th c 🅵🅲 *A*
16 Cut-glass celery vase, Bakewell, Page & Bakewell,

Pittsburgh, *c.*1825 🅱 *C*
17 Opaline vase with coralene decorations, late 19th c 🅱 *C*
18 Cut-glass compote, New England Glass Co., Mass., *c.*1872–6 🅱 ♀ *C*

---

five months in 1892 using an American coin of that year as part of the mould. (12)

About the middle of the century, many kinds of paperweight were made—including floral bouquets, fruit on a *latticino* base, *millefiori* and portraits based on coin and medal designs. Realistic fruit paperweights were made by the New England Glass Co., and in the latter half of the century pressed paperweights sometimes took the form of landmarks, books or animals.

"Opal-decorated" pieces—the contemporary name for opaque white glass—were made in large quantities from *c.*1855. A popular type of art glass was Pearl Satin Ware, or "satin glass". (15) Late 19th-C American glass, up to the heyday of Tiffany, followed English examples closely in the imitation of Bohemian wares, the revival of Venetian styles, and the fashion for ornate shapes, and colour produced by chemical means. (p 107, no. 2)

American cut glass from the earliest period (1771–1830) is unlikely to come the way of the average collector. Flute cutting was a common decorative technique of the middle phase (before *c.*1880), when elegant cased glass was also made, most popularly in ruby and dark blue. "Brilliant-cut" glass of great virtuosity was produced in the 1880s and 90s.

FIREARMS
=&=
EDGED WEAPONS

Firearms from before the mid-16th C are unlikely to come the way of collectors, but swords in good condition from the 15th C are comparatively common. Perhaps the term most likely to cause confusion to beginners is "rifle": it applies not to the shape or length of a firearm but to the grooves (rifling) cut on the inside of a barrel to give spin to the bullet in flight.

FIREARMS

The first hand guns (14th C) were difficult to aim, as the gunner needed a free hand to apply a light to the touch hole. In response to this difficulty the matchlock evolved: a movable arm (serpentine) which on pressure from a trigger swung forward to bring a lighted match into contact with a pan of priming powder. Because it was cheap, an improved matchlock musket was used for military purposes in Europe in the 16th and 17th C, even though more advanced guns were available.

The weakness of the matchlock was that it was temperamental in bad weather. This problem led in the early 16th C to the more weather-proof wheel lock. Pulling the trigger released a grooved wheel, held in tension, against a piece of pyrites, causing ignition. Wheel locks were used in early pistols (mostly German), which date from *c.*1530.

The first pistols were of forged metal, but by the mid-16th C it was usual for the stock to be wooden, with a ball-shaped butt. Inlaid decoration in ivory and stained horn was often applied. (3,8)

Around 1570 the snaphaunce appeared. It replaced the wheel lock in most of Europe, and was especially popular in Scotland, Scandinavia and Italy. The flint was held in the jaws of a cock which came down on a rough steel over the flash pan. (1)

France's importance as a gunmaking country in the 17th C owed much to Louis XIII, who encouraged the fashion for a plain wooden stock with an elegantly flared butt. The flintlock was

Firearm mechanisms

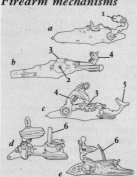

1 Serpentine
2 Revolving steel wheel
3 Flash pan
4 Cock
5 Steel
6 Combined steel and pan cover (known as the battery, frizzen or hammer)

a Matchlock
b Wheel lock
c Snaphaunce lock, shown with the steel drawn back
d Miquelet lock (Spanish type)
e French flintlock

developed in France c.1612. Later adopted elsewhere in Europe (but particularly belatedly in Germany), it was an advance upon the snaphaunce, with the difference that the steel and the pan cover were made in one. French firearms enjoyed their golden age in the reign of Louis XIV.

The paramount Italian gunmaking town was Brescia, where the Cominazzo family was dominant. (1) Spain and southern Italy favoured a variant of the flintlock known as the miquelet, identifiable by its exterior mainspring. (6) It fell out of use in Italy in the first half of the 18th C, but survived in Spain until well into the 19th. In the Baltic provinces of Germany in the 17th C, the *Tschinke* was a popular firearm: a sporting rifle with an outside mainspring. (10) In the Netherlands, Maastricht was well known for its ivory-stocked pistols. (2)

Gunmaking in England did not properly get under way until just before the Civil War. Long-barrelled sporting rifles were used in the later 17th C for shooting rising or stationary birds. The handier blunderbuss was a dumpy, bell-mouthed gun suitable for stage coach guards and boarding parties at sea. (12) English pistols of the early 18th C include a breech-loaded type with a cannon-like barrel and a mask on the butt-cap. Infantrymen of the period were equipped with "Brown Bess" flintlock muskets. Experiments with breech-loaders (first used in the 1530s) were stimulated by the American and Napoleonic Wars. Pistols replaced swords for duelling in the last quarter of the 18th C. Emphasis on duelling pistols soon shifted from decoration, which became subdued, to mechanical improvements. (5) Scottish pistols, generally with all-metal stocks and often decorated with Celtic motifs, are particularly sought by collectors. (4)

French styles were the predominant influence on high-quality Continental firearms for about a hundred years after c.1670. After

Pistols

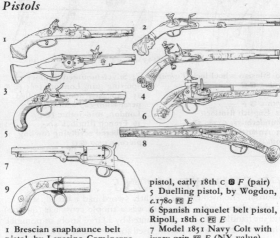

1 Brescian snaphaunce belt pistol, by Lazarino Cominazzo, 17th C **B** *I* (pair)
2 Dutch ivory-stock pistol, Maastricht, 17th C **B** ♀ *I* (pair)
3 Brescian wheel lock pistol, 17th C **B** ♀ *I* (pair)
4 Scottish all-steel flintlock belt pistol, early 18th C **B** *F* (pair)
5 Duelling pistol, by Wogdon, c.1780 **FC** *E*
6 Spanish miquelet belt pistol, Ripoll, 18th C **FC** *E*
7 Model 1851 Navy Colt with ivory grip **FC** *E* (NY value)
8 Saxon wheel lock pistol, the stock inlaid with staghorn, 1579 **FC** *H*
9 American percussion cap "pepperbox" revolver, mid-19th C **FC** *D* (NY value)

the Revolution Nicolas Noël Boutet was the supreme maker of elaborate presentation firearms.

In the early 18th C the first Swiss and German immigrants to America brought with them the short-barrelled rifle. Soon, long-barrelled rifles of the "Kentucky" type, with a patch box on the butt, were being made by Pennsylvanian Germans. (13)

Gunsmiths of the early 19th C experimented with percussion systems. In 1807 a Scottish clergyman named Forsyth patented a detonating lock, with a revolving magazine shaped like a scent bottle. By the 1810s a simpler version had been devised, using a copper percussion cap placed over a nipple. The percussion cap method greatly stimulated the evolution of revolvers. A popular type was the "pepperbox", with a cylinder containing five or six bores. (9) More efficient was the revolver introduced in America by Samuel Colt in 1848: as the hammer was cocked with the thumb the cylinder revolved to bring a new charge in line with the rifled barrel. A popular model was the 1851 Navy Colt, which took its name from an engraving of a naval battle on the cylinder. (7) In Britain similar revolvers were made, but with a hammer that could be cocked by pressure on the trigger.

Long arms

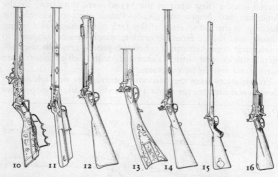

10 Silesian wheel lock *Tschinke*, 17th C 🅱 *G*
11 Norwegian snaplock rifle, 17th C 🅱 *F*
12 English flintlock blunderbuss, c.1780 🆖 *E*
13 American "Kentucky" rifle; 19th C 🆖 *F*

14 Silver-mounted flintlock sporting gun, London, 1785 🆖 *F*
15 Lancaster double-barrelled percussion cap sporting rifle, London, mid-19th C 🆖 *E*
16 French flintlock six-chambered revolving fowling piece, c.1700 🅱 *G*

EDGED WEAPONS

Swords. The medieval or knightly sword had a broad, straight, double-edged blade. The guard was a simple cross-bar (quillon) and the handle (hilt) was surmounted by a large knob, or pommel. This heavy cutting implement, used for combat against armour of mail, gave way in the 15th C to a longer, narrow, thrusting weapon made to counter plate armour. By mid-century the guard began to curve into an S shape, and somewhat later the knucklebow developed—a half loop extending from the quillon. The hilt with a complex arrangement of loops and bars to protect the hand reached its apogee in late 16th-C Europe with the light and elegant swept-hilt rapier. (7) The rapier was a fencing weapon used for duelling.

Edged weapons

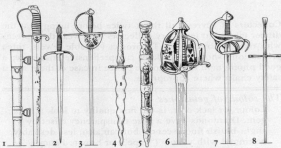

1 1805 pattern naval officer's sword, London FC F
2 Left-hand dagger, c.1600 FC F
3 Italian cup-hilted rapier, decorated with warriors' heads, birds, fruit and flowers, late 17th c FC E
4 English plug bayonet, late 17th c FC E

5 Scottish regimental dirk and scabbard, late 19th c C D
6 Scottish basket-hilted broadsword, 18th c FC F
7 Swept-hilt rapier, with blade made at Solingen, late 16th c FC F
8 German two-handed estoc, c.1500 B F

It was both a cutting and thrusting sword, and as it was worn with ordinary dress, more emphasis was placed on decoration. Two-handed combat using a rapier in the right hand and a dagger in the left, decorated *en suite*, was developed in the 16th c.

For extra protection, steel panels of stylized shell shape were added to either side of the hilt's base. From these developed the basket-hilted sword, favoured in Scotland. (6) Cup-hilted rapiers, popular in Italy and Spain, offered irresistible possibilities for embellishment. (3)

A new light, short-bladed rapier was introduced in the 17th c: the "smallsword". Its hilt, particularly on presentation swords of the 18th c, acquired jewel-like ornamentation. The hunting sword was introduced in the 15th c for giving the *coup de grâce* to wounded game. Its scabbard was sometimes fitted with smaller knives and other cutlery. Hilts could be of staghorn or ivory.

Most military swords are simple and robust. Regimental markings may add considerably to the value. (1)

The principal blade-making centres were Solingen in Germany, Toledo and Valencia in Spain, and Milan and Brescia in Italy. Many swords made before the 18th c are fitted with a later blade. Marks should be treated with caution: many blades purporting to be made by the best Italian bladesmiths or at Toledo in fact come from Solingen.

Daggers and bayonets. The dagger appeared as an accessory to the sword in the late 13th c. In the 16th and 17th c the left-hand dagger played an important role in duelling. (2) The ballock dagger, with a guard formed by two protruding lobes, was popular in the late 16th-early 17th c. Other collectable types include the rondel dagger, ear dagger and Scottish dirk. Dirks of the 17th and 18th c sometimes appear on the market, but much more common are 19th-c costume versions, often with a cairngorm on the pommel. (5) Early bayonets (plug bayonets) were fitted into the muzzle, but this encumbered loading, so from the late 17th c special sockets were used. (4) In the 19th c the sword bayonet evolved—a small hilted sword attached to a lug on the barrel by a spring catch.

JEWELLERY

Collectors of Sèvres will think twice before using it at the dinner table, but jewellery collectors may wear their pieces with relative unconcern. To protect valuable jewels, three precautions should be taken: comprehensive insurance; a good photograph to give to the police in case of theft; and a safety chain where appropriate.

The colour of gemstones

Colour, or lack of it, is the first quality to look at in a gem. Diamonds have a pure transparency offset by a slight bluish fluorescence, but can also, less desirably, be tinged with yellow ("cape") or brown. Fancy-coloured diamonds occasionally occur, and command high prices.

The colour of a stone is caused either by traces of impurity (e.g. in rubies and sapphires, which are both varieties of corundum) or by an element built into the crystal structure. Rubies improve their colour in artificial light, so it is wise to buy them in daylight. Topaz, in its familiar sherry-coloured form, superficially resembles citrine, but may be distinguished by its soapier feel. Turquoise turns a nasty shade of green when exposed to grease: for this reason, one should never wash one's hands while wearing a turquoise ring.

Weight and hardness

Gemstones are weighed by the "carat", which is one fifth of a metric gramme, subdivided into 100 points. The "grain" (one quarter of a carat) is the unit of weight applied to pearls.

The hardness of a stone is classified according to the Moh scale, which ranges from 10 (diamond) down to 1 (talc, which is only about as hard as a fingernail).

Fraudulent gemstones

An old trick with diamonds is to whiten a cape stone with a wash of indigo. More recently, low-grade diamonds have been turned into "fancy" ones by the colouring effects of radiation. White zircons are sometimes used as a diamond substitute.

Rubies and emeralds—the most valuable of gems—have been widely synthesized. Fake rubies and sapphires made by the Verneuil process give themselves away by curved colour zones visible under a lens: in the real thing the zones are straight or acute-angled. Soudé emeralds are made of two layers of quartz or colourless beryl fused together with green cement.

Turquoise has been successfully imitated, using glass, porcelain, chemical composition or turquoise dust bonded together by a resin.

Pearls

Pearls, whose lustre can be spoilt by chemicals in the atmosphere, are very soft and must be separated from faceted gemstones to prevent scratching. A string of pearls in regular use should last about 150 years, if they are restrung on silk at least once a year.

THE RENAISSANCE

The "rebirth" of the Renaissance affected jewellery just as much as the other arts, though styles owed a debt not to classical jewellery but to sculpture. Classical myths were a favourite subject, and classical columns and pediments were incorporated in jewel settings. The tradition of cameos stretched from classical times right through the Middle Ages to the 15th C and beyond. (2) Great Italian cameo-cutters of the Renaissance included Giovanni Bernardi, Domenico Compagni and Valerio Vicentino. There were some expert cutters of small portrait cameos in France, but their names are largely unknown.

It is often very difficult to fix the nationality of a piece of Renaissance jewellery. The style that spread from Italy became standard, and there was other cross-pollination too. Many of Henry VIII's jewellers had foreign names, and there was a constant traffic of merchants from abroad. Monarchs gave and received jewels as gifts and bought fine examples for their treasuries. Designs were spread internationally by engravings and pattern books.

Renaissance jewellery

1 French enamelled gold hat badge with head of St John the Baptist, early 16th c V͠R ⚲ I
2 Cameo of Ludovico Sforza, c.1500 V͠R ⚲ H
3 German enamelled gold pendant set with rubies and pearls, c.1600 V͠R ⚲ H
4 Cross found in Denmark, early 16th c V͠R I

5 Gold ring with uncut diamond crystal, c.1520 ⊞ G
6 Flemish enamelled gold and baroque pearl pendant (the hull is a pearl), second half of 16th c, ht 14cm ⊞ ⚲ I
7 Enamelled gold pendant of Prudence, the head and arms of chalcedony, probably French, mid-16th c V͠R ⚲ I
8 Italian enamelled gold eagle pendant, with baroque pearl and carbuncle, late 16th c, ht 7.2cm ⊞ ⚲ H

The pendant is the most distinctive ingredient of Renaissance jewellery, especially the pendant pearl. (7) Important pendant designers of the 16th C included Etienne Delaune, Pierre Woeiriot and architect Jacques Du Cerceau. A characteristic jewel type in non-Italian regions was the gold and enamelled *enseigne*, or hat badge. (1) Portrait badges and portrait pendants were especially favoured and sometimes sent as presents. Other portraits were made in enamelled gold: the finest surviving is of the Emperor Charles V. It was an age of personality cults, and these were also served by jewels formed of owners' initials; Henry VIII was particularly fond of this kind of ornament. Religious jewels bearing the sacred monogram "IHS" were also made—one was designed by Arnold Lulls for Anne of Denmark.

A fashion that originated in Italy was for massive gold chains, worn mainly by men in England, by women in Flanders and South Germany. Generally speaking, men were still the main clients for jewellery.

In most of the arts the early classical phase of the Renaissance had given way by *c.*1540 to mannerism, which blended virtuosity and fantasy. After *c.* 1560 jewellery was treated with more display and profusion. (3) The centres of craftsmanship shifted from Italy and France to Germany and Austria. In Italy the monumental style was kept up. In France, exhausted by religious wars at the end of the 16th C, the demand for luxurious jewellery decreased.

Augsburg was the leading German centre and Prague became important from *c.*1570 in the reign of Emperor Rudolph—a prosperity ended by the Thirty Years War. England and Spain were rich in jewellery at the time when Elizabeth I and Philip II were locked in rivalry. Nationalism was growing, but it was still hard to detect the country of origin of a jewel.

Jewels were now becoming a perquisite more of women than of men. (Henry VIII had worn more jewels than all his wives put together.) Aristocratic ladies owned magnificent *parures*—suites of jewels comprising a *carcanet* (collar for the neck), a matching chain outlining the neck of a dress, and a *cotière* (long chain with pendant). The fashion for *parures* probably originated at the court of Maximilian in Vienna. By the 1560s it had spread to Spain, and rich belts were popular in France by the 1570s. *Parures* gained favour more slowly in England.

Watches and pomanders were hung from belts. Pendants remained fashionable—sometimes of dragons, eagles, phoenixes, seahorses, chimeras. Erasmus Hornick of Nuremberg published designs for such pendants in 1562, incorporating the newly popular baroque pearls—*barocco* means "misshapen pearl". (6, 8)

A new taste of the last quarter of the 16th C was for pendants with architectural or geometric elements made up of square-cut stones. Pilasters, arches and arcades framed voluptuous mannerist motifs, depicting biblical or classical subjects or personified Virtues. Most of these jewels came from German workshops. In jewellery, as in literature, it was the age of "conceits"—of Gordian knots, rebuses and acrostics. But more commonplace subjects came in as the taste for emblems and allegories faded. Elizabeth I of England owned a brooch in the form of a warming pan, and in the National Museum at Stockholm there is a mousetrap brooch.

The importance of maritime supremacy in the 16th C is reflected in jewels taking the form of ships. (6) The medieval fashion for scented jewellery was continued, in pomander beads. Portrait cameos remained popular.

A new lightness and symmetry is seen in the designs (1596–1616) of the Huguenot Daniel Mignot, who worked at Augsburg. He was one of many designers who served the turn-of-the-century fashion for *aigrettes*—jewels supporting a feather worn in the hair or cap. Anne of Denmark introduced the fashion into England when she married James I.

THE *17th* CENTURY

In the 17th C the prodigal ornament of mannerism was succeeded by a cooler, self-consciously "tasteful" period, and then by the pomp of the baroque. Figures became less fashionable than geometric designs, and multicoloured enamels relinquished their importance to gemstones, especially diamonds. (1, 7, 8) Cases for miniatures and watches entered the realm of jewellery. (3) The new accent on gems is illustrated by the designs of Arnold Lulls, the

Dutch jeweller who worked in England for Anne of Denmark: he created formal arrangements of table-cut stones with a faint backing of enamelled scrolls. Jewel cutting was becoming more sophisticated, with rose cutting (triangular facets on a hemisphere) as well as table cutting (one main facet). (See p 80.)

Leaf, flower and pea-pod shapes became popular for the gold settings of pendants, in designs that were increasingly naturalistic after 1620. (2, 9) Van Dyck's portraits showing pearls illustrate an important current of taste. In Spain the fashion was for one huge jewel, sometimes with matching earrings—a *demi-parure*.

Jewellery, 17th C

beryl *girandole* earring FC *F* (pair)
6 Italian *verre églomisé* and rock crystal pendant with silver-gilt mount B *G*

1 Enamelled gold diadem with pearls, rubies and emeralds, South Germany, width 10.8cm B *G*
2 Cameo of Lucius Verus (reverse), *c.*1620 B ϱ *G*
3 Gold miniature case with champlevé enamel in white and black, *c.*1620 VR *H*
4 Enamel cross with Corpus Christi and skull B *F*
5 Spanish gold, emerald and

7 English necklace and pendant set with rubies, table-cut diamonds and emeralds, the pendant with a centre garnet, set in a scrolled silver and gold mount, the stones foiled B *H*
8 Spanish emerald and green beryl brooch, the stones foiled and set in gold FC *G*
9 French diamond and emerald cross, set with rose diamonds in silver, late 17th c B *I*

In the second half of the 17th C, in the Europe of Calvinism and the Counter-Reformation, death became an obsession. Skulls and other *mementi mori*—even coffin-shaped pendants—appeared in jewellery. (4) Mourning jewellery, often in black and white, included *carcanets* of jet "tears". Jewels were made to commemorate the death in 1649 of Charles I, mainly slides incorporating "CR" in fine twisted wire, worn on a ribbon at neck or wrist.

Louis XIV loved jewellery. In 1661 he introduced the fashion of a jewelled watch hanging at the waist, and gave up the traditional cross pendant. The great Paris jewellers Robert de Berquen and Gilles Légaré demonstrated the 1660s' trend towards lighter pieces. Almost all Légaré's designs for necklaces are formed of plaques threaded together with cords through narrow double tubes at the back. Bow-shaped brooches (later known as *Sévignés*) came into vogue, as did *girandole* earrings with three or more pendants. (5, 8) The *Brandebourg* (jewelled clasp for fastening a coat) began as a male fashion but was soon pirated by ladies.

Charles II's marriage to Catherine of Braganza in 1662 briefly introduced to England the Portuguese habit of wearing a knot brooch on the shoulder.

Towards the end of the century miniature cases were decorated with faceted gems. Few have survived; the diamonds have often been prized out. By the 1690s enamel work was sometimes very luxurious, but at the same time many gems were set without enamel, with a plain gold backing. (p 102, no. 1)

THE 18th CENTURY

The taste of the Age of Enlightenment was for jewels that would wink and glow in candlelight. A new distinction between daytime and night-time jewellery was becoming evident. From the 1690s, diamond buttons illuminated coats, and extra sparkle was added by diamond buckles, sleeve clasps and stars. Enamel was no longer fashionable for settings, except in conservative Spain. Jewels now became complementary to fine gold settings.

Paste jewellery, the *pis aller* of the badly off and the strategem of the security-conscious, was already being produced in the late 17th C, by Ravenscroft the glassmaker among others. (1, 5, 7, 8) Early paste was often rose-cut, like the diamonds it was imitating. So were the Bristol crystals ("Bristowes") of English and Flemish jewellery of the early 18th C.

Gem cutting

As interest became concentrated on the stone rather than the setting, cutting and polishing grew in importance. A major step was taken towards a new brilliance when open backs were introduced at the end of the 18th c.

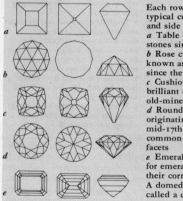

Each row of drawings shows typical cuts from top, bottom and side views

a Table cut, used for softer stones since the Renaissance

b Rose cut (when pear-shaped known as briolette). In vogue since the 17th c

c Cushion-shaped form of brilliant cut, also known as old-mine

d Round brilliant cut, originating in Venice in the mid-17th c and now the most common diamond cut, with 58 facets

e Emerald or step cut, used for emeralds to avoid chipping their corners

A domed, unfaceted gem is called a cabochon.

The Venetian Vincenzo Peruzzi invented the brilliant cutting of diamonds, *c.* 1700, as a way of achieving minimum weight loss with maximum exploitation of optical properties. The resulting multi-faceted stones put coloured gems out of fashion. Design and execution were becoming divorced at this time, a trend deplored (*c.* 1722) by the French designer Auguste Duflos. Women were now the main clients for jewellery.

Rococo was already coming into jewellery in the 1730s, but it influenced settings only for a brief period. By mid-century quite

Jewellery, 18th C

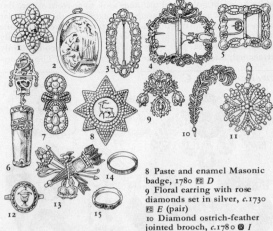

1 White paste flower brooch, pavé-set in silver, with foiled and closed back FC *E*

2 English memorial pendant, with miniature partially executed in hair, *c.*1785 G *D*

3 English cut-steel buckle, *c.*1775 G *B*

4 French waist buckle set with marcasites, *c.*1770 G *C*

5 Paste waist buckle G *C*

6 English châtelaine and *étui* mounted in gold, *c.*1770 GG

7 French paste and aquamarine earrings, *c.*1760 FC *E* (pair)

8 Paste and enamel Masonic badge, 1780 FC *D*

9 Floral earring with rose diamonds set in silver, *c.*1730 FC *E* (pair)

10 Diamond ostrich-feather jointed brooch, *c.*1780 ▣ *I*

11 English Maltese cross set with old brilliant-cut diamonds, *c.*1790 *G*

12 Memorial ring, ivory surrounded with amethysts, *c.*1780 FC *D*

13 French gold brooch, partly enamelled, set with cornelians, emeralds and pearls, *c.*1790 ▣ *F*

14 White enamel mourning ring (commemorating death of a bachelor or spinster), mid-18th c FC *D*

15 Mourning ring, mid-18th c FC *D*

regular *Sévignés* were shown in the drawings of Christian Taute, although rococo lingered on in the Iberian peninsula.

St Petersburg was a great centre of jewellery making in the 18th C, and the Russian Imperial jewels illustrated the new wave of naturalism which came in *c.*1760. Sprays and bouquets of diamonds, or sometimes of coloured stones, were made to sew on dresses. Semi-precious stones were originally for the bourgeoisie, but aristocrats occasionally had *parures* of garnets, smoked crystals, agates and cornelians—all strictly daytime jewels. In the Low Countries, amber was set in silver over red foil. Garnet jewellery became more geometric after *c.*1770.

Gold and pinchbeck (an alloy of copper and zinc) were used for châtelaines—girdles from which hung needle cases and other "necessaries". (6; p 102, no. 2) Classical and (from *c.*1760) *chinoiserie* decoration were common on such pieces. After 1760 chased gold was often replaced by gilt metal.

Buckles were another important type of daytime jewellery, worn at the throat and wrists as well as on shoes and belts. (4) They could be of cut steel, paste, silver and gilt metal. (3) In the neo-classical period, Wedgwood of England made some pottery jewellery, including jasper beads. Faceted steel jewellery was produced in England by Boulton & Fothergill of Birmingham and in Paris by a Yorkshireman named Sykes.

THE 19th CENTURY

Throughout the 19th C diamonds continued to be set in silver with the backs set in gold, until platinum took over from silver. But there was now also an increasing exploitation of the spectacular effects to be gained from open-back settings. Brooches became more naturalistic, aiming at a more exact imitation of flowers. By the 1860s a vogue for whimsical pieces had become firmly entrenched, leading to animal and insect motifs. (25) The import-

Jewellery, 19th C

1 French enamelled gold necklace set with chrysoprases (detail), c.1830 FC F
2 Amethyst and *cannetille* necklace, early 19th c C F
3 Victorian gold, diamond, ruby, emerald and sapphire ring, c.1850 C C
4 Victorian garnet and half-pearl cluster ring C C
5 Victorian turquoise and diamond cluster ring with gold mount, c.1840 FC C
6 Gold brooch with mounted hair, early 19th c C C
7 Victorian painted porcelain brooch in gilt metal frame, c.1870 C C
8 Victorian mosaic scarab pendant set in a gold frame FC E
9 Victorian lava cameo drop earring, c.1850 C C (pair)
10 Victorian jet earring, c.1850 C C (pair)
11 Celtic Tara silver-gilt brooch, c.1850 C C
12 Hollow-gold ram's-head brooch by Castellani B E
13 French pendant/brooch set

with a cameo in a frame of rubies, diamonds, pearls and lapis lazuli, late 19th c B F
14 *Pietra dura* brooch, set in gold, the enamelled silver frame set with pearls and rubies, in the centre a cornelian and glass cameo, c.1850 C D
15 Blue and white Wedgwood cameo, early 19th c FC C
16 French gold-framed shell cameo, c.1810 B E

ation of South African diamonds in the 1870s led to a new taste for flashiness. When supplies of diamonds were halted by the Boer War, pale stones such as amethysts and opals filled the gap.

One of the materials that was intermittently fashionable through much of the century was coral. (34) It was often left in its natural branches, but cameos were carved from it in the 1850s. Ivory was especially popular in the 1880s. Shell was the favourite of the vast range of materials used for cameos. (16)

In the second decade of the century *cannetille* work—a kind of gold filigree—was introduced, often used with amethysts, topaz and aquamarines. (2) The style was popular in France and England, but had declined by the 1840s, giving way to repoussé work.

Exotic and archaeological influences of the period included the Japanese craze (chrysanthemums, bamboos, storks and fans), the lotus motif of the ancient Middle East, Egyptian hieroglyphics and scarabs, and the metalwork of the Etruscans. (8, 19) It was an antiquarian interest too that partly accounted for an occasional tendency to use gold on its own. But silver was mostly worn instead of gold by the 1880s—its rise to temporary popularity was greatly helped by the discovery of the prolific Comstock Lode in Nevada, USA, *c.* 1860.

Piqué decoration (gold and silver on tortoiseshell or ivory) was revived for daytime jewellery in the second half of the century. (32) By the mid-1870s *piqué* work was being mass-produced.

British Victorian jewellery. Neo-Gothicism was a potent influence on Victorian taste until the 1870s, and early Victorian jewellery often incorporates cusps and quatrefoils. Another form of romanticism, partly inspired by Queen Victoria's fondness for Balmoral Castle, popularized Scottish jewels, including brooches set with cairngorms in the form of grouse claws and dirks. (30)

West's of Dublin re-created jewels of the Celtic period. The famous Tara brooch was much reproduced in silver. (11) And Irish bog-oak was used as a substitute for jet, a fossilized driftwood which became the basis of a thriving industry in Whitby, Yorkshire. (10) Other materials considered suitable for mourners were vulcanite (an imitation jet), *piqué* and black onyx. A passion for hair in jewellery reached a climax in the 1850s. (6)

Fine jewellers of the period working in England include Robert Phillips, John Brogden (active 1842–85) and Carlo Giuliano. The latter revived classical goldwork and invented his own neo-Renaissance style, using stones chosen for their colour; his mark —"CG"—has often been faked. (22; p 102, no. 3)

The removal of a tax on silverware in 1890 revived the flagging spirits of Birmingham jewellers, who now began to mass-produce love brooches, "Mizpah" brooches and bangles (given by parting lovers) and, in 1897, Diamond Jubilee brooches. (18)

French jewellery after 1800. The Paris Company of Goldsmiths was suppressed in 1791. The French Crown Jewels were stolen by revolutionaries and many were later sold off. By the early 1800s, when the jewellery trade was back on its feet again, serpents were a popular motif and cornelian had become a fashionable stone. Now, as Joan Evans has put it, "it was no longer an insult to democracy to wear diamonds". Some were mounted in branches of jasmine. Napoleonic classicism revived the popularity of cameos. (16) Inexpensive jewellery was made of *jaseron*—a fine Venetian gold chain, sometimes combined with small mosaic plaques made in Florence or Rome. In 1805 the Pope set a fashion for decorative rosaries, by presenting some to court ladies when he came to Paris for Napoleon's coronation. Commercial jewellery was made bearing Imperial emblems. After 1812, money went on campaigns, not jewels, and it was patriotic to have *parures* of faceted steel.

After the return of the Bourbons in 1814, luxury jewellery went out of fashion for a time—it was more chic to wear no jewellery at all. From 1815, ordinary Parisian wear was gold set with semi-precious stones, especially topazes and amethysts. *Cannetille* was popular, though aristocrats tended to think it vulgar.

By *c*.1820 France had recovered from war, and diamonds were back. They were soon used in a naturalistic style with cascades of stones, a mode popular until *c*.1855, when diamond *aigrettes* of corn, barley and feathers were worn in the side of the hair. Bouquets were made still more naturalistic (*c*.1845) by green enamel on the leaves. In 1855 Eugène Fontenay made a diadem of diamond blackberry leaves, blooms and fruit, partly set in the new light metal, platinum. Lifelike flower-sprays were made by Oscar Massin at this period, and were much imitated. The rival to naturalism was a style based on the French royal tradition of the 18th C—the *style Marie Antoinette*.

The main exponent of neo-Gothicism in France was F.D. Froment-Meurice. Around 1835 the motif of a bird defending its nest against a snake came into fashion, and stayed there for 20 years. The Algerian campaigns popularized Algerian knots and tassels.

After 1860, lizards, dragonflies and beetles became popular motifs, and absurd earrings in the form of hens, windmills, watering cans, etc., were worn. English-style "photograph" lockets came in during the 1860s.

After the wave of the individual revivalist jewellers in France came the rise of the great jewel houses: Cartier (from 1847), Boucheron (from 1858), Chaumet (which succeeded to the

Jewellery, 19th C

17 Victorian silver bangle, *c*.1880 © *B*
18 Victorian "Mizpah" silver bangle © *C*
19 Gold hinged bangle, set with a green stone scarab, *c*.1870 ⑧ *F*
20 Italian gold-mounted shell cameo bracelet, *c*.1840 © *E*
21 Italian mosaic plaque bracelet, mid-19th c ⑨ *E*

22 Bracelet of pearls, rubies and diamonds set in blue and white enamel on gold, by Giuliano, *c*.1880 ⑧ *H*
23 French bracelet of amethysts set in gold (part of a parure), *c*.1820 ⑨ *E*
24 Berlin ironwork bracelet, *c*.1820 ⑨ *D*

Jewellery, 19th C

25 Victorian ruby-eyed lizard brooch, set with diamonds and green garnets, *c.*1880 ⓕⓒ F
26 French cloisonné enamel pendant, by Falize ⓚ F
27 Victorian butterfly brooch set with turquoises and rose diamonds in gold, *c.*1820 ⓒ E
28 Paste head ornament ⓕⓒ C
29 Silver Jubilee brooch in silver, 1887 ⓒ B

30 Scottish dirk brooch, set with cornelian, jasper, agates, bloodstone and foiled citrines in silver, late 19th c ⓒ C
31 Gold locket with applied anchor, *c.*1850 ⓒ C
32 Victorian *piqué* tortoiseshell pendant, inlaid with gold and silver ⓕⓒ C
33 French convolvulus brooch set with small turquoises, *c.*1840 ⓚ G
34 Victorian coral hat-pin ⓕⓒ C

businesses of Etienne Nitot and Fossin), Falize (from *c.*1850; best known for cloisonné enamels in the Japanese style) (26; p 103, no. 1) and Fouquet (from *c.*1860).

German jewellery after 1800. A factory producing ironwork jewellery was set up in Berlin in 1804, but the most important group of ironwork pieces are those given in the Prussian revolt against France to wealthy patriots who contributed their jewels to the war effort. Such items, if they are inscribed "Gold gab ich für Eisen", are now rare. (24)

Italian jewellery after 1800. The first jeweller to be inspired by Greek, Roman and Etruscan jewellery was Fortunato Pio Castellani (1793–1865), who in particular was intrigued by the Etruscan technique of "granulation"—minute spheres of metal decoratively applied to a surface. (12) Sicily (*c.*1805) was the origin of the 19th-c revival of cameo carving. The tourist trade was served by lava cameos depicting Mount Vesuvius. Mosaic jewellery was made in Rome, notably by F.P. Castellani and his sons, and in Florence. (21)

P.C. Fabergé. Peter Carl Fabergé (1846–1920) is a figure whose name always dramatically increases the market value of a piece. His jewellery, though always outstandingly crafted, is less spectacular than his bejewelled "objects of fantasy". It is generally in the 18th-c French manner.

C.L. Tiffany. The first indication of an attempt to create a distinctively American jewellery style was seen at the 1876 Philadelphia Exposition: until then Paris and Italy had been the sources of the most fashionable jewels. Charles Lewis Tiffany (1812–1902) was a leading spirit of the new trend. From 1841 he sold imported Parisian pieces. He began to manufacture on his own account from 1848, after acquiring a stock of diamonds. Among his achievements was an original exploitation of a growing *japonaiserie*. His son Louis was largely responsible for bringing Art Nouveau to the USA.

ENAMELS

Enamels for the embellishment of metals are similar in principle to those used by the potter: powdered glass mixed with a flux (to encourage melting), and a metallic oxide if colouring is required. After application, usually to a copper, silver or gold base, the enamel is fused to the metal in a kiln.

Enamelling techniques

Enamelling may be transparent, translucent or opaque. The latter type is the most common and includes the cloisonné technique, by which thin strips of metal are soldered to the surface to form small cells into which the enamel is received. On melting the enamel shrinks. More is put in and the process is repeated. A related method is champlevé, by which recessions for the enamel are gouged out of the metal. When reliefs in metal are covered with transparent enamel the process is known as *basse taille*. *Plique à jour* is similar to cloisonné but involves removing the back plate to leave translucent or transparent enamels held together only by wires, giving the effect of miniature stained glass panels.

A cheap form of enamelling on brass was introduced in Europe in the 17th C. It was especially applied to andirons, candlesticks and horse harnesses, and in England was known as "Surrey" ware.

Painting in enamels

Painting with enamels was developed in Limoges from *c*.1470. An early kind, known as *en grisaille*, used white to grey tones on a dark background for cameo-like representations. In the early 17th C Jean Toutin introduced the technique of simultaneous polychrome painting on an enamelled ground. This superseded earlier methods and was much used in 18th-C Europe for portrait miniatures and for decorating small boxes and other objects.

Collecting enamels

The types most usually collected today are cloisonné and painted enamels from China (much of the painted work was made for export) and the vast range of small painted items made in Europe in the 18th and early 19th C. These include snuff boxes (made prolifically after 1740), patch boxes (with a mirror inside the lid), *étuis* (for holding scissors, tweezers, etc.) and *bonbonnières* (for breath-sweetening sweetmeats or cachous). The more luxurious types of enamelled objects, especially those with a gold base, belong to a category known as "objects of vertu". Collectors of modest means are more likely to be interested in copper-based enamels, although the best work of factories such as Battersea, Bilston and Birmingham commands high prices.

Copies

Samson of Paris, in the 19th and early 20th C, made superb replicas of late 18th-C English enamels. A tell-tale feature on some Samson boxes is a projection on the outside of the hinge.

ENGLAND

Boxes. English enamelled boxes had a copper base, and were decorated by hand painting in four colours, by transfer printing or by a mixture of both. Thus they offered an inexpensive alternative to the grander gold and enamel boxes from Paris. Many bore sentimental inscriptions: "Souvenir de L'Amitié", "A Lover's Gift" or "When this you see pray think on me, Tho' many miles we distant be". Others have a topographical interest: "A Trifle from Cheltenham" and so on. (2) A novelty of the late 18th C was a type of box with an inner lid depicting an erotic subject.

Until the 1920s it was assumed that all English boxes were made at Battersea, because the renown of that short-lived factory had overshadowed other factories in England. Now it is clear that most boxes were made in Birmingham, Bilston and other south Staffordshire regions, and elsewhere in London. The industry lasted from the late 1740s until the 1840s, but a decline in quality had already begun by the 1790s. There are few "documentary" (signed and dated) pieces. Experts often differ about attributions: but that is part of the fun.

Other items. In addition to boxes a variety of other objects was made. These include scent bottles, bodkin cases, *étuis, bonbonnières,* tea caddies, urns, candlesticks and caskets. (1, 7) Some of these enamelled items often look like porcelain to the novice. Indeed, many of the motifs were based on those of Continental porcelain factories such as Meissen and Sèvres.

Battersea. The factory at York House, Battersea, in London, flourished only from 1753 to 1756. Among the few enamels that can be attributed with certainty are snuff boxes, oval and rectangular plaques and bottle tickets or decanter labels in the form of wavy cartouches. All Battersea work is transfer-printed, sometimes with hand-coloured additions. Subject matter covers religious, classical and political scenes, and royal and aristocratic portraits.

The outstanding quality of engraving distinguishes Battersea printing. The most famous engraver was Simon François Ravenet, whose output includes a fine series of decanter labels depicting

English enamels, 18th C

1 Bilston candlestick, *c.*1775, ht 28cm ⏚ *E* (pair)

2 Bilston motto patch box, late 18th c ⏚ *C*

3 Snuff box depicting *commedia dell'arte* scene, south Staffordshire ⏚ *E*

4 Bilston urn, with blue ground, ht 24.8cm ⏚ *F* (pair)

5 Battersea bottle ticket, width 6.3cm ⏚ *E*

6 Boar's head snuff box, lgth 7.6cm ⏚ *E*

7 *Etui*, with yellow ground, ht 9.8cm ⏚ ⏚ *E*

cherubs. (5) On box lids and plaques the design invariably covers the entire area and seldom has a decorative border.

Other London enamels. Some 25 enamellers who are known by name worked in London in the period 1745–70. One was a Swiss, Anthony Tregent of Denmark St, whose work is usually signed. He specialized in monochrome-printed table snuff boxes, inscribed with almanacs, stanzas from songs, or Masonic insignia.

Birmingham. Edmund Burke described Birmingham as "the great toyshop of Europe"—enamelled boxes were often called "toys". The Birmingham producers probably acquired the plates formerly used at Battersea and continued to print from them in the 1760s. But a vast range of other items was also made. Small circular boxes with waisted sides were common. Decoration was usually on an all-over white background. Unmistakable signs of Birmingham origin are trailing flowers in a rococo cartouche, and insects painted on the underside of boxes.

Bilston and Wednesbury. A number of French enamellers had settled at Bilston in south Staffordshire by 1745, and we also know the names of some English enamellers of that time, including Dovey Hawkesford and the Bickley family. Small boxes with an inscription (sometimes in French) are typical of Bilston. (2) Sèvres porcelain motifs were an important influence, and the Sèvres *rose Pompadour* a frequent colour. Designs were often taken from Robert Sayer's *The Ladies Amusement* (1758–62), which included flowers, birds and fruit. Other subjects included landscapes, insects, ships, classical ruins, calendars and almanacs. When the lid of a box was pictorial, it was usually set in a white or gilt rococo border. Avidly collected today are scent bottles and *bonbonnières* made in the shape of animals, birds, human heads, vegetables and other forms. (6)

Wednesbury, close to Bilston, was another important enamelling centre. It is generally associated with a group of late 18th-C royal blue boxes with designs in raised white, like icing on a cake.

An ornamental effect peculiar to south Staffordshire is a pattern of white stars with red and white centres on a royal blue ground. It was especially used on tobacco jars, vases and ornaments for chimneypieces.

Liverpool. The Liverpool firm of Sadler & Green is well-known for its transfer printing, on enamels as well as ceramics. Notable colours are black or deep brown on white. Portrait plaques and medallions are the only common items.

THE CONTINENT

The early period. The first school of Limoges enamel painters began in the mid-12th C and flourished until the 14th. (1) Limoges enjoyed a second great period of enamelling in the 16th and 17th C. Nardon Penicaud (*c.*1470–1543) evolved a technique whereby a lightly fired black outline was filled in with a limited range of colours before a second firing. Later in the 16th C painting *en grisaille* was employed, with the addition of a red pigment for flesh tones. The master of this method was Pierre Reymond, who used it for mythological scenes on caskets, vessels, ewers, dishes and other items. (3, 4) Classical themes were first used by Léonard Limousin (*c.*1515–76), the finest of the enamellers.

In the early 17th C the Toutin family and the enamellers of the Blois school in France started to practise polychrome enamelling on small gold objects. Their influence spread to England, Germany and Switzerland. In Geneva the Huaud brothers specialized in watch cases painted with mythological scenes, landscapes and other subjects. Luxury enamelled items of great elaboration, such as

Limoges enamels

1 Limoges eucharistic dove,
c.1200, ht 19cm V̄Ř *I*
2 Polychrome salt, by Joseph
Limousin, c.1625. ht 9cm Ⓑ *G*
3 *Grisaille* plate, by Pierre
Reymond, c.1560 Ⓑ *F*

4 *Grisaille* ewer, by Pierre
Reymond, mid-16th c Ⓑ *H*

silver toilet sets, were produced at Augsburg.

The 18th and 19th centuries. The market for objects of vertu in
the 18th C was dominated by France until the Revolution.
Fantastically ornate small gold boxes were made in Paris, often
incorporating jewels or enamels. In the neo-classical period boxes
were set with *en grisaille* Grecian-style miniatures by Jacques-
Joseph de Gault, who collaborated with the celebrated goldsmith ·
Pierre-François Drais. Joseph-Etienne Blerzy sometimes used
enamels on boxes to simulate rubies and pearls.

Perhaps the most prolific producers of enamelled wares in the
early part of the 18th C were the Fromery family in Berlin. (10)
Alexander Fromery practised a style exploiting raised, often lattice-
like ornamentation in silver or gold on a white enamelled ground,
sometimes with additional colours. From the 1740s onwards cheap
trifles were made at Augsburg. Later, at the time of the Seven
Years War (1757–63), enamel boxes were used as propaganda for
the cause of Frederick the Great, whose portrait appeared on some
examples. Fine enamelling was also done at Dresden.

At Copenhagen (c.1760) enamel boxes were made imitating
earlier porcelain ones from Mennecy and Vienna. Playing cards,
popular songs, maps and *trompe l'oeil* copies of envelopes were
typical themes, and there was sometimes a portrait inside the lid.

Continental enamels, 18th and 19th C

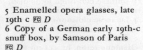

5 Enamelled opera glasses, late
19th c ꜰꜱ *D*
6 Copy of a German early 19th-c
snuff box, by Samson of Paris
ꜰꜱ *D*

7 Four-colour gold and enamel
snuff box, school of Petitot, 1774
Ⓑ *I*
8 Chocolate pot, by the von
Jüngers workshop, 1760s Ⓑ *E*
9 Jewelled gold and enamel
snuff box, Geneva, 1800–10 ꜰꜱ *H*
10 German enamel snuff box,
perhaps by Fromery, c.1750 Ⓑ *F*

Until 1790 the Swiss enamelling industry concentrated on watch cases, but from the turn of the century enamelled boxes were exported from the workshops of Geneva. (9) One of the few Swiss enamellers to sign his work was Jean-Louis Richter, who specialized in landscapes. Other artists often copied paintings by David and others. Mechanized gold and enamel boxes with singing birds that popped out from an oval lidded recess were also manufactured at Geneva.

The enamelling workshop of the von Jünger family in Vienna, which flourished from c.1764 to 1780, turned out a vast range of products, including jugs and coffee pots. (8) Embellishment imitated Sèvres styles. Vienna remained a major centre for enamels until the First World War.

From the 1840s to the 90s there was a revival of Limoges painted enamels in France, beginning at Sèvres and shortly spreading to Paris.

CHINA AND JAPAN

China. Enamelling is a rare instance of an art perfected in the West before it reached the Orient. The original Chinese term for it probably meant literally "from the devils' country". It is unlikely that the Chinese practised enamelling on metal much before the 13th C. The earliest work (and perhaps the best) was done just before and during the Ming dynasty, largely by the cloisonné method. Surviving pieces generally have a simple, often geometrical design, and the enamel surface is noticeably pitted. But most items seen in Europe today are from the reign of Qianlong (1736–95) or later, and are more fussily designed than Ming work. Cantonese painted enamel work on copper was often inspired by porcelain forms and designs of the same period.

Japan. The earliest Japanese enamels date from the beginning of the 17th C. The art may have been introduced from China via Korea. The best period is from c.1840 to 1900, when the Paris Exposition stimulated a heavy demand in the West which continued until the close of the St Louis World's Fair in 1900. The pressure to meet this demand caused a decline in quality.

The Japanese experimented with new techniques and with variations on the Chinese method, sometimes using temporary, removable *cloisons* (cells) or "rainbowing" colours.

Oriental enamels

1 **Ming cloisonné lotus box and cover**, 15th c, diam. 12cm v⅝ *I*

2 **Japanese cloisonné *tsuba* (sword guard)**, diam 7.4cm **B** *E*

3 **Chinese cloisonné lotus dish**, 17th c, diam. 40.6cm **B** *E*

4 **Japanese cloisonné vase**, 18th c, ht 17.8cm **FC** *D*

5 **Chinese cloisonné *ting***, Qianlong reign, ht 44.5cm **FC** *F*

DECORATIVE OBJECTS

"Decorative objects" is an amorphous category of antiques that embraces many highly specialized passions. Some collectors are fascinated by the mystique of a substance such as jade or ivory, while others cannot resist the appeal of miniaturized craftsmanship such as that lavished by the Japanese on netsuke and inro.

IVORIES

Ivory of the finest quality comes from the African elephant, but Indian and Asian elephant tusks have also been used. The Indian variety is densely white and easily carvable. Asian ivory tends to yellow quickly. Other animals, such as the walrus, hippopotamus and whale, have provided useful alternatives.

Western and oriental ivories

1 Chinese card case, 19th c 🄵 *C*
2 French diptych leaf, 14th c, ht 7.6cm 🄵 *F*
3 Pieces from Cantonese chess set, mid-19th c 🄵 *E* (set)
4 Ivory tankard, south Germany, late 18th c 🄱 *H*
5 Bust in the manner of Cheverton, ht 13cm 🄵 *D*
6 Japanese family group, late 19th c, ht 12.5cm 🄵 *D*
7 Chinese puzzle ball 🄵 *C*
8 Dieppe ivory bust of Marie Antoinette, opening to reveal her last hours in the Bastille, 19th c, ht 12cm 🄵 *E*

Europe and the United States. Carved ivory in the Gothic age was a medium for religious expression. Diptychs and triptychs—carved folding screens—were often given an architectural frame of traceried pointed arches. (2) Ivory was also used notably for pyxes (containers for consecrated bread), caskets for the relics of saints, and liturgical combs. The range of secular ivories included mirror cases and gaming pieces.

Italy was supreme in the 14th and 15th C, but with the Renaissance ivory production there entered a decline. Crucifixes made in 17th-c Europe often had an ivory Christ mounted on wood. Germany was especially well known for its massive silver-mounted tankards. (4) Low-relief portrait medallions, decorative plaques, tobacco graters, powder flasks and many other objects date from this period. Dieppe, Paris and Ste Claude (in the south-east) were important centres of production in France. (8) Chess sets were made in Europe by the 17th C (the best in Italy, France and Germany), but not in Britain until the early 19th.

English Victorian artefacts of interest to collectors include parasol handles and the miniature portrait busts machine-made by a method invented by Benjamin Cheverton. (5) American sailors were well-known for "scrimshawing"—engraving and carving whalebone, whales' teeth, shells and walrus tusks. Fakes abound.

China. Few Chinese ivories survive from the Han dynasty or earlier, although seals and dignatories' batons were made. But by Tang times (AD 618–906) the range of products had increased enormously, and the repertoire of decorative techniques included staining, painting and inlaying as well as carving.

Fukien was a famous region for ivory carving in the Ming era (1368–1644), when fine Buddhist statuettes were made, free of any colouring: these have been much reproduced. In the Kangxi period of the Qing dynasty, workshops in Peking supplied the court with wine-cup stands, cylindrical brush pots and other artefacts. Ivories of the female body were used by women to describe their symptoms to a physician.

In the late 19th and early 20th C, a speciality was virtuoso display pieces of pierced concentric spheres carved from a single block. The same treatment was often given to the bases of chess pieces made for export. (3, 7)

Japan. In the 8th C—an early highpoint of Japanese ivory art—Tang styles were commonly imitated. Characteristic objects included rulers, stones for the game of *go*, plectrums and small cylindrical vases. The 18th C was the great age of netsuke, inro (see below) and *okimono* (household ornaments, usually in the form of realistically carved figures). In the late 19th C, after Japan had opened up to commerce with the West, many larger items were produced for export, often carved and embellished with painted designs in lacquer. (6)

NETSUKE AND INRO

Netsuke. A netsuke was originally no more than a practical toggle for suspending small everyday objects—a purse, seal case (inro), pipe case or tobacco pouch—from a Japanese man's sash (*obi*), as the loose garment he wore lacked pockets. A shell, small double-gourd, bone or stick could be used. But by the 17th C objects were specially made for the purpose, in an amazing variety of decorative forms.

Wood, lacquer and ivory were mainly the commonest materials. Eyes were often of inlaid ebony, horn, amber, metal, glass or tortoiseshell. On wooden pieces the hole for the cord was frequently ivory-lined. A primitive form was the flat, round *manju*, either left plain or in later periods engraved, inlaid or carved. (4) A version of *manju* especially favoured in Tokyo in the later 19th C was the *kagamibuta* ("mirror lid"), which bore an ornamental metal disc. The earliest carved netsuke produced in quantity were tall humorous figures (sometimes up to 15 cm long), reflecting Chinese taste and mostly made in Osaka. (1) Most popular of all kinds were the *katabori*: three-dimensional carvings of deities, humans, myth-ical figures, plants or animals, or objects. Among the typical themes were: Amma, a blind masseur, often depicted servicing a client (3); the immortal Chokaro who carried a gourd in which his magical horse slept; and Shoki the demon-queller, with a long sword. (5)

Netsuke

1 Chinese merchant, ivory, 18th c, ht 11cm ⑧ *F*
2 *Sennin* (old man), ivory, 19th c, ht 10cm ⑯ *E*
3 Blind masseur lifting boulder, 19th c ⓒ *C*
4 Small ivory *manju*, mid-19th c ⑯ *D*
5 Shoki the demon-queller, ivory, 18th c ⑧ *F*
6 Rat, by Okakoto, 18th c ⑧ *G*
7 Mermaid with child, ivory, late 18th c ⑧ *F*

Mask netsuke represented ceremonial Buddist masks and the characters of No drama.

The best netsuke belong to the late 18th and early 19th C, after which their forms become stereotyped or overelaborate. After the end of the Edo period (1601–1867) their use declined with the adoption of Western dress, but "art carvers" such as Koseki continued to produce them. The signature of one of the masters of the golden age, such as Masanao, Okatomo, Tomotada or Okatori, will increase the value of a piece enormously. Novelty netsuke with moving parts are keenly collected: examples include rattles, and worms that pop out of mouldy fruit. Forged netsuke are common. They often have too conspicuous a hole for the cord. Some forgeries have been made by putting a hole through a genuine example of small ornamental carving.

Inro. Towards the end of the 16th C in Japan it became the fashion among men of the aristocratic class to carry their seal and the red pigment used for printing it in a small case dangled from their

Inro

8 Sheath inro, showing lakeside scene, late 18th c ⑯ *D*
9 Four-case inro, with netsuke, Koma school ⑯ *E*
10 Large four-case inro, lacquer, with wood netsuke, Kajiwara school ⑧ *F*
11 Three-case ivory inro, signed Fuji Masanobu ᵛ̃ᴿ *F*
12 Five-case inro, early 19th c ⑯ *E*
13 Red lacquer inro, signed Matsuda Hokei, 19th c ᵛ̃ᴿ *G*
14 Five-case inro, early 19th c ⑯ *E*
15 Three-case inro, signed Jokasai and Yosei ᵛ̃ᴿ *G*

girdle, held in place by a netsuke. This case, usually of lacquered wood but sometimes of ivory, carved wood, metal or pottery, was called an inro. It was increasingly used also as a miniature travelling medicine chest and receptacle for aromatic spices and tobacco.

The inro was made up of from three to five compartments, cleverly fitted together one on top of the other and held in place by two silk cords which were knotted at the bottom and passed up through holes or runners at the sides. The cords were threaded through an ornamental bead or *ojime* (these are now collected too) and then tied to the netsuke through its cord hole or sometimes a natural gap in a carving—between the stems of a plant, for example. (9, 10) The loose cords allowed segments to be raised or shut at will. The most common shape of inro is a rounded rectangle in profile, a flattened oval in section.

Inro display the highest form of the lacquerer's art. The earliest, dating from the Momoyama period (1574–1602), were black with subdued, refined designs, but during the Tokugawa régime (1603–1867) they became increasingly decorative.

The numerous techniques included raised lacquer, carved or incised lacquer, addition of gold or silver dust, and inlays of metals (including gold or silver), ivory, shell, mother-of-pearl or ceramics. Decorative themes include historical scenes, deities, poets, scholars, scenes from contemporary life, real and mythical flora and fauna, and abstract motifs. Inro with matching *ojime* and netsuke are especially valuable. Among the famous masters of the earlier period, whose examples fetch very high prices, are Korin, Ritsuo and Tachibana Gyokuzan.

JADE

Confusingly, the term "jade" is applied to two unrelated minerals, both very hard. The first, nephrite, is the commoner, and was prized in China from the third millenium BC onwards. The second, jadeite, was known to the Olmecs and the Mayans in central America from *c.*1500 BC, and later in China, where it was imported from Burma. The word "jade" comes from the Spanish *piedra de la ijada*, meaning "stone of the loins": the stones brought from Mexico by the Spanish conquistadors were believed to be a cure for colic. This legend of curative properties lingered on, and the Mexican stone was given the name *lapis nephriticus* ("kidney stone"): hence "nephrite". It was not until the looting of the Summer Palace in Peking in the 1860s that specimens of the other type were identified and the name "jadeite" applied to them.

Although "jade" is synonymous with certain shades of green, both nephrite and jadeite can have various colours. Jadeite has the more vivid tones. Nephrite is usually a subdued green, but also occurs in a cloudy white variety known as "mutton fat". The more distinct colours a piece displays, the greater its appeal to collectors.

Jade cannot be carved in the ordinary way, but needs to be cut by abrasives. Treadle-operated cutters were used from the 16th until the late 18th C. Sawing and drilling by treadle power produce a pitted surface that is visible through a magnifying glass.

Ming jade is often of marvellous quality. Ritual vases were frequently modelled on ancient bronzes. The Kangzi period (1644–1722), so rich in fine ceramics, is not noted for jades, but in the Yongzheng and above all the Qianlong (1736–95) periods, craftsmanship reached heights of excellence. Ornamental pieces were produced in extravagant and intricate shapes, often with decoration in high relief. (2) Elegant animal carvings were made, as well as table screens and brush pots. (4) The *tours de force* of the jade-workers' craft often incorporated interlocking chains of separate rings or links. (1) From the late 17th C pedestals for jade objects were carved from Sinhalese eagle-wood.

As well as Chinese jades, collections are also formed of Olmec, Aztec and Mayan figures, Moghul Indian vessels of the 16th and 17th C (mounted with precious stones), and Maori New Zealand pendants, ornaments and toggles.

Chinese jade

1 White jade vase and cover, 18th c ⓑ *G*
2 Dark green nephrite carving, Qianlong mark, ht 14cm ⓑ *F*
3 Pale celadon jade boulder, 18th c, ht 11cm ⒻⒸ *F*
4 Translucent green nephrite screen, Qianlong reign, diam. 22.5cm ⓑ *G*
5 Translucent jade incense burner, in form of a Dog of Fo, Qianlong reign, ht 24.4cm ⓑ *F*
6 Translucent emerald green libation cup, with carved

phoenix on cover, Qianlong dynasty, ht 13.8cm ⓑ *F*
7 Pale celadon and brown jade vessel, Ming, ht 17cm ⓑ *F*
8 Green nephrite carving of Guanyin, 19th c, ht 47cm ⒻⒸ *F*

PAPIER MACHE

The term "papier mâché" was coined in the mid-18th C to describe pulped paper mixed with a binding agent and dried in moulds. Many objects made in this way were painted with floral designs or japanned in imitation of oriental lacquer. In 1772 Henry Clay of Birmingham revolutionized the industry in Britain with a new heat-resistant paperware, so hard that it could be sawn, chiselled or screwed. In 1825 Jennens & Bettridge, the best-known manufacturers, patented a method of "inlaying" papier mâché with mother-of-pearl. Products of the time included trays, tea caddies, small boxes, writing cases, chairs, tables, hand screens and pole screens. (3, 5, 6) Birmingham and Wolverhampton were the main production centres. Enthusiasm for papier mâché began to wane in the 1860s, by which time decoration had become vulgar and overdone. Jennens & Bettridge closed down in 1864.

Continental manufacturers included George Sigismund Stobwasser of Germany, notable for his signed snuff and tobacco boxes (from the 1760s).

Between 1850 and 1854 the Litchfield Manufacturing Co. made papier mâché in Connecticut. Clock cases were their speciality, but they also produced daguerrotype cases, boxes and screens. (1, 2)

Papier mâché, 19th C

1 Clock, by the Litchfield Mfg Co., Connecticut FC *C* (NY value)
2 Card tray, by the Litchfield Mfg Co. FC *A* (NY value)
3 Small tray, painted with a rural scene FC *C*
4 Japanese-inspired match-holder, Wolverhampton, 1880–1900 FC *A*

6 Tea caddy, painted and inlaid with mother-of-pearl, Wolverhampton, c.1860 FC *C*

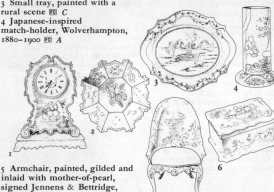

5 Armchair, painted, gilded and inlaid with mother-of-pearl, signed Jennens & Bettridge, 1844 ® ९ *E*

WOOD

Antique small wooden objects are known as "treen". Lathes used for turned wares were treadle-operated at first, but wheel lathes were later introduced. Good decorative turned objects were made from the 17th C. But often treen were incised with a knife or chisel—an activity for sailors and rural folk, whose love tokens made by this method have a special charm. (6, 7)

On the Continent snuff rasps (*râpoirs*), snuff boxes and knife handles were delicately carved in relief, while intaglio work was applied to butter and gingerbread moulds and other wares. (1)

Collectors often specialize: for example, in smoking paraphernalia. Drinking vessels form the largest category. (2)

Objects in wood

1 French *râpoir* (snuff rasp), late 17th c ⱽ℞ *F*
2 Olivewood goblet, 18th c, ht 15.9cm FC *C*
3 Scandinavian butter tub ® *E*
4 Welsh butter mould, c.1790 FC *A*
5 Norwegian sycamore tankard, early 19th c, ht 22cm ® *E*
6 Carved stay busk ® *C*
7 Welsh love spoon ® *C*

8 Tunbridge ware box with geometric top and mosaic sides, 19th c FC *B*

1 Scottish *caqueteuse* (or
caquetoire: chair with a
trapezoidal seat), 16th c Ⓡ *F*
2 English wing armchair,
early 18th c Ⓡ *B*
3 Detail of 17th-c marquetry,
the Netherlands
4 German parquetry bureau-
cabinet, *c.*1730 Ⓡ *H*

Opposite page
1 Louis XIV marquetry bureau, with hinged top enclosing a kingwood fitted interior, width 114cm ⑬ ♀ *I*
2 Detail of Boulle marquetry (i.e. tortoiseshell and brass)
3 Detail of English japanned writing cabinet, *c.*1730
4 Florentine *pietra dura* table-top, 18th c

This page
1 Danish walnut *bombé* commode, with marble top, 18th c, width 78cm ⑬ *H*
2 French kingwood and marquetry *bombé* commode, with marble top, *c.*1900 ꜰꜱ *E*
3 American secretary in cherry and mahogany, Connecticut or Rhode Island, 1790–1810 ᵛʀ *I*
4 Detail of inlay and ormolu by J.-H. Riesener, on back of a magnificent desk, 18th c

FURNITURE

1 Chippendale mahogany side chair **B** *E*

2 Chippendale mahogany settee, *c.*1760 *VR* *I*

3 Red-Blue Chair by Gerrit Rietveld, 1917–18 *VR* *♀* *I* Rietveld was a member of the Dutch De Stijl group, whose principles are reflected in his use of straight lines and primary colours

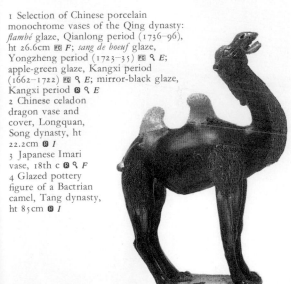

1 Selection of Chinese porcelain
monochrome vases of the Qing dynasty:
flambé glaze, Qianlong period (1736–96),
ht 26.6cm FC *F*; *sang de boeuf* glaze,
Yongzheng period (1723–35) FC ♀ *E*;
apple-green glaze, Kangxi period
(1662–1722) FC ♀ *E*; mirror-black glaze,
Kangxi period B *E*
2 Chinese celadon
dragon vase and
cover, Longquan,
Song dynasty, ht
22.2cm B *I*
3 Japanese Imari
vase, 18th c B ♀ *F*
4 Glazed pottery
figure of a Bactrian
camel, Tang dynasty,
ht 85cm B *I*

1 Enamelled and bejewelled gold pendant, 17th c **Ⓡ** *G*
2 French châtelaine *c.*1795 **Ⓡ** *G*
3 A selection of 19th- and 20th-c jewellery: all the pieces are fairly common, except that in the middle of the bottom row—an enamel, garnet and moonstone pendant, signed CG (Carlo Giuliano) **Ⓡ** **ⵞ** *F*
4 Victorian enamel mourning brooch, with pearls **Ⓒ** *D*

1 Gold and cloisonné enamel bracelet, by
Lucien Falize, c.1890 ® *I*
2 Three 18th-c *étuis*: Dutch, c.1755; German,
c.1720; English, c.1720 FC *F* (each)
3 Ruby, diamond, enamel and gold brooch, by
Luis Masriera, before 1915 ® *I*
4 Swiss gold and enamel snuff box, with
border of split pearls, c.1830, lgth 9cm FC *I*
5 Swiss gold and enamel snuff box, early
19th c, lgth 9.25cm FC *I*

1 Kazak prayer rug
(Caucasian), late 19th c 🄵🄲 *H*
2 Tiflis runner carpet
(Caucasian) with meandering
boteh designs (detail) 🅁 *G*
3 Kashan silk embossed prayer
rug (Persian) (detail) 🅁 *H*
4 Soho tapestry covering a
chair (detail), *c.*1700 🅁 *F*

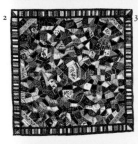

1 Brussels tapestry of *The Meeting of the Generals* (detail), *c.*1640 ⓡ *I*

2 American "crazy" patchwork quilt, 19th c ⓡ *C*

3 Stuart laidwork casket in coloured silks ⒡ⓒ *F*

4 Uzbek "Bokhara" *suzani* (bedspread, made by a bride as part of her dowry), worked on linen with rich silks, 19th c ⓡ *F*

1

2

3

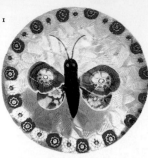

Opposite page
1 Venetian *latticino tazza*, early 17th c v̸ʀ 9 *F*
2 Bohemian coloured glassware, mid-19th c FC *D* (maximum)
3 Three English 18th-c enamelled glasses with opaque twist stems, two on left by the Beilbys v̸ʀ *G* (average)
This page
1 Baccarat *millefiori* paperweight, dated B1847 ® *F*
2 A selection of American glassware: Peachblow bowl, Mt Washington Glass Co., 1886–90 ® *E*; vase, New England Glass Co., 1886–8 FC *D*; coral cruet, 1886–91 FC *D*; Amberina vase, New England Glass Co., 1886–8 ® *E* (NY values)

3 Webb's cameo glass vase, ht 12.5 cm ® *F*
4 Gallé cameo table lamp, ht 59.5 cm ® *G*

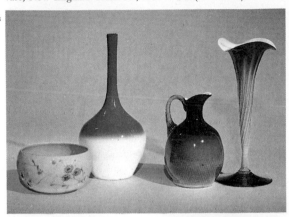

Opposite page
1 Bristol enamelled glass scent bottle, 1770–90 V̂R *F*
2 Chelsea porcelain group, red anchor mark, *c*.1755 🅱 *F*
3 Worcester "Brocade" pattern porcelain dessert plate, *c*.1755, diam. 24.1cm 🄵🄲 *C*
4 Pair of Derby porcelain botanical plates, with crown, crossed batons and D mark, late 18th c 🄵🄲 *E* (each)

This page
1 Staffordshire salt-glazed teapot, 18th c, ht 11.4cm V̂R *F*
2 A selection of Wedgwood Queen's Ware, *c*.1785: "Green Water Leaf" tureen 🄵🄲 *C*; "Brown and Blue Barley" custard cups 🄵🄲 *B*; tray 🄵🄴 *B*
3 English delft posset pot, 18th c 🅱 *G*

109

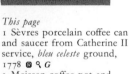

This page
1 Sèvres porcelain coffee can and saucer from Catherine II service, *bleu celeste* ground, 1778 **◙ ⚲ G**
2 Meissen coffee pot and cover, decorated by J.G. Höroldt, *c.*1735 **◙ ⚲ G**
3 Marseilles faience bowl and cover, with "VP" monogram, *c.*1765 **◙ ⚲ F**

4 Vincennes soft-paste porcelain bowl, cover and stand, with *bleu royal* ground painted by Capelle, 1754 **◙ ⚲ F**
Opposite page
1 Meissen "Greeting Harlequin" by J.J. Kändler, *c.*1740 ᴠʀ ⚲ *I*
2 St Cloud soft-paste biscuit group, mid-18th c **◙ E**
3 Italian maiolica dish depicting Death of Lucrece **◙ G**
4 Dutch delft plaques, 18th c, ht 25cm **◙ F** (each)

1 Two vases, painted in coloured slips under the glaze,
Rookwood, Cincinnati, Ohio, *c.*1900: (left) ht 26.4cm Ⓡ *D*;
(right) ht 21cm Ⓡ *D* (NY values)
2 Japanese Kinkozan earthenware vase, ht 74.5cm Ⓡ *F*
3 Selection of earthenware tiles by William De Morgan

CLOCKS
= & =
WATCHES

Clocks and watches often combine the appeal of beautiful cases with the fascinating mechanical aspects of timekeeping. The finest pieces are a perfect collaboration of art and science.

CLOCKS

It is not known when mechanical clocks first came into use. But Dante describes a clock's motion in his *Paradiso* of 1321, and an astronomical clock was in use at Strasbourg by 1350. The motive force of a clock comes from either weights or springs. These actuate a system of meshing toothed wheels which turn the hand or hands. An essential device is the escapement, which releases the power at a controlled speed (see diagrams below).

The verge escapement was universally employed until *c*. 1670. The regulator in the earliest form of this system was a horizontal bar (foliot), with adjustable weights on the ends, and mounted on a vertical rod (verge). The verge had two flags (pallets) set at right angles to each other, which released the escape wheel at the rate of one tooth per swing of the foliot. In a later version the foliot was replaced by a balance wheel. (*a*)

The use of a coiled spring as a motive force (recorded as early as the 15th C) led to the development of the portable table (or bracket) clock. The difficulty with spring-driven clocks was that the force of the uncoiling spring had to be equalized. Early German makers used a device called a "stackfreed" to achieve this, though a simpler and more efficient means was a cone-shaped gear known as a "fusee". (*c*)

Escapements

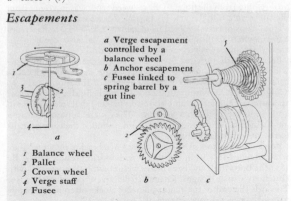

a Verge escapement controlled by a balance wheel
b Anchor escapement
c Fusee linked to spring barrel by a gut line

1 Balance wheel
2 Pallet
3 Crown wheel
4 Verge staff
5 Fusee

Until the mid-17th C few clocks were accurate to within a quarter-hour per day, and the minute hand was not used. Timekeeping vastly improved with the introduction of the pendulum by the Dutchman Christiaan Huygens in 1657. (Most old clocks were converted to the new method, and few retain their original foliot or balance.) English makers shortly afterwards devised a new escapement, the anchor, which allowed for a longer pendulum, with a consequently slower swing, thereby reducing cumulative error. (b) Hence the rise to popularity of the longcase (grandfather) clock. Among the various types of pendulum specially designed to stay at a constant length regardless of temperature were the "mercury" and the "gridiron".

Bracket clocks generally had handles, to move them from room to room: this explains the survival of the verge escapement for a hundred years or so after the invention of the anchor escapement, which required more accurate levelling.

The creation of an efficient mechanism for striking the hour also exercised the ingenuity of clockmakers. The "count plate" system continued in use well into the 19th C, despite its great weakness— that the striking sequence could become increasingly out of phase with the hands. This problem was conquered in 1676 by Edward Barlow's "rack and snail" construction. The *grand sonnerie*, which came in *c.*1660, is a type of striking in which the hours and the quarters are struck at each quarter.

Lantern clocks are one of the few types that have been extensively forged. However, movements have been frequently altered, and false signatures added. Arches have been commonly added to square dials.

England. The earliest clocks generally available to collectors date from the reign of Elizabeth I. By *c.*1600 the familiar "lantern clock" had become popular: the name was a corruption of *latten*, meaning brass, but also conveniently describes the lantern-shaped frame. (6) The engraved dial was equipped with one hand, and there was usually a hemispherical bell for striking the hours. The escapement was normally of the verge and balance variety until the pendulum was introduced.

In 1631 Charles I allowed the London clockmakers to form their own "company", with strict enforcement of quality control. The first English pendulum clocks were made in 1658. Longcase clocks until *c.*1680 were generally in oak cases veneered with ebony or walnut. Walnut remained a fashionable material until *c.*1770, by which time the favourite wood was mahogany. Marquetry, progressing from the floral to the seaweed type, was in vogue from the late 17th C until *c.*1715. (7) Japanned cases were popular until *c.*1760. Tops of cases evolved from gabled (*c.*1660–70) to flat (from *c.*1670, when spiral columns flanking the dial also came in) to crested (from *c.*1675) to arched (from *c.*1720).

From the early 18th C a "break-arch" dial, arched at the top, came widely into vogue, used to accommodate a strike/silent lever, a name-plate or, somewhat later, the phases of the moon. (2)

Night clocks, incorporating an oil lamp behind a semicircular aperture, and generally an elaborately painted dial, were made in both longcase and table versions. They were superseded by a mechanism which, at the pull of a cord, sounded the time on bells to the nearest quarter-hour.

Bracket clocks sometimes originally had a bracket by which they were attached to a wall, but this is seldom still present today. By 1675 the brass dials and back plates were commonly engraved with Dutch-style tulip designs. Enamelled dials were introduced *c.*1750. Towards the end of the century bracket clocks often had ornately pierced gilt-metal tops known as "basket tops".

The golden age of English horology was the period 1650–1740, and the giant among craftsmen was Thomas Tompion (active 1671–1713), whose achievements included work with perpetual calendars (i.e. with corrections for short months and leap years). Other makers whose clocks command high prices are Daniel

English clocks

1 Bracket clock, by J. Knibb, 1680 B ♀ H
2 Bracket clock with break-arch dial, 18th c FC ♀ F
3 Dial and hood of longcase clock, c.1690 B ♀ G
4 George III "Act of
Parliament" wall clock, signed W. Clement B F
5 Skeleton clock, 19th c FC D
6 Lantern clock, 1660 FC ♀ F
7 Marquetry and veneered walnut longcase clock, 17th c B ♀ G

Quare, the Fromanteel family, Edward East, George Graham, Joseph Windmills and Joseph Knibb. (1)

In the Regency period, when the clockmaker's and case-maker's arts had polarized, identical cases were given movements by many makers. A leading early 19th-c London clocksmith, the last of the old breed, was Benjamin Lewis Vulliamy, who adopted a succession of Gallic styles from Louis XIV (Boulle marquetry and ormolu mounts) to neo-classical (porcelain and marble).

A favourite ornamental type of the 19th c was the skeleton clock, with a mechanism under a glass dome. (5) The Gothic Revival influenced clock design from the 1830s.

France. Some small spring-driven clocks made in France survive from the 16th c. Silver, and even gold, were often used by clockmakers, but most early examples of such pieces have been dismantled for their yield of precious metals. The most popular 16th-c timepiece was hexagonal in plan, with a column at each corner and a pierced dome over the bell. This type was replaced by the square form in the period 1590–1610. Early pendulum clocks copied Dutch examples, but under Louis XIV the so-called *pendule réligieuse* was embellished with intricate tortoiseshell veneers and silver and brass inlays. The most magnificent decoration was by André-Charles Boulle. The 1690s saw the introduction of an enamel plaque for each hour numeral.

In the early 18th c the pedestal clock came into vogue, and was often a superb piece of furniture. The French never made many longcase clocks (*régulateurs*); most existing specimens are of provincial origin. Much more typical were bracket clocks (with specially made consoles, and characteristically waisted) and wall-hung cartel clocks (now rare). (8) Another type was the clock incorporated in a piece of luxury furniture. Cases were almost always topped by an ormolu figure, favourites being Time with his scythe, or Diana.

Continental clocks

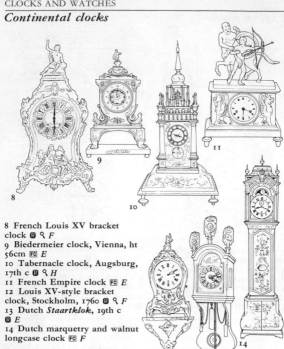

8 French Louis XV bracket
clock Ⓡ ♀ *F*
9 Biedermeier clock, Vienna, ht
56cm Ⓕ© *E*
10 Tabernacle clock, Augsburg,
17th c Ⓡ ♀ *H*
11 French Empire clock Ⓕ© *E*
12 Louis XV-style bracket
clock, Stockholm, 1760 Ⓡ ♀ *F*
13 Dutch *Staartklok*, 19th c
Ⓡ *E*
14 Dutch marquetry and walnut
longcase clock Ⓕ© *F*

In the reign of Louis XV, rococo scrolls, shells and flowers were
disposed in a wealth of intricate forms over a mechanism that by
now had become standard: a count wheel system, with power
supplied from "going barrels". Porcelain cases were often used,
with ormolu mounts. In the neo-classical age of Louis XVI marble
or unglazed (biscuit) porcelain made an appearance in clockmaking, and urns and human or animal figures were among the most
fashionable motifs. Bracket and cartel clocks were gradually
superseded by mantel clocks. A particularly elegant variety took
the form of a lyre. In the Empire period decoration often included
Egyptian and classical forms in low relief. (11) Great technical
innovations were made in the 18th c by Julien Le Roy (1686–1759),
his son Pierre Le Roy (1717–85), Jean André Lepaute and others.
France is particularly known for its carriage clocks, made
throughout the period 1770–1910. Their antecedents were the
round-dialled *pendules d'officier* used mainly by military officers
while travelling.·Carriage clocks proper had a rectangular gilt case,
glass panels, a rectangular face and a fairly large handle, and were
sparsely ornamented. Miniature examples are the most desirable,
especially if they have an alarm. Some of the earliest ones were
made by one of the most talented of France's horologists, Abraham
Louis Breguet (1747–1823).
A notable provincial design was the wall-hung Morbier clock,
made in large numbers from the end of the 18th c in the Jura region
of eastern France. An inverted verge escapement was characteristic
of this type during most of its long career. The striking was double
at each hour (the second time two minutes after the first), and the

usual French practice of striking once on the half-hour was followed.

The Netherlands. A characteristic type of 17th-C Dutch clock, which resembles the French *pendule réligieuse*, has a movement fixed to the dial, which is hinged to the case. Longcase clocks of the early 18th C often have projecting scrolls at each corner of the base, and triangular calendar panels in the dial. (14) Striking took place on the preceding half-hour on a higher pitched bell, as well as on the hour itself.

Three distinctive types of wall-hung clocks later developed: the *Zaanse* (with an elaborate box-like bracket containing the pendulum, pear-shaped weights on ropes, and ornate brass crestings); the *Staart* (with a long tail-like backboard housing the pendulum) and the *Stoel* (with the movement sitting on a wooden stool supported by the wall bracket). (13) Many *Stoel* clocks were made in Friesland.

Germany. Germany was a supreme clockmaking region during the Renaissance. Augsburg clocks, which often bear the town stamp "AG" or a pineapple, were unrivalled throughout Europe. A speciality of the town was the tower-shaped "belfry" or "tabernacle" clock. (10)

In the ages of the baroque and the rococo, cases reached great heights of elaboration, especially in Bavaria. Factories such as Meissen, Höchst, Berlin and Frankenthal made porcelain rococo cases. David Roentgen's graceful longcase clock cases often had fine marquetry on trunk and base, and generally accommodated movements by Kinzing.

Clockmaking of a less sophisticated character was practised in the Black Forest, where the verge and foliot continued in use in wooden clocks until well into the 18th C. The wooden dials were painted with flowers, birds, animals or figures.

Austria and Switzerland. Horology expanded greatly in Austria in the 18th C, especially in Vienna, where French and German influences combined. The Biedermeier style (1815–48) was particularly fruitful in clock design. (9) Vienna, in the 19th C, became well known for its "regulators" (i.e., non-striking clocks made to a special degree of accuracy). Early 19th-C examples often had a severe but elegant ebony case with stringing of lighter wood. Inferior clocks passed off as Vienna regulators were later made in Silesia and the Black Forest. In Switzerland in the 18th C, P. Jaquet-Droz of Neuchâtel made magnificent French-style bracket clocks.

The United States. The work of clockmakers in America before 1750, many of whom were English, is to be found mostly in museums. David Rittenhouse (active *c.* 1750–90) is the best-known of a group of early makers in Philadelphia. Clocks of the 18th C are mainly of the longcase type, and made to order with a brass eight-day movement. From the mid-1740s wood was used to replace brass, which had become expensive, by some Connecticut craftsmen: examples by Benjamin or Timothy Cheney, Gideon Roberts or John Rich are eagerly sought.

The Willards of Boston were a prominent clockmaking family in Massachusetts. In 1802 Simon Willard patented the (non-striking) banjo-shaped clock, which acquired a long popularity and became the most commonly faked of all American clock types. (18) (Many genuinely old ones have forged labels.) Simon's brother Aaron is notable for shelf clocks, while his son, Aaron Jnr, is credited with the introduction of the lyre-shaped clock, a rare type made in Massachusetts *c.* 1820–40. Other styles of the period include the lighthouse shelf clock (patented by Simon Willard in 1822) and the girandole wall clock (designed by Lemuel Curtis). The girandole, a

American clocks

Value symbols refer to New York estimates expressed as pounds

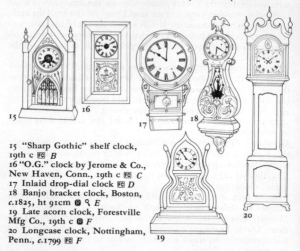

15 "Sharp Gothic" shelf clock, 19th c FC B
16 "O.G." clock by Jerome & Co., New Haven, Conn., 19th c FC C
17 Inlaid drop-dial clock FC D
18 Banjo bracket clock, Boston, c.1825, ht 91cm B ♀ E
19 Late acorn clock, Forestville Mfg Co., 19th c B F
20 Longcase clock, Nottingham, Penn., c.1799 FC F

very rare type, was an elaborately decorated banjo clock with a circular box at the base.

Thomas Harland, an English clockmaker, settled at Norwich, Connecticut, in 1773. His ability was surpassed by that of his apprentice Daniel Burnap who worked at East Windsor. He in turn was outshone by his famous pupil Eli Terry, who in the early 1790s began making wooden clock movements in the town that is now Plymouth. These were sold uncased, and many were left that way, to serve as "wag-on-the-wall" clocks. Terry's major contributions were the use of standardized wooden parts, and the evolution with his brother Samuel of the influential pillar-and-scroll shelf clock, which had slender side pillars, a scrolled pediment and urn-shaped finials.

Chauncey Jerome initially made cases for Terry's shelf clocks, but by 1827 had formed a partnership with Elijah Darrow at Bristol, Connecticut. In the 1830s he was absorbed in the manufacture of cheap 30-hour brass movements. (By c.1840 wooden movements were obsolete.) Jerome & Darrow produced Empire-style clocks, sometimes stencilled with bronze powders (replacing the gold leaf used earlier) and fitted with a looking glass beneath the dial.

Joseph Ives made rapid strides in brass and steel movements and introduced a "wagon spring" clock c.1825—the basis for numerous examples later made by Birge & Fuller of Bristol. He also developed the rectangular "O.G." style case (c.1830), so-called because of its ogee (s-shaped) mouldings. (16) This type soon became ubiquitous. Ives' "hour-glass" shelf clocks were powered by means of a coiled spring. Other Connecticut styles include the rare "acorn" shelf clock, and the commoner "beehive" shape. (19) Neo-Gothicism spawned the "sharp Gothic" case (with pointed gable and pinnacles) and the "round Gothic" case (sometimes with a rippled effect along the round arch). (15) Both innovations have been credited to Elias Ingraham. Sharp Gothic clocks are now generally known as "steeple clocks".

WATCHES

The natural sequel of the spring-driven portable clock was the *personal* portable clock—the watch. Early examples made in France and Germany in the mid-16th C were spherical. Before long the familiar circular shape had come in, but stars, ovals, octagons, crosses, even skulls and birds, also gave their form to watches. (1) As early as the start of the 17th C, striking mechanisms, alarms or calendars were sometimes built in. But watches were essentially items of jewellery. Materials used for cases included gold, silver and gilt metal, while the repertoire of embellishment covered embossing, damascening and, above all, enamelling, which was most expertly practised in France. Dials and backplates were often superbly engraved, and even winding keys were decoratively treated.

Important early centres were Nuremberg and Blois. (At Blois the best enamelling was done.) Paris and Geneva dominated by the early 17th C (4), but the lead later passed to England. Here, the

Watches

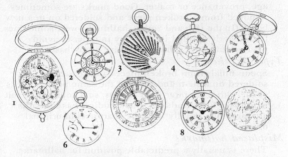

1 Engraved silver watch, by Hubuer of Bremen, early 18th c VŘ *I*
2 American Waterbury-type watch, with revolving movement, *c.*1878 ꜰꞬ *C*
3 *Montre à tact* by Breguet VŘ *I*
4 Swiss enamelled gold verge watch, *c.*1800 ꜰꞬ *F*

5 English pair case verge watch, *c.*1750 ꜰꞬ *F*
6 Gold watch showing the date, by Breguet VŘ *I*
7 Watch by Lucas, Amsterdam ɴ *G*
8 Pair case verge watch by William Warren, London, early 18th c ꜰꞬ *F*

"pair-cased" watch, with both inner and outer case, was popular until *c.*1830. (8).

Two late 17th-C inventions increased the popularity of watches: the balance spring, which made them more accurate, and the waistcoat, which provided a convenient place to carry them. Thomas Mudge devised the "detached lever escapement", which gradually displaced the verge and became universal for pocket watches. Its achievement was to liberate the oscillations of the balance from continual interference by the escapement.

Queen Elizabeth I of England had a wrist watch, and so did the Empress Josephine. But wrist watches first became widely accepted after 1850. Examples from this time are mainly Swiss. By the late 19th C, Swiss watches were of unrivalled excellence.

The outstanding watchmaker of all time was Abraham Louis Breguet (1747–1823), a Swiss who worked in Paris. He produced an automatic winder from 1780, and many other complex pieces, including *montres à tact* for telling the time in the dark. (3) He also gave his name to a characteristic style of hands. (6)

SILVER

Quality in silver is the sum of many attributes, including balance, patina, weight and sensitive use of the fashionable stylistic repertoire. A piece can only be described as first-rate if it is undamaged and unaltered, retains the original decoration and armorial engraving (if there is one) and has a full set of well-positioned marks (see pp 182–3) whenever applicable.

Detecting alterations

Repairs or alterations are easiest to see on plain pieces. Erasure of an armorial causes a patch of thin silver, detectable by a shiny interruption in the patina. If you breathe on a piece and a line shows up it may indicate a transposed armorial or a repair. Sometimes the tamperer may have tried to hide this line by decoration. The "breath test" will also show up transposed marks intended to deceive the buyer about age, provenance or maker. Good marks are sometimes removed from a broken piece and soldered on to a new body. (In the 18th and 19th C, hallmarks were sometimes fraudulently applied in this way in order to avoid paying duty rather than to deceive a purchaser.)

Types of fake

Spoon finials from broken pieces are frequently soldered on a stem and bowl of the same period. Forks of the 18th C are rarer than spoons, so a common deceit is to place fork heads on spoon bodies. Faked marks are rare: they usually lack the sharpness of original ones.

Misplaced hallmarks

There is usually a predictable position for hallmarks, depending on country, date and type of wares. Unusual placing—you will need to consult specialist books before you can detect it—is a cause for suspicion. The general rule is that marks should follow the line of a piece, but beneath a round object should be grouped in the middle. In England, which has the most consistent hallmarking system, lids and other separate parts had to be stamped, as well as the main body.

Hallmarking irregularities

Marks are never an infallible dating guide. Marking was not invariably required and there have always been pieces that have been marked erroneously. Even in England, commissioned luxury silver of the 16th–17th C bore only a maker's mark. Early provincial silver often escaped the attentions of the assay office. Sometimes heavily decorated pieces were exempted in case punching caused damage.

Armorials

Heraldic armorials often appear on antique silver, and the style of a decorative surround (cartouche) to an armorial can be a good clue to dating. Scrolled foliage (c.1675–1700), baroque scrolling, brickwork, scallop shells and masks (c.1700–35), rococo asymmetry (c.1735–70) and neo-classical ribbons and husks (c.1780–1800) are among the most obvious indicators. In Europe the armorial was generally embossed, stamped or cast and applied, but in England usually engraved.

Prices

Price fluctuations in silver can be bewildering. A characteristic type of complication occurs when a craftsman becomes so fashionable that his pieces are priced way above those by even the most skilful of his contemporaries. Slight damage can devalue an article by 50% to 75%, as can the absence of a lid.

Sets or pairs

When buying sets or pairs always check every detail of decoration to ensure a perfect match. A slight mismatch would bring down the price considerably.

Care of silver

Avoid abrasive cleaning, which will damage the patina as well as the marks. The best maintenance rule is to hand-wash in warm soapy water (or a gentle detergent) and then rub dry with a soft cloth.

ENGLAND

During the Civil War a great deal of plate was melted down for coinage, and surviving pieces of pre-Restoration workmanship are rare. Early drinking cups can sometimes be found. The earliest kind, known as mazers, were of wood, often with a silver lip and base. Mazers were superseded by standing cups—tall cups raised on a stem and with a tall cover. Salts, one of the most important types of secular plate, became large and ornamental in Elizabeth I's reign, but this type virtually disappeared in the 1680s.

English silver, Restoration—Queen Anne

3 William III column candlestick, 1689 Ⓑ F (pair)
4 Small Queen Anne caster, 1705–15 Ⓑ F
5 Queen Anne chocolate pot, with cut-card decoration, 1706 Ⓑ H
6 Queen Anne teapot, 1713 Ⓑ G

1 Beaker, c.1660–80, ht 8.9cm Ⓑ F
2 Charles II porringer with chased acanthus-leaf decoration, lacking a lid, 1678 Ⓑ F

By the 1680s, after the immigration of French Huguenots into the country, a decline in craftsmanship was halted, and some native goldsmiths were making fine pieces in French styles. Gadrooned edging, embossed acanthus leaves, spiral or vertical flutes and flat-chased *chinoiserie* were popular. In 1697, to prevent the melting down of coin for manufacturing, the silver standard for plate was raised to 95.8%, distinguishable from sterling (92.5%) by the marks of Britannia, the lion's head erased, a date letter and the first two letters of the maker's name (see p 134). In 1700–01 five provincial towns were appointed to assay silver of the Britannia standard, each using its own town mark. The use of soft silver encouraged a sparsely decorated style, "Queen Anne", sometimes enlivened by cut-card work. (5) This gave way to greater elaboration after 1720, when the sterling standard was restored. By 1730 the English were taking cautious steps towards rococo asymmetry. Chinese-style decoration came in c.1745. (7, 11)

The greatest silversmith of the 18th C was Paul de Lamerie (active 1712–49), a Huguenot craftsman: his mark adds between 300% and 1,000% to the value of a piece. (15) To the period 1765–95 belongs what is now generally called "Adam silver", in the neo-classical style. Oval shapes were favoured, and tall pieces often took their form from the narrow-necked urn, generally without decoration after 1780. (12) Bright-cut engraving came in during the 1780s. Writers on silver usually inveigh against the "dis-proportionate" reputation of the neo-classical silversmith Hester Bateman (active 1775–90), but her pieces are certainly of unusual grace. (13)

From the later Georgian period, silver becomes heavier, a fashion reaching its height in the early 19th-C wares, of Rundell, Bridge & Rundell. Benjamin Smith and Paul Storr, whose marks appear on much of Rundell's plate, ran workshops for them before going on to found their own outstanding businesses. Smith excelled in relatively small pieces, while Storr (1771–1844), the leading Regency silversmith, was versatile enough to produce charming beehive honeypots as well as more monumental wares.

Favourite models for designers in the Victorian era, when pieces were often preposterously showy, were Cellini, the Renaissance master, and, nearer at hand, John Flaxman, the neo-classical artist and sculptor. The Victorian period began with a rococo revival and the rise of an exuberant naturalism; vines became more lifelike, convolvulus more convolved. Towards the end of the 40s there were signs of a neo-classical revival, and some designs based on Italian Renaissance metalwork.

Tankards and mugs. The tankard was the most popular vessel from the 16th to the 18th C. Under Charles II the usual kind was large and plain, with a low, flat-topped cover in two steps, a splayed, moulded base and a thumbpiece. Some late 17th-C tankards are embossed round the base with acanthus leaves or spiral fluting—the only genuine types of embossing applied to tankards before c.1810. Others of the period are engraved with *chinoiserie*. In Anne's reign the flat cover was gradually superseded by a domed one, and before the middle of the century a baluster-type tankard with a high moulded foot came in. A mug is essentially a small tankard without a lid (note that every vessel with a capacity of over a pint was lidded).

Porringers. The porringer was a two-handled covered cup with two main variants: the caudle cup and the posset cup. Early Restoration examples often had embossed decoration on the lower half. As with tankards, acanthus or spiral-fluted embossing or (less often) *chinoiserie* engraving were found in the late 17th C, echoed on the covers, although plain porringers were also made. (2) Other items associated with drinking include beer jugs, wine coasters (circular stands for a bottle or decanter, made from c.1760) and punch bowls, which are comparatively rare.

Coffee and chocolate pots. Chocolate pots are distinguishable from coffee pots only by their hinged or removable finial, revealing a hole for stirring. Early coffee pots had conical lids, straight spouts and rounded handles which until c.1720 were either opposite the spout or at right angles to it. By 1700 the spout had become curved, the lid was rounded, and handle and spout joints were sometimes treated with cut-card decoration. (5) Side handles went out of fashion c.1715. Before 1730 the only ornament, apart from cut-card work, was engraved armorials. The cylindrical body gave way at the turn of the century to polygonal. Around 1725 lids became

English silver, Georgian–Victorian

7 George III *chinoiserie* tea caddy, in the manner of de Lamerie, 1761, ht 15.2cm FG F
8 George II cow creamer, by John Schuppe, 1764 FG F
9 Kettle, *c.*1735 FG F
10 Victorian cast candlestick, in mid-18th c style, 1840, ht 33cm FG G (pair)
11 George III *chinoiserie* coffee pot, 1767, ht 30.5cm FG F
12 George III tea urn, 1783 FG G
13 George III oval teapot, by Hester Bateman, London, 1790, ht 15.2cm FG F
14 Salver, 1890, diam. 32cm G E
15 George II silver-gilt cream jug, unmarked, attributed to Paul de Lamerie, *c.*1735 FG F
16 Victorian mustard pot and ladle, London, 1846 G C

flatter and *c.*1730 the pear form was introduced, sometimes with flat-chased or embossed work. (11) The typical coffee pot of the 1780s and 90s was urn-shaped, sometimes with bright-cut engraving. In the 19th c examples were squatly pear-shaped, often on feet and frequently standing on a spirit-lamp.

Teapots and associated items. Early teapots are generally small, as tea was expensive. Teapots are rarer than coffee pots up to 1780. The egg-shaped body of the later 17th c gave way to the Queen Anne pear shape, often octagonal after 1710 and gradually becoming higher. (6) Handles were of wood. The bullet-style teapot which became popular *c.*1720—round with a flattened top and a straight spout—was followed by the inverted pear. The sequence of neo-classical forms went from cylindrical to flat-topped oval to dome-topped oval, and *c.*1800 to a variety of rectangular forms. All had a straight spout rising from near the base. (13)

Tea or coffee urns, introduced *c.*1760, more often had neo-classical than rococo embellishment. (12) Cream jugs were made in a variety of styles, including the realistic cow creamers made (1757–68) by John Schuppe. (8) Caddies of the mid-18th c were commonly embossed with *chinoiserie*. (7)

Sauceboats. The earliest sauceboats, which are rare, have low oval bodies with two lips and two handles. In the second quarter of the 18th C this form was discarded for a boat on three legs with a handle opposite the lip. Most examples date from before 1780.

Salts, casters and peppers. The earliest salts which frequently appear on the market are of the "trencher" type, with a central depression for the salt. Salts became three-legged after *c*.1735, and from *c*.1760 pierced oval ones occur, with a blue glass liner. Boat-shaped salts came into vogue *c*.1785, and oblong tubs at the end of the century.

Casters, used for sprinkling condiments, were made in sets of three, the largest for sugar. The cylindrical "lighthouse" caster gave way (*c*.1705) to the pear shape set on a moulded foot. (4) About 1715 the upper part of the body became distinctly concave.

Flatware. Spoons are the only items of pre-Restoration silverware available to most collectors. Decorative finials are found in great variety, but seal-top spoons are commonest, with a flat seal on a baluster. (17) Apostle spoons survive in surprising quantities, and are immensely popular. (21) Trefid spoons, with two notches in the end, have an elongated "rat-tail" down the back of the bowl, sometimes surrounded by a lacy pattern echoed on the front of the stem. (22) The Hanoverian spoon has a ridge along the front of the stem and an upward-turning end. The Old English pattern, in contrast, has the ridge along the back and the end turned the other way. A trend of the 1760s was the scrolled Onslow end. Patterns of the early 19th C include the fiddle-and-thread and the hourglass. (25) The mote spoon had a pierced bowl, for removing foreign matter from liquids. (20) Handles of knives and forks tended to follow spoon styles.

English flatware, 17th–19th C

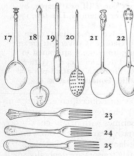

18 William and Mary basting spoon, *c*.1690 FC F
19 Early George II marrow scoop, 1729 FC C
20 George II mote spoon, of dessert size, by Edward Jennings, London, *c*.1730 FC C
21 Charles II provincial apostle spoon (St Jude), by Thomas Dare, *c*.1680 FC F
22 William and Mary trefid spoon, London, 1694 FC D
23 Albany pattern dessert fork, 1890 FC C (set of six)
24 Old English Thread fork, 1790–1810 FC F (half-dozen service)
25 Victorian Fiddle-and-Thread fork FC B (F for set of six)

17 Charles II seal-top spoon, 1665 FC E

Candlesticks. Charles II candlesticks are not uncommon. The characteristic type until *c*.1700 was made from sheet, with a clustered or fluted column on a square or polygonal stepped base. (3) The cast type was introduced by the Huguenot silversmiths *c*.1690 and became standard until *c*.1760. Height gradually increased. The "Queen Anne" style (*c*.1700–15), with a baluster stem echoing the wide base, was the basis for many later variations. Mid-century figure candlesticks included caryatids and kneeling blackamoors. The Corinthian column form, made from sheet, came in with the classical revival. A typical design of the Adam period was a concave column with festoons on the base and ram's heads on the four-sided shoulder.

Other silverware. Luxurious toilet services of up to 30 pieces were made in the reign of Charles II. The new table silver of the 18th C included the epergne, a centrepiece with detachable stands or hanging baskets for fruit and sweetmeats. Inkstands, also known as standishes, were rare before George II. Wine labels are a large specialist subject, made in silver from *c.*1734: the earliest were of shield shape, followed by crescents. Baskets for bread, cake, fruit or sweetmeats became common in the late 1720s.

SCOTLAND AND IRELAND

Scotland. Scottish silver tends to be more austere than English. As in Europe, the beaker became a popular vessel in the 17th C, its shape introduced by traders from the Netherlands and by Protestant refugees. Tankards were rare before 1700, and then tended to be large, superbly made and still fairly uncommon. Characteristic of the last decade of the 17th C is the "thistle cup", a small lobed mug of inverted bell shape, with an S-shaped handle and simple decoration of thin lobes rising from the base—a rare and expensive type.

Quaiches are very much a Scottish speciality. Originally a quaich—the word is adopted from the Gaelic for bowl or cup—was made of a solid block of wood, like the English mazer, or of small wooden staves held together with hoops. It had two or more handles. Although silver quaiches, with engraved representations of staves, were made for the aristocracy (*c.*1660–1725), they are less frequent than silver-mounted wooden ones. (1) Teapots are among the most treasured 18th-C items. The typical Scottish bullet teapot is totally spherical, instead of slightly flattened in the English manner. (3) Examples after *c.*1730 frequently have flatchased or embossed decoration.

Scottish mulls—large or small horns—were often mounted in silver for snuffboxes, especially in the early 19th C. In the

---

Scottish and Irish silver, 18th and 19th C

1 Small quaich, Scotland, *c.*1740, diam. 5.1cm **Ⓝ** *F*
2 Three-legged sugar bowl, Dublin, *c.*1750 **Ⓝ** *F*
3 Scottish bullet teapot, *c.*1740 ⒻⒸ *F*

4 Scottish bowl, *c.*1825 ⒻⒸ *F*
5 Scottish snuff mull (silver-mounted ram's horn), *c.*1800 ⒻⒸ *C*
6 Dish ring with farmyard decoration, Dublin, 1763 **Ⓝ** *F*
7 Dish ring pierced in arabesques and quatrefoils, Dublin, *c.*1775 ⒻⒸ *F*
8 Irish three-legged cream jug, 1730–70 Ⓔ *E*
9 George IV tea urn, Dublin, 1824 ⒻⒸ *F*

Highlands such boxes were commonly made from a curled sheep's horn with silver mounts and hinge. (5)

The Edinburgh hallmarking system was introduced in the mid-15th C. The date letter was added after 1681 in both Edinburgh and, more erratically, in Glasgow, and from 1784 the sovereign's head duty mark was used (discontinued everywhere in 1890). Glasgow was not established as an assay office until 1819.

Ireland. Until recently, the usual opinion of Irish silver was that the earlier, Celtic-style pieces were beautiful but unobtainable, while the later pieces were indistinguishable from English plate. Irish tankards after 1660 cannot be told apart from English, except by the marks. Quintessentially Irish, however, is the "farmyard design" used on many objects, but especially on sugar bowls and dish rings, between 1760 and 1780. Early Irish coffee and chocolate pots were identical to English ones, but from the mid-1730s some national features appear, such as a transverse band on the spout, with slanted grooves above it. A particular type of wide-lipped, helmet-shaped cream jug has no exact parallel among English wares. The central-foot type dates mainly from the mid-1730s; later a three-legged model was introduced with the third leg under the lip (not the handle, as in England). (8) About 1740 the feet of these helmet-shaped jugs changed to lion masks or human masks (the human type was favoured especially in Cork and Limerick).

The dish ring (c.1740–1820) is an Irish speciality. Its function was to raise a bowl above a mahogany table, to protect the surface from heat. The common early form is made from sheet silver, pierced and decorated, and dates from c.1740, just before the "rococo revolution". In the later 1740s the diameter of the bottom became larger than the top, and this style persisted until the 1770s. The "farmyard design" became common on dish rings in the 1760s. (6) In the 70s chasing and *repoussé* decoration gave way to geometric piercing and bright-cut engraving. (7)

FRANCE

In the France of Louis XIV, nobles were required to send their plate to be melted down as subsidy for wars. And in the French Revolution church and secular plate was seized and turned into bullion for the benefit of the Republic. So French silver wrought before 1790 is rare and valuable except for small, lightweight pieces. Examples from the 16th C and earlier hardly ever appear on the market, although occasionally a grandiose item such as a *nef* (silver ship centrepiece used at ceremonial banquets) will find its way to one of the larger auction houses.

During the 17th C a dramatic change took place in French silver. The strong, simple traditions of the medieval world were abandoned in favour of showy baroque, with lambrequins, vicious-beaked bird masks and elaborate chased decoration. Towards the end of the century craftsmanship became more restrained, and with the death of Louis XIV in 1715 there began a period of simplicity, when piercing was the fashionable ornament. This brief spell gradually modulated, via the Régence style, into 40 years of florid rococo. The silversmith Juste-Aurèle Meissonnier (1695–1750) is generally credited with inaugurating the rococo style with a candlestick he designed in 1728. Another genius among rococo silversmiths was François Thomas Germain, who had many royal commissions—among others, to make a gold rattle for every royal birth from 1726. (3, 7) Madame de Pompadour was the human embodiment of the rococo, as Louis XIV was of the baroque. Only four pieces of silver known to have belonged to her survive—a pair of sauceboats and two mustard barrels.

The French Revolution snuffed out the rococo (already dying of neo-classicism) and encouraged pedantic imitation of the Roman and Greek. In 1797 the craft was reorganized, and marks, hitherto regional, now became common throughout the country: the maker's mark in a lozenge and a tax mark indicating first- or second-class silver. Annual marks were introduced in 1818. The most successful silversmiths of the neo-classical First Empire of Napoleon were Martin-Guillaume Biennais (1764–1843) and Jean-Baptiste-Claude Odiot (1763–1850). After the Empire, French silverware closely resembled English for about 30 years.

French silver, 18th and 19th C

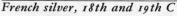

1 Louis XV ewer and basin, Paris, 1733 Ⓑ *I*
2 Fluted neo-classical candlestick, Paris, 1782 Ⓕ*C* *G* (pair)
3 Ewer by François Thomas Germain, c.1760 Ⓥ̄Ʀ *I*
4 Chocolate pot with hinged finial, 1774 Ⓕ*C* *F*
5 Table seal, c.1850 Ⓕ*C* *C*
6 Ecuelle, by Paul Soulaine, 1747 Ⓕ*C* *F*
7 Candelabra, by François Thomas Germain, c.1758 Ⓥ̄Ʀ ♀ *I*
8 Louis XVI oval soup tureen, Paris, 1770 Ⓑ ♀ *I*

No comprehensive collection of French silver is complete without an *écuelle*, a vessel akin to the porringer, but shallower. (6) Most were made in the period 1714–70 and were decorated with cut-card work and complex finials. After c.1730, *écuelles* were often supplied with stands. Wine tasters, surviving from the 18th and early 19th C, are small bowls, normally with a single s-shaped handle, a thumbpiece or a pierced lug with a ring beneath it. France was the first country to introduce double-lidded oval or rectangular spice boxes on four feet, at the end of the 17th C. Coffee pots commonly had a wooden handle at right angles to the spout. (4) Candlesticks progressed from late 17th-C restraint to rococo flamboyance, becoming asymmetrical by 1740, although some examples of the same period were quite plain.

GERMANY

The two great centres of the goldsmith's art in the 16th C were Augsburg and Nuremberg. The Jamnitzer family dominate the history of 16th-C German silver. Wenzel Jamnitzer (1508–85), who has been called the Cellini of Germany, practised in Nuremberg from 1534, producing some superb centrepieces and cups. His work is covered with relief ornament, such as realistic lizards and insects. His grandson Christoph was also a fine craftsman.

Beakers were popular in Germany from the 16th to the 18th C,

German silver, 17th and 18th C

1 Embossed tankard, south Germany, 1620 Ⓒ *F*
2 Double beaker, 1610 ⒻⒸ *F*
3 Silver-gilt rococo *trembleuse*, with engraved blue glass but lacking its Meissen cup, by Andreas Schneider, Augsburg, 1753–5 Ⓑ *F*
4 Oval sugar casket, Dresden, *c.*1760 ⒻⒸ *F*

5 Silver-mounted coconut cup, Maintz, 1656 V̄R̄ *H*
6 Small pineapple cup, Nuremberg, 1650 ⒻⒸ *F*
7 Coffee pot, by Johann Christoph Engelbrecht, Augsburg, 1749–51 ⒻⒸ *F*
8 Bowl, by Johannes Schuelten, Düsseldorf, *c.*1735 Ⓑ *F*
9 Tureen, Hanover, 1770 Ⓑ *G*

16th-C examples being often covered with plain bosses. Some 17th-C ones were made in imitation of German wine glasses. The typical beaker of the 17th C is heavily embossed and stands on a moulded base, although an earlier type on plain ball feet was still frequently made. Double beakers in the form of barrels occur. (2)

Trends in German tankards run parallel with those in English examples: in the 16th C, small tapering bodies; from the 17th C, tankards of larger capacity, often with *repoussé* designs from the Bible or from classical mythology. (1) Bacchanalian subjects and tankards set with coins were popular from the mid-17th C. Tankards were often parcel-gilt.

Double cups are typically German, often covered with large bosses. The top cup is frequently smaller than the lower, and was intended for use by the ladies. The later cups have larger and rounder bosses separated by foliage and other ornament, and sometimes the bosses too are decorated in relief. Alone among the silversmiths of Europe, the Germans made standing cups and covers of great height, intended for display rather than use. The supremely characteristic German vessel was the pineapple cup, covered in lobes or bosses. (6) These were introduced in the later 16th C and reached their greatest popularity between *c.*1600 and *c.*1650. Much ingenuity went into the design of the stems of these vessels: some are treetrunks, with or without attendant woodmen, others are figures. Typical of the German Renaissance too are what might be called fantasy cups of the mannerist school: ostriches bearing real ostrich eggs on their backs, Atlases holding globes, silver-mounted coconuts (5) and nautilus shells, and charging equestrian figures, all belong to this group. Wager cups—double cups often with one bowl in the form of a long-skirted woman, the other pivoted above her head—were produced in great numbers from the late 15th C until the 1850s, especially in Augsburg.

Sweetmeat dishes were a very popular 17th-C product. Early German *écuelles* were given small button feet, giving way to claw supports in the mid-18th C. *Trembleuses* (frames for holding a teacup or glass) were among the showpieces of rococo exuberance. (3) A date letter system was introduced into German hallmarks in 1735, but it was not used after the mid-19th C.

THE NETHERLANDS

In the Netherlands the characteristic early drinking vessel was the silver or silver-mounted horn. Costly cups were presented by members of the Dutch guilds for use at banquets. The commonest Dutch vessel after the age of the drinking horn was the beaker. (1) Some were engraved with bands of arabesques and flowers, others decorated with sacred subjects.

The 17th C is the great period of Dutch silver. Some magnificent embossed work was done, the depth of the relief cunningly varied to indicate perspective. The van Vianen family were the outstanding silversmiths of the late 16th C and the 17th C. Adam van Vianen (*c*.1555–1627) introduced an extreme mannerist style of ornament known as *Kwabornament*. (2) The opportunities for *kitsch* in such a style were obviously immense, and at times nothing more than a gross playfulness is achieved. But in its asymmetry, *Kwabornament* was a true forerunner of the rococo, and today pieces in the style are eagerly collected. *Kwabornament* spread throughout the Netherlands, but by the mid-17th C was petering out, to be replaced by primarily floral decoration. Tulipomania was at its height *c*.1745.

Dutch standing cups of the 17th C follow German 16th-C examples, but sometimes the decoration is distinctively Dutch (for example, chased saints after designs by Hendrik Goltzius). Cups were popular gifts to Dutch naval heroes, such as Admiral Michael de Ruyter, but silver tankards are rare.

Dutch silver, 17th and 19th C

1 Small beaker, Groningen, 1650–1 🄵 *F*
2 Salt in the van Vianen style, Utrecht, *c*.1620 Ⅴꝝ ♀ *I*
3 Melon-shaped teapot with flower finial, Middelburg, *c*.1770, ht 13.6cm 🄵 *F*
4 Oval brandy bowl, by van Helsen, Bolsward, 1762, width 24.1cm 🄵 *F*
5 Tobacco box with engraved rim, by Jan Buysen, Amsterdam, 1791, diam. 12.7cm 🄖 *E*
6 Spoon, Leiden, 1701 🄖 *D*
7 Violin-shaped embossed snuff box with English import marks of 1900 🄖 *C*
8 Windmill cup, *c*.1620 🄑 ♀ *H*

Peculiarly Dutch are silver-gilt stands for holding wine glasses made in sets of a dozen. Coconuts and nautilus shells were sometimes set in silver mounts, and bridal cups, on the principle of German wager cups, were a speciality: the bigger, fixed bowl, in the form of a woman's skirt, was filled with wine and the drinker had to drain it and then reverse the cup and empty the pivoted smaller bowl without wetting his doublet. A still more ingenious wager cup was the windmill cup: by blowing through a tube, the sails were set in motion, and the cup had to be emptied before they stopped. (8) Then there was the cup known as *Hansje in den kelder* ("Hans in the cellar", 16th–19th C) which was brought out to celebrate news of a child on the way. In the centre, under a domed lid, was the figure of a baby which popped up when the vessel was filled with wine. Another Dutch drinking vessel of the 17th and 18th C, closer to the Scottish quaich than to the English porringer, was the brandy bowl. (4) Dutch candlesticks of the 17th C, which are rare, tend to have bulbous hemispherical bases, and the main shaft is often "wrythen" like barley-sugar.

Domestic silver of the 18th C was influenced by French styles, with much use of gilding. Tobacco boxes, teapots, kettles, tea urns (from 1760) and other practical pieces were in great demand at this time. (3, 5)

SCANDINAVIA

Denmark. The most popular early drinking vessel of Scandinavia was the horn, often mounted in gilt copper and sometimes silver. Beakers succeeded horns, and in both Denmark and Norway (united until 1814) commonly had an open band of flowers and foliage encircling the body.

Scandinavian silver, 17th and 18th C

1 Swedish beaker, Stockholm, 1692, ht 13cm **⑧** *F*
2 Norwegian tankard, 1585, ht 19cm **⑧** *I*
3 Danish rococo coffee pot with bird finial and dragon's-head spout, Copenhagen, 1756 **⑧** *G*
4 Swedish parcel-gilt tankard, *c.*1690, ht 19cm **FC** *G*
5 Norwegian bowl, Bergen, *c.*1660, diam. 12.7cm **⑧** *F*

6 Swedish coffee pot, by Rehr Zethelius, Stockholm, 1799, ht 26cm **⑧** *F*
7 Norwegian beaker, *c.*1740 **FC** *E*
8 Norwegian spoon, by Michel Plumeion, Bergen, 1618 **FC** *E*
9 Norwegian spoon, by Lucas Steen, Bergen, *c.*1620s **FC** *E*
10 Swedish kettle, by Andreas Wall, Stockholm, 1720, ht (with handle) 23cm **⑧** *G*

Shallow two-handled silver bowls, for serving hot brandy and liquor, were made in Denmark, as well as in Norway, Sweden and Holland, in the 17th C. (5) Often they are engraved all over with formalized, baroque-style arabesques. Scandinavian tankards of the 16th and early 17th C, sometimes lightly engraved, had tall cylindrical bodies which later became shorter and wider and came to be fitted with three feet or in rare cases four. The distinctive,

Scandinavian peg tankard, made from c.1650, had eight pegs evenly spaced behind the handle, as a guarantee of equal shares.

Charles II English cups were copied, including the granular finish sometimes favoured. The French rococo influence affected Denmark in the early 18th C, while the English influence continued alongside it. Scandinavian pieces of the rococo period often have twisted ribbing. (3)

Norway. Norwegian tankards are similar in design to Danish but usually bolder. (2) Examples of the late 17th C often have a flat-topped cover, larger in diameter than the tankard itself, and sometimes set with a medal or coin. Romanus Fridrichsen Möller of Christiania was one of the makers of these. Another Christiania tankard-maker was Berendt Platt. Albret Groth (active 1706–17), of the same city, favoured acanthus foliage on his tankards and imitated English wares.

From the early part of the 18th C onwards, complete sets of marks (townmark, maker's and warden's marks, and marks for year and month of production) are occasionally found.

Sweden. Sweden was great in the 17th C under Gustavus Adolphus, the hero of the Thirty Years' War, but his exploits were celebrated more in German silver than in Swedish. Much Swedish domestic plate of the 17th C is German in style. Tankards of the late 17th C and 18th C differ from those of Denmark and Norway in that the bodies are shorter and tend to taper downwards, while the covers are lower and broader and project outward over the lip. The ball feet and thumbpieces are larger and much decorated—again in line with German example. (4) Beakers were also popular in Sweden, usually tall with wide mouths and narrow bases. (1) In the second half of the 17th C vessels were often made in filigree work, by makers such as H.V. Torell of Gothenburg, and Rudolph Wittkopf and John Stahle of Stockholm.

RUSSIA

Three distinctive vessels—the *bratina*, the *kovsh* and the *charka*—are essentially Russian, and one decorative technique, *niello*. The *bratina* was a covered handleless loving cup. At the death of a royal prince or princess, a favourite *bratina* was placed on his or her tomb in a church and was sometimes afterwards consecrated for use as an incense-burner. The *kovsh*, with a boat-shaped body and a bent handle extending from it like the prow of a Viking ship, was

Russian silver, 17th–19th C

1 Large parcel-gilt *nielloed* beaker and stand, c.1680 VR *I*

2 Vodka cup, with scrollwork on a matted ground, Moscow, mid-18th c ▣ *D*

3 Schnapps beaker, Kiev, 1899–1908 ▣ *B*

4 Chocolate pot, Leningrad, 1804 ▣ *E*

5 *Kovsh*, by Fabergé, Leningrad, c.1890, lgth 11.4cm ▣ *F*

originally used for ladling and drinking but later acquired a commemorative or symbolic function. Numerous 19th-C copies of 17th-C styles can be encountered. (5) The *charka* is a small cup, usually with one handle, for strong liquors or brandy. Some are entirely of precious metal, others ornamented with rock crystal and semi-precious stones. Coloured enamels were sometimes used as decoration in the 17th C.

Niello, a black inlaid enamel, was used to decorate and letter Russian gold and silver in the 16th and 17th C, but especially at Tula, St Petersburg and Novgorod in the 18th C. (1) The most frequently encountered 19th-C *niello* work is on Russian silver snuffboxes. Filigree was another Russian speciality.

Peter the Great introduced the compulsory hallmarking of plate in 1700. Under his influence the old traditional vessels declined in popularity, and English and other European silver was imitated. Some English craftsmen even settled in Russia, including the London goldsmiths Robert Hogg and William Donarth.

ITALY

Italian silver is often showy and fantastical—vases have animal handles, river gods sprawl over tureen covers. Something of the sculptural tradition of Renaissance gold and silver work lingers on in beautifully executed reliefs and in boldly modelled domestic wares.

The five leading centres of silver production were Rome, Turin, Venice, Genoa and Naples: silver was almost always hallmarked in these towns in the 18th C. Roman silversmiths naturally specialized in ecclesiastical plate. They also made silver statuettes more often than the other centres, and the neo-classical style took root there more quickly. Genoa was famous for its silver filigree, and was also the only place in Italy where *trembleuses* were made. French influence is strong in Turin silver. Venetians went in for highly embossed ornament and made superb silver book-bindings and picture-frames.

THE UNITED STATES

Silver was the first of the European arts to flourish in the New World. Plate was more desirable than coin, as it could be identified, in wills or after robberies, by shape, makers' marks or engraved arms. It was used for pledge and even to buy real estate.

The port towns of Boston and New York were the main silversmithing centres of the 17th C. In Boston English precedent inevitably had a strong influence in the early days, and much silver was imported from England. Some London goldsmiths brought their skills to America. In New York, naturally, the predominant influence was Dutch. The names of the early silversmiths—van der Burgh, Onkelbag, Kierstede—reveal their origin. (2, 3)

Gradually, though, a home-grown distinctly "American" style began to emerge in both Boston and New York, and in Philadelphia and Charlestown, which had their own craftsmen. Not that English styles died out. The new, plainer style of Queen Anne's reign reached America, partly through gifts of plate to colonial churches, partly by émigrés from and visitors to England. The rococo style came to America about five to ten years later than to England.

Just at the point at which one might have expected America to free itself from English example—after the Declaration of Independence—the prevailing style in England happened to be irresistibly seductive to revolutionaries setting up a new society:

neo-classicism, which relied on classical precedent as much as did the politicians with their Capitol and Senate. So bright-cut ornament in the Adam style became the vogue. The classical urn shape was widely favoured. Philadelphia's own unmistakable idiom at this time was characterized by bold pineapple finials, small beading on most edges, and pierced galleries on the shoulders of urn-shaped pieces, such as coffee pots and covered sugar urns. The most renowned silversmith of the period is Paul Revere (1734–1818), who worked in Boston. (8, 11)

Until recently, the serious collector of American silver was expected to stop taking an interest after c.1800 (when spoons with

American silver, 17th–19th C

Value symbols refer to New York estimates expressed as pounds

4 Candlestick, by Jeremiah Dummer, 1686 VR *I* (pair)

5 Candlestick, by George Ridout, 18th C VR ♀ *I* (pair)

6 Coffin-end spoon, c.1800 FC ♀ *B*

7 Coffee pot, by Simeon Soumain, 18th C VR *H*

8 Commemorative urn, by Paul Revere, 1800 ⓑ ♀ *I*

9 Teapot, by Jacob Hurd, Boston, c.1738 ⓑ ♀ *H*

10 Acorn-grip sugar tongs, early 19th C FC *A*

11 Covered cream jug, by Paul Revere, 1784, ht 17.8cm ⓑ ♀ *F*

1 Porringer by John Coney and Peter van Inburgh, Boston, early 18th C ⓑ *F*

2 Punch bowl, by Cornelius Kierstede, c.1600–25 VR ♀ *I*

3 Caudle cup, by Gerrit Onckelbag, 1696 VR *I*

their ends clipped in a coffin shape were made to commemorate George Washington's death). (6) Scholars wrote of the "coarsening" of classical ornament during the 19th C and of the "vagaries" of the 19th-C taste. But as more and more early pieces are received into museums, and prices rise, collectors have begun to take seriously the "manufactured" silver of the 19th and early 20th C.

Among the 19th-C firms whose wares are most collected today are Galt & Brothers, Inc., of Washington DC (founded 1802), who had Abraham Lincoln and Jefferson Davis among their clients; the Ames Mfg Company, Chicopee, Mass. (founded 1829); and D.C. Bromwell, Inc., of Washington DC (founded 1873), who discovered how to plate baby shoes with precious metals.

METALWARE

Some base-metal or alloy articles once overlooked by collectors are now fetching increasingly high prices. Dating of the humbler kinds of domestic ware can be difficult, owing to the long continuation of traditional designs.

SILVER-COLOURED METALS

Sheffield plate. This is copper plated with silver by a method which fuses the metals inseparably. It was allegedly invented *c.*1743 by Thomas Bolsover, a Sheffield cutler. He used the technique mainly to make buttons (which remained an important part of Sheffield plate production), but it was another cutler, Joseph Hancock, who first employed the new medium for candlesticks, coffee pots and other domestic wares.

Some of the earliest manufacturers, whose marks were entered at the Sheffield Assay Office in 1773, the year it was founded, were Henry Tudor, Thomas Leader, Thomas Law, John Winter & Co., Richard Morton, Matthew Felton & Co., John Littlewood and John Hoyland & Co. Matthew Boulton at Soho, Birmingham, was making fused plate by 1762, and three years later founded the Matthew Boulton & Plate Co. Styles drew heavily upon silver

Sheffield plate, 18th and 19th C

1 Telescopic candlestick, by A. Goodman & Co., 19th c, extended ht 40cm **B** *D*
2 Adamesque candlestick, Soho Works, Birmingham, *c.*1775, ht 27cm **B** *D*
3 Orange and lemon strainer, 1778 ᴠ̊ʀ *D*
4 Tea urn, by Richard Morton & Co., *c.*1790 **FG** *E*
5 Tray, early 19th c **FG** *D*

6 Wine cooler, 1820 **FG** *E*
7 Cheese toaster, *c.*1805 **FG** *D*
8 Cake basket, 1820s **C** *C*
9 Tea caddy, *c.*1870 **B** *C*
10 Octagonal teapot, late 18th c **B** *D*
11 Tea caddy with bright-cut engraving, 1780s, ht 8.8cm ᴠ̊ʀ *D*
12 Soup tureen, *c.*1820 **FG** *E*

Electro-plated and silver-coloured metals, 19th C

13 Dutch vase in the late 18th-c
style, 19th c, ht 26.7cm FG C
14 American boat-shaped fruit
bowl with servers, c.1870, lgth
28.5cm G E
15 German double beaker, 1896,
ht 8.5cm FG C
16 German candelabra, late 19th
c, ht 20cm FG E

17 English electro-plated wine
ewer, goblets and tray,
elaborately chased, 1879, ht
29.5cm FG D
18 Austrian teapot, late 19th c
G C
19 Scandinavian peg tankard in
17th-c style, mid-late 19th c, ht
26.5cm FG E

forms, often copying the grandest and most elegant designs. (2, 4, 11) Since Sheffield plate was only a third the price of silver, competititon with silversmiths was intense.

"Double plating" (plating on two sides of the copper instead of one) came in c.1763 and was used particularly for drinking vessels, and dishes which came into contact with food. Methods of decoration included flat chasing, "swaging" (the swage, a kind of pincers, was used for moulding edges) and piercing. By c.1780 it was customary to apply silver bands or shields to the plated ware to provide a suitable metal for engraving. Silver wire was sometimes added to sheared edges from 1787.

The most collectable smaller items still to be found are wine coasters, salt and mustard pots, inkstands, and candle-snuffers with trays. Among the larger articles were epergnes, soup tureens (12), entrée dishes, salvers, ice pails and wine coolers (6). Teapots, coffee pots, hot-water jugs and cake baskets were also made, and plated wire toast racks appeared c.1780–85. Tankards were much in demand—Nathaniel Smith, John Love and Joseph Smith were among the most prominent makers of these. Candlesticks continued to be an item of immense popularity, and some were telescopic. (1, 2) Some church vessels were made, notably by Robert Gainsford, who produced handsome communion flagons.
Marks. In the early days of Sheffield plate production, makers unscrupulously used marks to suggest that the wares were silver. In 1773 the silversmiths of Birmingham and Sheffield asked Parliament to establish an assay office in those cities so that some control could be exercised over this abuse. The Act of 1773 forbade letters to be punched on plated articles, which unfairly prevented platers marking their wares; another Act was passed in 1784 allowing them to sign their wares as long as silver assay marks were not used.
Electro-plating. By 1830 the introduction of "German silver", an alloy of copper, zinc and nickel, was already causing the decline of the Sheffield plate industry. It was finally ruined by the growing

use of electro-plated utensils, which could be produced at a far lower labour cost. (17) Electro-plated reproductions of Sheffield plate are all too common. Look for differences in condition and colour: Sheffield is usually more worn and the silver used for it has a bluish-grey tone, in comparison with the purer silver colour created by electro-plating. Note that the joint pins in Sheffield plate hinges end in a small ornamental cap. Seams should show some sign of solder: an electro-plated article naturally has no such trace as it has been dipped in the plating vat.

TINWARE AND TÔLE

British and Continental tin. The tinplate (tinned iron) industry was introduced into Britain from Saxony about the middle of the 17th C. In the early 18th C John Hanbury of Pontypool, Monmouthshire, developed the process of flattening iron bars between rollers.

Tinware, 19th C

1 American japanned coffee pot ⓑ ℞ C (NY value)
2 Pontypool chestnut urns in "Chinese red", c.1790, ht 33cm ⓑ F
3 English tôle bowl and cover with gilded handle, c.1810, ht 29cm ℣℞ F
4 American tin coffee pot ꜰᴄ B (NY value)
5 Dutch tea caddy ⓑ C
6 English tôle teapot, black with gilt decoration, 19th c ⓑ D
7 French *tôle peinte* plate, c.1800, diam. 25cm ꜰᴄ C
8 American candle mould (24-candle size), ⓑ D (NY value)
9 American japanned coffin tray, lgth 21cm ꜰᴄ ℞ C (NY value)
10 English small chocolate tin exported to South Africa ⓖ A
11 American tin chandelier ⓑ D (NY value)

Tinplate was popular in those days because of its resistance to rust and the ease with which it could be cut, bent and soldered. It could also be printed upon.

Japanned ware (or "Japan", or sometimes "tôle") was an attempt to produce from asphaltum (a coal by-product) a lacquer similar to that used by the Japanese. Japanners working on metal were active in the late 1690s at Bilston, Staffordshire. The most celebrated centre in the 18th C was Pontypool. Around 1763 a rival factory was started at nearby Usk. Less costly work was produced in Birmingham, Wolverhampton, London and elsewhere.

Early japanned wares were of thinly rolled sheets of iron, but tinplate was later substituted and was the basis for "Japan" until papier mâché took over in the mid-19th C. Trays and salvers, urns for carrying hot chestnuts (2), knife boxes, tureens, candlesticks, clock-face plates, tea urns, teapots (6), hot-water kettles, tea caddies, coffee pots, chafing dishes and snuffboxes were some of the items made in japanned ware. At Usk, cheese cradles were produced. A popular form of decoration in imitation of tortoiseshell was widely used for trays.

French japanned ware (*tôle peinte*) is of unrivalled quality, the principal Parisian centre of production being "Au Petit Dunquerque" in the Faubourg St Honoré. (7) The preference was for monochrome decoration over light grounds. In north Germany tôle was manufactured in Brunswick *c*.1800.

American tinware. Tinware was imported into America from England by 1737. William and Edward Pattison in Berlin, Connecticut, began to produce plain wares, decorated by others, *c*.1740. Thereafter Connecticut became the centre of the industry.

The greatest amount of tinware was made after the Civil War. Typical products included tin kitchens (roasting ovens), biscuit ovens, skewers, kettles, plate-warmers, grid-irons, poppers (tin boxes with long handles for popping corn over the hearth) and coffee-bean roasters. Also in demand by collectors are food-warmers, lanterns, pipe racks, graters and recherché pieces of kitchen equipment such as meat-loaf pressers and sausage guns. Cream-whippers, butter churns, pie-crimpers, maple-syrup skimmers and pudding moulds were all made of tin. So were scales, tinder boxes, hatchels (used in spinning), chandeliers (11) and candle moulds. (8)

In addition to stencilled pieces, some wares were painted by Oliver Buckley, who favoured orange circles surrounded by smaller spots. More realistic was the decoration of Zachariah Stevens of Maine who made painted tinware from 1798 until 1842. Anne Butler in Greenville, New York, decorated in a tight, busy style, using dots to fill in spaces; her initials sometimes appear, framed in heart-shaped borders. Tinware painted in Pennsylvania tended to be red, while black was the usual colour in New England. (1, 9) Punched tinwares date mainly from the period 1830–60.

COPPER

Many people prefer the glowing reddish colour of copper to the more showy ersatz gold of brass.

In the 16th and early 17th C copper was often used for caskets, clock cases and scientific instruments, though usually in combination with brass or bronze. Craftsmen in Italy used the metal for ewers, basins and other vessels, either engraved or embossed. In the Netherlands in the 18th C copper coffee pots and teapots were made with brass-gilt handles and knobs. Other specialities of coppersmiths were "Herrengrund cups" (decorated drinking cups originating in Hungary) and "Iserlohn boxes" (small fancy-lidded boxes given as gifts, produced at Iserlohn, Westphalia, and in large numbers in the Netherlands).

Cornwall was the great copper-mining county of England. There was a burst of activity after *c*.1700, led by John Coster, son of a Gloucestershire ironsmith. Other mines were opened in Anglesey (1768) and at Ecton in Staffordshire. Steam power was introduced. But the Anglesey mines were exhausted by the end of the 1700s and the Cornish mines a century later, after which imported copper was used. Copper was being mined in Connecticut from *c*.1700.

Antique domestic copper wares are quite plentiful from the mid-

Copper, 18th and 19th C

1 "Ass's ear" type of ale
warmer, lgth 26cm ⓒ A
2 Boot-shaped ale warmer, lgth
44cm ꜰꜱ B
3 Ale measure, lgth 25cm
ⓒ ♀ B
4 Kettle, tinned inside, c.1800–20
ⓒ B
5 Wine cistern, 18th c, lgth
62.4cm ⓑ D

6 Four-gallon haystack jug,
c.1790–1810, ht 50cm ꜰꜱ C
7 Loving cup, early 18th c, ht
20.5cm ꜰꜱ A

18th C onwards. Among the most common articles are ale and
spirit measures in sets ranging from a half-gallon to a "drop", and
ale warmers in the "ass's ear" or "boot" shape. (1, 2, 3) Copper was
a favourite material for coal scuttles, kettles and saucepans. (4)
Vessels were usually lined with tin to prevent poisoning (though
some tin alloys contained much lead, another health hazard).

BRASSWARE

English brass. It may surprise those familiar with English
medieval church brasses that no brass was made in England until
the late 16th C: it was imported from Flanders and engraved by
English artists.

Brass is an alloy of copper and zinc. In the 1560s copper mines
were opened at Keswick in the Lake District, with German
expertise and financial help, and zinc mines in Somerset. Manufacture took place at Tintern and Rotherhithe. James I also
encouraged brass production, but output was virtually halted by
the Civil War. In 1689 the Mines Royal Act freed all mines from the
yoke of royal ownership. This was the signal for real investment in
copper mining and brass making by private enterprise. Huguenots
who had fled from France in 1685 lent their skills.

The best period of English brass is from the late 17th C until the
early 19th C. In 1704 Abraham Darby and his partners opened a big
brassworks at Bristol, using copper from Cornwall and calamine
(zinc ore) from Somerset. Bristol was a good place to manufacture
the alloy, as brass wool-cards were needed in nearby Gloucester.

In 1781 the great Birmingham Brass Co. was founded. Steam
engines powered rolling mills and stamping machines. Mass
production was on the way, and with it the deterioration of brass
goods. Brass was imitative, a substitute. In colour it imitated gold;
in shape it often mimicked silver or pewter. One finds few designs
used for brass alone.

Candlesticks head the list of collectable brass. (9, 10) Other
objects frequently made were wax and taper jacks; snuffers and

douters (scissors-like instruments for putting out candle flames) (3); hall lanterns; chandeliers; fire tools; a wealth of kitchen utensils including bowls, pestles and mortars, and strainers; locks and keys; irons; warmers and servers; rococo tea kettles over burners; a few chamber pots (possibly for travellers); warming pans (7); much-faked horse brasses (1); and coffin handles.

Continental brass. The town of Dinant in Belgium was an important centre of brassware manufacture from the 10th C. Pieces from the area are known either as "Mosan brass" (after the River Meuse) or "Dinanderie".

American brass. The most commonly found article made in America from sheet brass was the spun-brass kettle, produced in large quantities in Connecticut from the mid-19th C. Brass buttons were made in the 18th C by Caspar Wistar in Philadelphia and by his son Richard. Early cast-brass andirons (firedogs) are fairly rare. Other items include candlesticks, furniture mounts, door knockers and mathematical and surveying instruments. (8)

Brass, 18th and 19th C

1 English horse brass ⊗ ⚲ *A*
2 Dutch tobacco box engraved with a view of Amsterdam, 18th c, lgth 15.5 cm ⅤⓇ *C*
3 Douter with stand, *c.*1720, lgth 15.9 cm ⅤⓇ *C*
4 American horse brass, 19th c ⊗ ⚲ *A*
5 Victorian trivet (for standing a kettle close to the fire) ⅎ⊑ ⚲ *A*

6 Kettle and stand, *c.*1810, ht 43.3 cm ⊗ *C*
7 English warming pan with pierced top and walnut handle, mid-18th c ⊗ *C*

Brass candlesticks. Brass candlesticks were made in many areas of Europe from medieval times, but few before the mid-17th C fall into the hands of collectors. The pricket candelstick, with a spike for fixing the candle, was ousted by the socket candelstick *c.*1650, although the socket type was known as early as 1500.

The earliest pieces, in solid brass, have a wide grease pan half-way up, and a flat, spool- or trumpet-shaped base. One type had a slot in the side of the socket, for removing stubs more easily. The Huguenots in the late 17th C introduced a type made of two hollow-cast halves brazed together, with a visible join. The grease pan disappeared, replaced by an enlarged rim to the socket; this became a detachable sconce by the 1720s. Plain octagonal bases gave way to more elaborate ones, and stems acquired a greater number of knops.

A single seam is evidence of manufacture from sheet brass—a rare type, characteristically found with a rod in the stem to adjust the candle's height. Sticks became taller *c.*1770, and seams disappeared, thanks to a new casting technique. Neo-classical stems are often slender, fluted and gadrooned. Genuinely antique candlesticks have a patina on the underside, which forgers can never simulate.

Candlesticks, 17th–19th C

8 American chamber stick, c.1800 Ⓑ ♀ B
9 Sheet-brass candlestick in three sections, Dutch or English, c.1690, ht 44.5cm Ⓥᴿ E (pair)

10 English "trumpet" candlestick, c.1640–50, ht 17.8cm Ⓥᴿ E (pair)
11 French gilded brass candlestick, c.1720–30, ht 25.4cm Ⓑ C (pair)
12 German pricket candlestick, 17th–18th c, ht 50cm Ⓥᴿ ♀ E (pair)
13 English ormolu wall light,

c.1755–60, ht 33cm Ⓑ ♀ G (pair)
14 Italian baroque altar candlestick, in the alloy paktong, c.1680, ht 87cm Ⓑ ♀ F (pair)

PEWTER

Pewter is a grey alloy, usually containing mostly tin, with some copper or lead, and sometimes antimony. Unlike silver or copper, pewter is not easily shaped by hammering: articles made of it were generally cast. Decoration could be either cast with the object in relief, or engraved. One form of engraving was "wrigglework", created by rocking a pointed tool against the metal to form a series of dots. (6) Particularly in north Germany, brass mounts or brass inlays were sometimes applied on high-quality pieces. Marks, an invaluable aid to identification, took the form of craftsmen's "touches", which were registered at the guildhall. On the Continent it was usual for the touch to be accompanied by a town mark. The earliest surviving domestic pewter objects are jugs for wine or beer. Styles sometimes followed those of silverware, especially in France, but some very individual forms were also evolved.
British pewter. Although pewter has existed in Britain since Roman times, it was not until 1349 that it was recognized and controlled by a London guild. In 1503 marking of wares was made compulsory. The Great Fire of 1666 destroyed Pewterers' Hall and the records housed there, but the system was revived in 1668 and continued until the early 19th C. The Scottish Hammermen's Guild

and other guilds such as York also kept touch plates. The dates which appear in many touches are the years of registration, not of manufacture. From *c.*1550 a rose and crown mark was applied to the finest-quality wares. From 1671 this device was applied to export pewter, and from 1690 it was also added to items for native use.

At first pewter was a material for the nobility. By the end of the 15th C it had generally replaced wood on the tables of ordinary folk, and gradually it began to be used in taverns. Crockery had outpaced it by the 17th C, but good pewter continued to be made until the 19th C.

British and American pewter, 17th–19th C

1 English pear-shaped tankard, late 18th c, ht 19cm 🅵🅲 *C*

2 Charles I or Cromwellian flagon, ht 26.6cm 🅱 *F*

3 Scottish tappit hen, 18th c 🅵🅲 ⚲ *D*

4 American tankard, by Frederick Bassett, New York, 18th c 🅱 ⚲ *F* (NY value)

5 American coffee pot of Britannia metal, Cincinnati, *c.*1850 🅵🅲 *C* (NY value)

6 English "wrigglework" marriage plate, Bristol, *c.*1730, diam. 21cm V̆R̆ ⚲ *E*

7 American hot-water plate, by H. Will, New York, 18th c 🅱 *F* (NY value)

8 American porringer, by Gersham Jones, Rhode Island, late 1700s 🅱 *E* (NY value)

9 English alms dish, *c.*1730, ht 34.3cm V̆R̆ *F* (pair)

"Sadware" is the pewterers' term for plates (up to 12 inches in diameter), dishes (12–18 inches) and chargers (over 18 inches). "Hollow ware" covers flagons, tankards, measures, pots, mugs, beakers, porringers (shallow vessels with a flat, horizontal handle), "bleeding bowls" (porringers marked with liquid capacities), barbers' bowls (shaped to fit round the shaver's neck), loving cups (two-handled) and quaiches (Scottish porringers with two lugs). (1, 2, 3)

Baluster jugs were made from the 16th C right through to the early 19th. The most valuable English pieces, though, are 36-inch dishes and flat-lidded Stuart tankards of the 17th C. Open-top tankards, used in ale houses long after pewter had become obsolete in the home, are worth very little in comparison. Spoons, with finials that followed silver patterns (apostle, seal-top, etc.) are a good subject for the new collector.

Continental pewter. Early French wine jugs belong to a type known as the *pichet*. (10) The most valuable early pewterwares are the large Silesian flagons of the 15th-16th C. Flagons are especially associated with guild banquets. Polygonal, conical and cylindrical examples were peculiar to Germanic regions.

Continental pewter, 16th–19th C

10 French *pichet*, Arras, 18th c,
ht 28.5cm ♀ *E*
11 German "wrythen" coffee pot
with wooden handle,
Nuremberg, *c.*1770 *C*
12 German apostle spoon, 16th c
VᴿR *D*
13 German *chinoiserie* tea caddy,
Augsburg, 1750–67, ht 16.5cm
VᴿR ♀
14 German hot-water bottle,

1749, diam. 23cm FG *B*
15 Flemish or Dutch pot belly
measure, *c.* 1760 ♀ ⊡ *C*
16 German relief-pewter dish,
by Paulus Öham the Younger,
Nuremberg, late 17th c ♀ *E*
17 German covered goblet,
*c.*1890, ht 45cm *C*

Display pewter is best represented by the relief-decorated work of François Briot from Lorraine. His pieces inspired some superb pewter bowls made in Nuremberg by Albrecht Preissensin, Nikolaus Horchhaimer and others. (16) In the first 40 years of the 18th C relief pewter attained a new-found popularity at Strasbourg, Lyons, Bordeaux and Rouen.

In France and Germany (whose main centre of production was now Augsburg) the luxurious table silver of the rococo was faithfully copied by pewterers. (17) Neo-classicism also made an impact.

American pewter. The earliest mention of a pewterer in America is in connection with a shop in Salem, Massachusetts, which opened in 1635. But records have revealed no more than ten in the trade by the end of the century, and very few surviving pieces date back further than 1725. One reason for the low output was lack of tin ore in the Colonies. Limitations in moulds and materials (often old imports that had to be reworked) led to a pleasing simplicity of style. A particularly popular type of ware, which survived into the 19th C, was the porringer, either with pierced or lug handles. (8)

Britannia metal. Britannia metal is a compound of tin, antimony and copper invented in the late 18th C. It could be machine worked, was harder than pewter and had a bluish sheen. By the mid-19th C over 100 factories in the Sheffield area of England were producing wares of this metal, mainly teapots. James Dixon & Sons made the finest pieces.

IRON

The four main methods of working iron are forging (shaping the metal while hot); benchwork or locksmithery (working the cold metal with file, chisel or drill); casting, in a mould; and sheet work, in which the iron is rolled out and cut like pastry, and sometimes given repoussé decoration by hammering from underneath. The term "wrought iron" is used to describe a ductile, easily forged type containing almost no carbon but quite a lot of slag, giving it a grainy appearance.

Among the iron antiques often sought today are andirons (or firedogs), fire irons (tongs, brushes, fireforks, pokers, shovels) and firebacks. When the fireplace was in the centre of the room the andiron was simply utilitarian; but decoration was added when the hearth was moved to the wall. Other collectable items include trivets, spits, tools and lighting devices. To see whether a firedog or fireback is a genuine antique examine the soot deposit, which should be hard-caked and difficult to remove.

Wrought ironwork commonly had a profusion of scrolls and curlicues, but in America in the early 18th C a more severe style developed. Even the pieces made by the Pennsylvanian German smiths were comparatively restrained.

In France in the 18th C, benchwork was predominant. Many fine pieces were recycled in the Revolution. In Italy forged work was more common at this period. Fine sanctuary lamps were made in Spain and Portugal.

In 18th-C Germany iron snuff boxes, seals and *bonbonnières* were among the small items made by benchwork. Some were damascened (i.e. the surface was encrusted with gold or silver, a process more especially associated with Milanese ironwork). German 19th-C cast iron was of good quality.

BRONZE

Bronze is an alloy of copper and tin. It scores over other copper alloys in being more readily melted and more easily cast in moulds, without sacrificing hardness. An important variant, introduced in the late 17th C in France, was ormolu, or gilt bronze, which was extensively used for furniture mounts, chandeliers, wall lights and for mounting porcelain. In England the Birmingham company of Boulton & Fothergill made ormolu vases, candlesticks and perfume-burners in the 1760s and 70s. (See p 140, no. 13)

European bronzes, 16th–18th C

1 French andiron, late 18th c, ht 40cm **◻** *F* (pair)
2 Florentine bull, probably by Susini, 16th c, ht 22.5cm **◻** ९ *G*
3 South German table fountain, 1550–60, ht 16cm **◻** ९ *I*
4 "Lo Spinario", on marble base, by Severo da Ravenna, Padua, 17th c, ht 16cm v̊ ९ *H*

European bronzes. Sculpture in bronze was a major art of the Renaissance. Donatello, the Italian sculptor, was probably responsible for reviving the fashion for small statuettes of gods with which humanists now decorated their rooms. Under his influence a school of bronze-casters grew up in the mid-15th C in Padua, where Riccio and his followers realistically depicted crabs, snakes and other aspects of nature, as well as making hand-bells, caskets, statuettes, etc. The style was copied in the smaller courts of

Italy. Common themes for statuettes were the "Youth Removing a Thorn from his Foot" ("Lo Spinario") and "Hercules Resting on his Club". (4)

Sansovino settled in Rome in 1527 and formed an important mannerist school of sculpture there. Apart from Benvenuto Cellini, the genius of the medium, other important bronze-workers include Giovanni Bologna (or Giambologna; 1524–1608) and his pupil Antonio Susini. (2) The Renaissance statuette declined in favour at the end of the 16th C with the rise of the baroque, which demanded grandiosity. However, large sculptures were often reproduced in miniature.

Two distinct traditions developed in baroque sculpture: extremist, deriving from Italy and Bernini, and more restrained, deriving from Brussels, Antwerp and François Duquesnoy. The latter designed some delightful small bronzes, and there were to be countless imitations of his angelic cherubs.

The 18th-C rococo revived a taste for intimacy of scale. With the coming of the French Revolution sculptors like Claude Michel (known as Clodion) promptly redirected their oeuvre towards neo-classicism in line with the left-wing severity of the times. (1)

Animalier sculptures

5 Emu by Rembrandt Bugatti, ht 26cm Ⓑ *H*
6 Seated hound, by Antoine-Louis Barye, ht 26.7cm Ⓑ *F*
7 Bull, signed by Rosa

Bonheur, 1843, ht 31.8cm Ⅶ *F*
8 Arabian dromedary, stamped by Emmanuel Frémiet, 1847, ht 27.9cm Ⅶ *F*

Animaliers. Like many terms coined by art historians, *animalier* was first used derogatively. It was applied to the French sculptor Antoine-Louis Barye in the 1830s by a critic who argued that he was good for nothing but turning out trivial models of beasts—a crime in those neo-classical times. But the *animalier* sculptors were in fact making a refreshing return to nature.

Barye (1796–1875) was the most accomplished among the early exponents. His best work dates from 1837 to 1848. He was ruined by the 1848 Revolution and lost his bronzes and equipment to a bronze-founder named Martin, who made inferior casts signed with Barye's name. Eventually he was able to buy them back. His sculptures are signed, in block letters. (6)

Emmanuel Frémiet (1824–1910) is best known for sculptures of orang-outangs strangling men, and gorillas making off with negresses. But he also made some striking bronzes. Rosa Bonheur (1822–79) made marvellous horses. But the greatest of all was Rembrandt Bugatti (1885–1916), who departed from realism to bring out the abstract qualities of beasts. (5, 7, 8)

Three early American masters were represented at the Columbian Exposition of 1893: Edward Kemeys, whose favourite subject was wildcats; Edward D. Potter; and Phimister Proctor, who portrayed bison, bears, wolves and buffalo. Later American artists of note include: Solon Hannibal Borglum, a horse sculptor; and Frederick Remington, Charles Marion Russell and Robert Farrington Elwell, all known for Wild West pieces.

Chinese bronzes. The great period of Chinese bronzes is that of the Shang (*c.*1600–1027 BC) and Zhou (*c.*1027–256 BC) dynasties. In subsequent periods quality declined and earlier models were followed.

When bronze founding first took place in China, it was applied at once to the making of ritual vessels, used for offering food and wine to ancestral spirits. All surviving examples have been recovered from tombs. In the Zhou period such vessels were awarded by kings or by feudal lords to their subjects.

An important type of ritual food vessel was the three-legged *ding*, the earliest type taking the form of a loop-handled bowl with a rounded bottom on pointed, slightly splayed legs. Straight column legs were usual in the later Shang period. (14) From *c.*900 BC hoofed legs were introduced. Lids were always provided after the 9th c BC.

The *li* was a *ding* with hollow legs. For holding food after cooking, a notable vessel was the *gui* (round bowl on ring foot, often with zoomorphic handles). (10)

Ritual drinking vessels included the strange-looking *jue*, a one-handled, spouted tripod cup with two short columns rising from it. (9) Related to this is the *jia*, with columns but no spout. Other drinking wares are the *gu* (wine goblet with trumpet-shaped bowl) (12), *yu* (wine bucket), *zun* (often like a squat *ku*) and *hu* (tall baluster vase). (13)

Casting was by the difficult *cire perdue* (literally, "lost wax") method, which required a clay model to be made for each bronze to be cast. A typical Shang and Zhou motif was the formalized monster mask known as *taotie*. (10)

In Han times the emphasis shifted to utilitarian wares. Sculpture in bronze became more frequent after the introduction of Buddhism in AD 67.

Through long burial in earth, ancient Chinese bronzes have acquired a patina, ranging from the dull green of old jade to spectacular reds and greens. Patina has been vigorously faked.

Chinese bronzes

9 *Jue*, 12th–11th c BC, ht 19.7cm
FC ♀ H
10 *Gui*, with simple *taotie* decoration, Western Zhou dynasty, width 27cm ❽ ♀ I
11 Rhinoceros *zun*, late 11th c BC, ht 17.6cm VR I
12 *Gu* in the Shang style, 12th–11th c BC, ht 31.1cm ❽ ♀ I
13 *Hu*, late 9th or 8th c BC, ht

51cm VR I
14 *Ding* in the later Shang style, 11th c BC, ht 25cm ❽ ♀ I
15 Bronze mirror, Han dynasty, diam. 11cm FC F
16 Archaistic baluster vase, Ming–early Qing dynasty, diam. 21.5cm ❽ E

CARPETS & RUGS

Carpets and rugs present notorious difficulties to the collector. There is probably no field in which experts disagree more about attributions, or where there are subtler distinctions between the products of nearby regions.

The pieces most available to collectors today are Persian and Caucasian. Because most floor coverings have had a relatively short lifespan, the notion of antique may be revised to cover items made before, say, 1920.

Techniques

In the making of "knotted" carpets or rugs, rows of knots are tied to a series of "warp" threads on a loom. After completion of one or more rows, one, two or three "weft" threads are woven into the warps, and the work is pushed tightly down with a comb. This process is repeated until the desired length is reached. In general, the finer the quality, the denser the spread of knots.

The two main knots in oriental weaving are the Turkish or Ghiordes and the Persian or Senneh. In the former (used in Turkey, the Caucasus and some parts of Iran) the yarn is wrapped around two adjacent warps to form a collar. The Persian knot (found in Iran, Turkestan, Egypt, India, China and in some court rugs of Turkey) is more like a twist: the yarn encircles one warp thread and then passes behind the adjacent thread. (See p 150.)

The Spanish knot differs from these two in that it is tied to a single warp thread: knots are tied to alternate threads in each row, giving a serrated effect to the lines of the pattern.

Kelims—used in the East as curtains and sofa or divan rugs—are woven without a pile ("flat-woven"), like tapestry carpets. Most kelims are reversible, but some types, including the Soumak, have the loose ends showing at the back.

Knotted carpets should be distinguished from those made in the West with a pile formed as part of the weave. These include moquettes (e.g. "Wiltons" and "Brussels carpets"), which are woven in the same way as velvet. An earlier type of European carpet was made by needlework on a canvas ground.

Names and designs

Nomad rugs are often known by the name of their tribal group, but other oriental pieces are named according to their place of origin or their marketing centre. Spellings are not standardized.

Oriental designs are generally based on a central field framed by borders. The field may have a central pattern (a floral or geometrical "medallion", alone, or repeated, or with subsidiary elements in the corners of the field) or it may be fragmented into various main patterns, frequently joined by tendrils. Typical motifs include the palmette (like a cross-section of a flower), the rosette (a flower seen from above), the *boteh* (stylized palm leaf leaning sideways), the cloudbank and the *gul* (an octagon, common in Turkoman and Afghan work). (See p 150.) Natural forms are often represented with stylized angularity. Kufic inscriptions sometimes occur in the borders, and it is not unusual to find a date.

Moslem prayer rugs have a pointed arch (*mihrab*) at one or both ends of the field, and sometimes a hanging lamp and flanking pillars. The *hatchli* is a carpet design with a large cross quartering the field.

Materials of knotted carpets

Dyed wool is normal in the East for the pile, though silk was often employed for luxury work. In Turkish-type rugs, wool was generally used for both warp and weft, but in the weft it was sometimes replaced by cotton, especially in the Caucasus. In Turkey and related areas the weft was often dyed, usually red. Silk was at first a common material for warp and weft in Persia and India, though cotton was later substituted.

Antiquity and condition

Only experts are properly equipped to judge the age of a carpet or rug. Genuinely old pieces in good condition are extremely rare, and a good but damaged one can often be worth considerably more than an almost perfect late example. The most desirable and expensive rugs are generally those which were made before aniline dyes were introduced as a replacement for vegetable dyes (*c.*1870).

The ideal for a comparatively recent rug is to have a pile of regular height, an undamaged base weave and intact borders. Excessive fading should be avoided, and the colours should be clear. Cuts and tears are not usually such a serious weakness as a worn pile, as they can be mended. Some stains (e.g. dog's urine) cannot be removed. Beginners may be put off by variations in a field colour or by an irregular shape, but in rugs by nomads these are quite usual.

Forgeries

Dangerous copies of Eastern carpets have been made (e.g. in Rumania by Tuduc), and modern pieces woven in the East are often "antiqued" by subjecting them to artificial wear and to a process known as "old-washing".

IRAN

The golden age. The earliest Persian pile carpets seem to have followed Mongolian traditions. The conquest of Persia by the Seljuks (early 11th C) brought in stylized, geometric, floral patterns, which flourished until the late 15th C, when rugs veered towards floral asymmetry under the impact of the Mongol invasions.

The Safavids came to power in 1502, a date that marks the beginnings of the great age of Persian carpet-making. One of the new designs of the period was the vase type—a carpet with a one-directional pattern containing vases in a floral lattice. A group of densely floral designs is attributed to Herat. (7) A main theme of Safavid work was the garden: trees, flowers, water and animals conjured up the notion of a bountiful landscape. Some carpets showed layouts of gardens divided by canals. Others had tree designs with flowering branches. Of the silk "Polonaise" carpets made in the reign of Shah Abbas I (1587–1629) about 300 examples survive. (8) Another notable group is the "Portuguese" pieces,

Persian carpets and rugs

1 Heriz tree-of-life silk carpet, c.1840 ⊗ I
2 Senneh rug from Kurdistan, with *boteh* motifs ⊗ H
3 Kerman portrait mat, 79 × 61cm ⊗ F

4 Senneh kelim, c.1920, 198 × 132cm ⊗ E
5 Isfahan rug, inspired by Safavid patterns ⊡ F
6 Tabriz carpet, c.1930, 386 × 290cm ⊡ F
7 Herat rug, late 16th-early 17th

c 269 × 145cm V⊗ I
8 Shah Abbas "Polonaise" carpet, 206 × 145cm V⊗ I
9 Hamadan rug ⊡ E

with a large and elaborate central medallion.

Later weaving. There are two main types of 19th- and 20th-C Persian carpet: tribal village pieces and town-made factory pieces. The main weaving area in the north-west was around Tabriz. Here, Kurdish tribes continued to follow Safavid styles, but a big export industry evolved from the late 19th C, also dependent on ancient traditions. During the last half-century Tabriz has produced busy floral and animal pieces, and copies of vase carpets. (6) Heriz, in the same region, is famous for superb craftsmanship in silk. (1) To the south of the Tabriz area, Hamadan, in Kurdistan, is the centre of a major group of weaving villages. Hamadan products are generally hard-wearing, and often have a medallion and escutcheon pattern, or several such motifs linked by "poles". (9) Few colours are used on them, the main one being camel. Senneh and Bijar are associated with high-quality Kurdish work. (2, 4)

Central Iran has some of the most famous weaving areas. Outside Isfahan the Bakhtian group of carpets was made by semi-nomads, with medallions or all-over repeats. Kashan, a great Safavid centre, enjoyed a revival in the early 20th C, when very large, fine-quality floral carpets were woven. From the plains of Fereghan came sought-after carpets with apple green in the borders. Kerman's weavers imitated Safavid patterns, and in the late 19th C produced portrait rugs of characters from history. (3)

THE CAUCASUS

Caucasian rugs were woven in the mountainous area between the Black Sea and the Caspian. All pile rugs from the area have the Ghiordes knot, usually on a foundation of wool. Designs are quite severely geometric, with a preponderance of stars and squares.

The earliest carpets from the Caucasus (perhaps late 16th C) are the dragon rugs, based on Persian vase rugs. The original pattern, based on a lozenge diaper of serrated leaves, became coarser and more stylized as the centuries progressed. Floral rugs were also made in the earliest period. Some are adapted from Persian vase designs, while others make use of rows of shield-like palmettes.

Of the many rugs woven in the Caucasus in the 19th and 20th C, those with a long, heavy pile and "hot" colours come mostly from the mountain areas (Kazak, Gendje, Lesghi and Karabagh). Medium piles were produced in Talish, Lenkoran and Daghestan. And a fine low pile is a feature of Shirvan, Kuba and Baku rugs.

Kazak is one of a great number of important weaving areas. It favoured stylized floral motifs, with large expanses of plain colour—a typically Caucasian feature. A common arrangement is one or two octagonal medallions (incorporating stars or hooks), with a smaller geometric motif at each end of the field. Many rugs described as "Kazak" in the West were in fact woven elsewhere. The best-known pieces from the region of Karabagh are the Chelaberds, sometimes known as "eagle Kazaks". They have one or more large white cruciform medallions, which resemble the double-headed eagle of Russia. (6) One of the favourite designs of the Gendje area, also found elsewhere in the Caucasus, was a background embellished with diagonals of different colours, sometimes containing floral shapes.

Caucasian carpets and rugs

1 **South Caucasian kelim**, c.1900, 325 × 208cm ℻ ℺ E

2 **Karatchoph Kazak rug** ℻ G

3 **Shirvan rug**, c.1880, 190 × 130cm ℻ F

4 **Daghestan prayer rug**, 1826, 152.5 × 106.5cm ℻ G

5 **Perepedil rug** with ram's horn motif on a blue ground, 19th c ℻ ℺ F

6 **Chelaberd Kazak rug** with red field, c.1860 ℻ ℺ H

7 **Shirvan *sileh* carpet** (i.e. with S-shaped motifs) ℻ ℺ F

149

Shirvan rugs, woven on the shores of the Caspian, are a common Caucasian product. A great range of designs was employed, including naturalistic flowers in an overall lattice, and rows of shield-like palmettes. Large geometric medallion rugs were made in great numbers. The best Shirvans date from the period 1900–20 or earlier. (3, 7) Baku rugs, made further south along the coast, use a more subdued palette than elsewhere in the Caucasus. The field is dark blue, and has on it rows of rectilinear pear motifs, which look rather like fir cones.

The most prolific centre of Caucasian weaving is Kuba. The great variety of patterns and colours deployed in this region precludes generalization. Most Kuba rugs of the 19th C, however, are densely packed with floral motifs. Pieces from Perepedil often bear rows of "ram's horn" motifs, like handlebars. (5)

Soumaks are flat-woven, instead of having a knotted pile. Small animals often appear among their geometrical medallions.

Some French-influenced rugs made in the Caucasus for Russian clients in the 19th C had floral medallions incorporating bouquets of roses, in a very un-oriental style. Caucasian prayer rugs sometimes have humans and animals in the design. The *mihrab* arch, typically six-sided, often looks like an afterthought. (4)

Knots and motifs in oriental weaving

a Turkish or Ghiordes knot
b Persian or Senneh knot
c Kelim weaving
d Herati design
e Turkoman *gul*
f Cloudband
g Boteh

TURKEY

The earliest carpets of the Ottoman Empire, dating from *c.*1400, include the famous dragon-and-phoenix carpet in the Berlin Museum. Animal rugs were popular in the early period, but in the later 15th C geometric pieces became increasingly common. Those incorporating octagon motifs are known as "Holbein" carpets. Related to them is the so-called "Lotto" group, with alternating rows of yellow octagons and crosses of formalized foliage on a red ground.

Through conquest, the Ottomans absorbed Persian influences. Ushak in west Turkey produced fine work in the 16th and 17th C, when it was a centre of Ottoman court weaving. The main designs of Ushak were the double- or single-ended *mihrab* prayer rugs, star rugs, red and blue medallion rugs, and pieces with either the "bird" pattern (actually showing stylized leaves) or the "balls and lines" ("Arms of Tamerlane") pattern.

By the 18th and 19th C prayer rugs were being made largely in villages, most notably in the areas around Ghiordes, Ladik and Bergama. There are two types of Ghiordes rug, both characterized

Turkish carpets and rugs

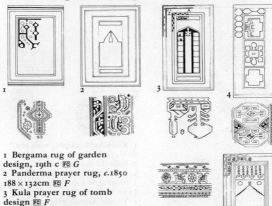

1 Bergama rug of garden
design, 19th c FC *G*
2 Panderma prayer rug, *c.*1850
188 × 132cm FC *F*
3 Kula prayer rug of tomb
design FC *F*
4 Yuruk rug, with red field,
*c.*1900, 264 × 114cm FC *F*
5 Ladik prayer rug, with red
mihrab, 18th c FC *G*

by baby carnations in the design. One has a red horseshoe-topped
mihrab containing a hanging lamp and formalized columns. The
other type has a squarish *mihrab* with an inverted V-shaped arch.
The border is very wide and has a delicate, rather feminine feeling.
Weaving in Ghiordes virtually came to an end in the 1920s, but
Ghiordes designs have been widely copied since at Panderma. (2)

Ladik is associated with two types of prayer rug, with tulip motifs
top and bottom. The first has a triple-arched niche, with six
columns in the *mihrab*, plus one at each side. More recent in origin
is the pattern with only two columns, or none at all, and a *mihrab*
that is mostly only one third of the length of the rug. (5)

Mejedieh (or Mejid) rugs have a distinctive style but not a
particular place of origin: they were woven in many areas of
Turkey in the 19th C. Pastel shades are characteristic, and the floral
decoration has a European origin. (Sultan Adb ul-Mejid I, who
ruled from 1839 to 1861, was a Europhile.)

Yuruk ("mountain nomad") rugs were woven mostly in eastern
Anatolia. They have a shaggy pile and bold geometric designs.
Late examples are often distorted in shape. (4)

In the 19th and 20th C magnificent silk carpets were made in
Turkey. The main source of patterns was Persian Safavid work of
the 16th C. The principal looms were at Hereke (from 1844) and
Koum Kapou.

CENTRAL ASIA

Turkoman rugs. Weavings by the warlike Turkoman tribes were
made mainly in the modern Soviet states of Turkmenistan,
Karakalpatstan and Uzbekistan. No completely authenticated
examples can be dated before the 19th C. The main colour schemes
are red, red-brown and red-blue, and the principal motif is the
octagon, or *gul*—a tribal symbol, probably serving a function
similar to that of clan tartans in Scotland. One of the most
commonly encountered Turkoman tribes is the Tekke. Other
important weavers include the Yomut, the Salor and the Saryk. The
term "Bokhara" is often used to cover all types. As well as

Central Asian carpets and rugs

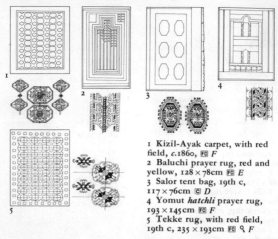

1 **Kizil-Ayak carpet, with red field**, *c.*1860, FC *F*
2 **Baluchi prayer rug, red and yellow**, 128 × 78cm FC *E*
3 **Salor tent bag, 19th c**, 117 × 76cm C *D*
4 **Yomut *hatchli* prayer rug**, 193 × 145cm FC *F*
5 **Tekke rug, with red field**, 19th c, 235 × 193cm FC ♀ *F*

carpets, collectors value other woven items such as tent hangings and saddle covers. (3)

The main *gul* of the Tekke was an ovalized stepped octagon quartered by four blue lines which join up the emblems on both the vertical and horizontal axes. (5) Tekke carpets have wide red kelim sections at the ends, but these are often missing.

Weavings of the Yomut tribe differ from Tekke work in having a heavier structure, bolder colouring and a design based on a lozenge-shaped division of the field. An attractive type of Turkoman rug was made by the Beshir, who often favoured floral motifs.

Afghan pieces, woven by Turkomans in Afghanistan, are popular in the West owing to their warm red tones, simple patterns (variations of a repetitive octagonal design across the field), deep, resilient pile and moderate price.

Baluchi rugs. Baluchi tribal weaves, once considered to be of poor quality, are now treated more respectfully. Most were made in an area bestriding the Iranian-Afghan border.

Baluchi carpets are generally small. The wool is soft and velvety, and dyed to give deep blues and reds, with some decoration in black, brown and touches of white. No examples date from before the mid-19th C. The "Meshed Baluchis", named after their distribution centre, are of especially fine quality.

Baluchi prayer rugs often have a square-topped *mihrab* occupied by a leafy tree-of-life. Above the niche are two rectangles which sometimes contain stylized hands. (2)

CHINA

The first evidence of rug weaving in China is in the years after the Yuan dynasty (1206–1368). But no Chinese carpets survive from much before the 18th C. The patterns antedate the techniques, and are derived from other media such as porcelain and bronze. Chinese carpet style is quite unlike that of areas further west. Symbolism played an important role, and often operated punningly. Bats and butterflies suggested prosperity, stags official rewards, peonies riches and love—and so on. The swastika is the

Chinese character for 10,000: hence, a continuous border of swastikas meant "ten-thousandfold happiness". Other devices found on carpets include flutes and chessboards (symbols of gentlemanly accomplishment), fans and castanets (associated with Taoism) and pearls and coins (with Buddhist meanings). Blue is the predominant colour and the pile is often very thick. To the 19th C belongs a group of Peking rugs of silk and metal thread, made for the Imperial courts of the Heavenly City. (1)

East Turkestan. The carpets known to Europeans as "Samarkands" were made in east Turkestan. Because they have been comparatively unappreciated, such pieces are inexpensive in comparison with Turkoman rugs. One of the most characteristic designs, in either silk or wool, is the all-over pomegranate pattern with one or more vases, attributed to the areas of both Khotan and Yarkand. (2)

Chinese carpets and rugs

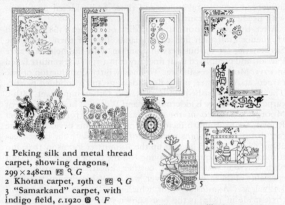

1 Peking silk and metal thread carpet, showing dragons, 299 × 248cm FC ♀ G
2 Khotan carpet, 19th c FC ♀ G
3 "Samarkand" carpet, with indigo field, c.1920 B ♀ F
4 Peking carpet, 19th c, 189 × 125cm FO ♀ E

5 "Samarkand" pictorial rug, c.1920, 239 × 170cm B F

INDIA

The Moghul dynasty of India began in 1526. The painting style used in Moghul miniatures blended Persian sophistication with Indian vitality, a combination found also in carpets. Akbar the Great (1556–1606) established workshops in Agra, Fatephur and

Moghul carpets and rugs

1 Moghul rug, late 17th-early 18th c VR I
2 Moghul prayer rug, early 17th c VR I

Lahore, but the finest work belongs to the reign of Shah Jehan (1628–59). Most Moghul carpets are floral, but there are also animal rugs, some depicting elephants. Designs are naturalistic and asymmetrical. Some of the best 17th-C pieces came from Lahore—the so-called "Indo-Persians".

Agra carpets, which generally came in large sizes, were woven in Agra Fort in the second half of the 19th C. They mainly adapted Persian designs, and were finely knotted and very hard-wearing. Indo-French carpets based on Savonnerie patterns have been produced since the early 18th C, when the French established workshops at Pondicherri.

EUROPE

England. In the 17th C many oriental carpets were imported by the East India Company. Home-produced pieces of this period were of two kinds: those made on looms, with a Turkish knot, and influenced by oriental styles; and those embroidered on frames with needles, on a canvas ground.

After the Revocation of the Edict of Nantes (1685) French Huguenot craftsmen fled to England. Two of them, from the Savonnerie, set up business in London with the help of Pierre Parisot, and completed their first carpet in 1751. The venture failed in 1755. More successful was Thomas Whitty's production of pile carpets at Axminster, using floral designs and a subdued palette. The factory flourished until 1835. (4) Other important 18th-C carpet centres were Kidderminster and Wilton. Thomas Moore, of Moorfield, worked in the neo-classical style for the architect Robert Adam. English factories benefited at this period from the fact that oriental designs were out of keeping with the latest ideas about décor. Wilton bought up the Axminster looms in 1835 and turned from "moquette" weaving (on the principle of velvet, but with coarser materials) to costlier knotted-pile work. The speciality of the factory, however, was mechanically woven carpets known as "Axminsters", of which the "Chenille Axminster" (first made in 1839) is the best-known type.

After the 1851 Exhibition, carpets became more naturalistic. Owen Jones, much influenced by Persian patterns, designed for the firm of Jackson & Graham. William Morris worked for Wilton and for the Heckmonwike Co. in Yorkshire. (1) Some excellent designs were done by C.F.A. Voysey for a number of firms, including Tomkinson & Adam and Heal & Son.

France. France was liberated by the Edict of Nantes (1598) from a period of religious wars, and in the following century grew to be the main carpet-making region of Europe. In 1626 Simon Lourdet was appointed by Louis XIII to start a carpet factory in an old soap works: this humble origin accounts for its name—the "Savonnerie". The establishment was later placed under the charge of Charles Le Brun, who also ran the Gobelins. Its products (made with a Turkish knot) were sent to furnish Versailles, the Tuileries and the Louvre. Motifs included sun or sunflower emblems, classical ornaments, lilies, sphinxes, military trophies and highly naturalistic flowers. Throughout the 18th C the style became more heavily floral, with a strong rococo influence in mid-century. Neo-classical Empire carpets were woven under Napoleon, and Gothicism made an impact c.1850. (7)

In 1743 a carpet factory was established at the old tapestry-making centre of Aubusson, near Limoges. Some pieces made here were of the same type as the Savonnerie, with a thick pile; but most employed a tapestry weave, like Caucasian Soumak carpets. Aubussons were simpler in design, and cheaper, than their

European carpets and rugs

1 "Hammersmith" carpet, by William Morris, 1880 🔲 G
2 Spanish Cuenca carpet, 17th c ⓑ I
3 Tapestry-woven Aubusson carpet, 19th c 🔲 ♀ F
4 English "Axminster" carpet, 19th c ⓑ ♀ H
5 Finnish rug, dated 1799 Ꝟ ♀ G

6 English carpet, 19th c 🔲 ♀ G
7 Empire period Savonnerie carpet ⓑ ♀ I

Savonnerie rivals. Gradually, the style of a central motif surrounded by garlands of flowers evolved. The most important pieces were made in the early 19th c. (3)

Spain. The earliest pile rugs in Europe were made in Spain. The best period (though not for collectors!) is that of the Moorish domination (AD 710–1492), when oriental patterns were followed. (Later, in the Gothic period, these were mixed with European elements to produce what is known as the *mudéjar* style.) The "Admiral" carpets of the early period are so named because they usually bore the arms of admirals. Motifs at this time included pomegranates, stars, sacred trees and calligraphic script.

By the 16th c the weaving industry had moved from Letur to Alcaraz. Both places used the "Spanish knot" (see p 146), but when the craft was established at Cuenca during the 17th and 18th c the Ghiordes knot was substituted. (2) The last phase of important Spanish production began early in the 18th c, at Madrid and Cuenca under royal patronage. A version of the French Savonnerie style was now adopted and was copied throughout the 19th c. Spanish "Aubussons" often used black and a very bright red.

Scandinavia. The *rya* or *ryiji* rugs of Finland are sought-after items. (5) The term generally refers to a non-reversible kelim-type piece, used as a horse cloth, sledge rug, coverlet, wall tapestry or house rug. *Ryas* were an important part of a family heritage, handed down from mother to daughter.

In the 17th and 18th c the *rya* was the most significant of all Finnish folk arts. *Rya* rugs were also made in Sweden and Norway. Foreign motifs such as the Dutch tulip were invading Scandinavian rug design by the mid-18th c.

THE UNITED STATES

Hooked rugs were produced in America as a country craft from an early date. They were made on a frame over which was stretched coarse linen (or, after 1850, burlap). The design was hooked in using strips of cloth, and the loops so formed (which were sometimes cut) formed the pile. The main motifs included diamonds, stars, overlapping circles, mosaics, leaves and flowers. Picture rugs depicted barnyards and snow scenes, and animals were also a popular subject. (1, 4) Thousands of patterns for amateur rug-makers were sold by Edward Frost, whose factory was still in operation by the early years of the 20th C.

The most elaborate early American rugs were embroidered with two-ply yarn, a technique that was common in the late 18th-early 19th C before hooked work superseded it. Braided rugs were made with plaited bands of cloth sewn together. New Hampshire ones were usually shaded with light colours in the middle modulating to darker ones at the edges. Rag rugs, for which waste pieces of fabric were used as the weft, were woven on hand looms using bright materials.

In the mid-18th C Peter Sprague of Philadelphia set up looms to make Axminster-type carpets, which unlike real Axminsters were made up of narrow strips. A developing native industry was boosted in the 1820s by taxation on imported carpets. The Lowell Manufacturing Co. was especially successful, and reached a large market with "ingrain" carpets (pileless loom-woven pieces of double construction). E.B. Bigelow of Boston invented a power

American rugs

Value symbols refer to New York estimates expressed as pounds

1 Hooked rug, with "Lion and Palm" pattern, 1880s FC *D*
2 "Bigelow Axminster" rug, c.1910–14 FC *C*
3 Navajo Germantown rug, c.1890, 206 × 134.5 cm FC *D*
4 Hooked rug, 19th c FC *D*
5 Shaker rug with braided edges, late 19th c FC *D*

loom for this type, and in 1850 opened his own factory. (2) As mechanization grew, Axminster, Wilton and tapestry weaves succeeded the ingrain, which had the disadvantage of a limited pattern range.

Navajo Indian rugs. The Navajos of New Mexico were taught to weave blankets by the Pueblo Indians c.1700. Their "classic" period was 1850–75, but floor coverings were not produced until c.1890, when pieces for the trading posts and the tourist market began to be made. Gaudy colours, a cotton warp and a loosely spun, boldly patterned weft were characteristic features. (3)

TEXTILES

For collectors who are willing to meet the challenge of displaying their pieces, textiles are a rewarding field. Not least of their attractions is the possibility of contributing to an under-researched subject.

Tapestries

In the Middle Ages tapestries were hung to serve an insulating as well as a beautifying and status-asserting purpose. By definition they are woven fabrics in which the design, usually pictorial, is an integral part of the weave. They may be in wool or silk or both, and sometimes have gold and silver threads for extra luxury. In "high-warp" tapestry the warp is stretched vertically on the loom, whereas by the cheaper "low-warp" method it is horizontal and the "cartoon" (preliminary design) is placed against it during weaving. Low-warp tapestries are generally smaller and have sharper definition. Until the 18th C one of the staple products of most north European factories was the *verdure*—a leafy landscape.

Lace

Lace—a decorative openwork fabric, usually of linen—was also made by two distinct methods.
"Needlepoint", made with a single thread, was a development of embroidery. The other, cheaper type, "bobbin lace" (or "pillow lace"), was made by twisting and plaiting multiple threads around pins which staked out the design. Needlepoint is firm and crisp, whereas bobbin lace is softer, and is at its best when hanging in folds.

Embroidery

Stitches like the satin stitch, chain stitch and cross stitch (see p 162) have been used almost universally to decorate woven fabrics such as linen, muslin, silk, cotton, wool and canvas. Most surviving early European embroideries were made for the Church. Since the range of embroideries is vast, collectors will mostly specialize in either a type of article (e.g. framed pictures, samplers, caps) or in a particular technique (e.g. whitework, quilting, blackwork, crewelwork).

Woven silks

Silk weavings include taffeta, satin, sarcenet and velvet—the latter differs from the others in having a pile, created by the introduction of rods during weaving. Damask is a reversible textile with a pattern formed by weaving the threads in opposite directions, giving a contrast in glisten. Lampas is similar to damask, but heavier, and with the reverse side plain. What is loosely termed a "brocade" is often a lampas embellished with gold and silver threads. Brocatelle is a stiff silk and linen damask with a pattern in pronounced relief, often brocaded.

Printed cotton

Painted cottons were first imported in quantity from India in the 17th C. In the early 1700s experiments showed that it was possible to imitate them by block printing, a technique superseded after 1750 by plate printing and later by roller printing. The term "chintz" now generally applies to Western printed and glazed cottons with characteristic floral designs, but was originally used to describe the Indian products that inspired them.

Copies and forgeries

Copies, made with no intention to deceive, are more of a pitfall to the textile enthusiast than forgeries. Old tapestries were widely copied in the 19th C, but close examination will reveal a regularity unattainable by early looms. Genuinely antique and newly woven fragments have sometimes been combined in a convincing "marriage". Collectors of lace should note that no lace was made of cotton before the early 19th C, though copies of earlier work sometimes are.

TAPESTRIES

France. In the mid-15th C Tournai overtook Arras as the great tapestry centre of France. The *mille-fleurs* tapestries, depicting figures against a sprinkling of little flowers, are generally attributed to the Loire region and dated *c.* 1490–1520. In the Renaissance, free interpretation of cartoons gave way to strict copying. François I established a workshop at Fontainebleau *c.*1540.

There was a tremendous weaving revival in Paris in the 17th C. The famous Gobelins workshop, set up in the mid-15th C, was taken over for the Crown in 1662. Baroque classical subjects were in favour, as were religious scenes, Elements and Seasons, and paintings by Old Masters. J.-B. Oudry, director from 1735, insisted on faithful copies of the cartoons. In the 18th C Gobelins work became more lighthearted in the designs of François Boucher and Claude III Audran. Elaborate borders known as *alentours* took up more space than the framed central panel. (3)

The other major workshop, at Beauvais (founded 1664), was a private enterprise. Low-warp weaving was the rule here. The best period began in 1726, when J.-B. Oudry was appointed chief designer. In the 19th C the factory specialized in furniture covers.

Aubusson, near Limoges, produced tapestries as well as carpets. Its best-known products were representations of La Fontaine's fables in the 18th C.

The Low Countries. Flanders is pre-eminent in the history of tapestries, its greatest period being the 14th and 15th C. In the 16th C, Pieter van Aelst's superb pieces based on cartoons by Raphael established Brussels as the principal European tapestry centre, and from now on the designers of cartoons, often great painters, assumed more importance than the weavers. In the early 17th C some Brussels weavers worked to designs by Rubens. Standards were lower in the later 17th C, but some fine genre scenes after paintings by David Teniers III enjoyed a long popularity. (2)

England. The founder of the first important English tapestry workshop was William Sheldon, who set up an establishment at Barcheston (Warwickshire) in the early 1560s. Better known, however, is the Mortlake factory (founded 1619). It was staffed by Flemish weavers, and Flemish or Italian designs were predominant in its *oeuvre*. Quality dropped just before the Civil War, and the establishment closed in 1703. The Mortlake mark was a red cross on a white shield.

"Soho" is a general term for post-Mortlake tapestries, and refers to the area of London where some of the best examples were made. Finest of all were the pieces of John Vanderbank, whose most intriguing work (*c.* 1700) incorporated *chinoiseries*. (4; p 104, no. 4)

Tapestries

1

2

3

4

2 Brussels Teniers tapestry,
mid-18th c, ht 286cm **B** *I*
3 Louis XVI Gobelins tapestry,
with *alentours*, signed "Neilson
Exit", ht 523cm **B** *H*
4 Soho *chinoiserie* tapestry
(detail), by J. Vanderbank, *c.*1710,
lgth 204cm **B** **9** *I*

1 Flemish *verdure* tapestry
(detail), 17th c **B** **9** **▢** *F*

Tapestries were revived in the late 19th C as an aspect of the Arts and Crafts Movement. In 1881 William Morris set up the Merton Abbey workshops to execute his own designs, as well as those of Rossetti, Burne-Jones, Ford Madox Brown and Walter Crane.

Italy. Important tapestry factories flourished at Ferrara from 1536 to 1580, and at Florence from 1546 to 1744. The famous Barberini factory in Rome (founded 1627) began production with a set depicting great European castles. Most striking of all 18th-C pieces in Italy were those made at Turin from the 1730s.

Spain. Under the patronage of Philip V, a tapestry centre was established at Madrid in 1720. Between 1774 and 1791 tapestries were woven after cartoons by Goya.

LACE

The 16th and 17th centuries. Forerunners of true lace include "cutwork", made in Italy from the 15th C: holes were simply cut in linen and then embroidered round. From "reticella", an advanced version of this, evolved the type known as *punto in aria*, the first needlepoint made without a linen or net foundation. (1)

Venice led in needlepoint production in the 16th and 17th C. The best-known type was *gros point*, which had huge scrolls. (3) Gradually the scale of motifs diminished, leading in the later 17th C to *rose point* (also termed *point de neige*). In addition to these raised laces some flat types were made. Copies of Venetian lace were made in England and elsewhere. A French lace centre was installed near Alençon in 1665, and the work made here—*point de France*—was promoted by Louis XIV. Pillow lace, which originated in 16th-C Italy and flourished at Milan and Genoa, was perfected in Flanders.

The earliest lace was principally for the Church, but later examples followed the vagaries of secular fashion.

The 18th century. Lace in the 18th C was of the finest linen thread. In the early part of the century the tone was still baroque, with

Lace

1 *Punto in aria* handkerchief (detail), late 16th c ⑧ *C*
2 Border of Brussels needlepoint appliqué on machine net, *c.*1865–75, width 72cm ⓕⓒ *B*
3 Venetian *gros point* border, 17th c, width 12cm ⓕⓒ *C*
4 Honiton cuff, late 19th c ⓕⓒ *A*

5 Border of cream silk Maltese lace, *c.*1860, width 24cm ⓕⓒ *B*
6 Argentan lace cap, with Alençon border, *c.*1755, 25 × 33cm ⓕⓒ *B*
7 Border of Binche bobbin lace, end of 17th c, width 7cm ⓕⓒ *B*

swaggering flounces. Before long motifs shrank and were set against expanses of mesh. Rococo was happily absorbed, but neo-classicism put the frills in retreat.

"Hollie point" lace, geometric and very flat, was peculiar to England. In France, Alençon and Argentan lace grew out of *point de France*. (6) Argentella was a variant of Alençon with a large dotted mesh. These were all "winter laces". For summer the lighter pillow work of Flanders and France was preferred, e.g. the types known as "Binche", "Valenciennes", "Lille" and "Mechlin". (7) In Flemish lace of the period (called *point d'Angleterre* to facilitate smuggling past the English customs) the motifs were made separately and the mesh joined to the back of them. Brussels was a major centre for both pillow and needlepoint, as well as combinations of the two. Honiton lace, the earliest and best in England, resembled that of Flanders.

The 19th century. In France in the early 19th C unashamed laciness came back into vogue. Silk lace (*blonde*) was fashionable. Black Chantilly lace was at first made mostly for Spain.

Machine-made nets, introduced in the later 18th C, were used as a ground for appliqué motifs (e.g. at Brussels). (2) By the 1840s it was possible to make inexpensive imitations of some types of handwork by machine. Hand craftsmanship now served a luxury market. A fine new Brussels lace was introduced—*point de gaze*. In Malta a silk pillow lace was made from 1833. (5)

EMBROIDERY

From the Middle Ages to the 17th century. The finest embroideries of the medieval period, known collectively as "Opus Anglicanum", were made in England for the Church in the 13th and 14th C. The ground was generally silk or satin, delicately worked with gold and silk threads. Chasubles and copes continued to be richly embellished but by the 15th C there was an increasing emphasis on secular needlework.

Embroidery in black silk on linen (blackwork) was popular in the 16th C for costume and household objects, especially in Spain and England. Coiling stem designs were common, and sometimes gold and silver threads were incorporated.

Embroiderers in Elizabethan England were particularly versatile, and embellished bed hangings, cushions, wall panels and garments, either in silk on linen or wool on canvas.

The earliest surviving samplers are from the 17th C. They began as panels embroidered with a variety of stitches or motifs to serve as models, but later they were made by young girls as test-pieces. In the 18th C samplers began to include letters of the alphabet, religious texts, a date and the name of the pupil. (7)

In the 17th C—the great age of pictorial embroidery in England—needlework pictures, caskets, cushions and mirror frames were worked in coloured silks. (1; p 105, no. 3) A characteristic technique was stumpwork (or raised work), by which the ornament was raised over padding. The popularity of quilting at this period was stimulated by Oriental coverlets. Crewelwork, using gaily coloured wools, was favoured for bed hangings and curtains.

Embroidery

1 English embroidered cushion, c.1660s, 21 × 30cm **B** F
2 Berlin woolwork picture, after Landseer, c.1850, 58 × 70cm **C** C
3 American patchwork quilt (detail), 19th c **B** D
4 Offertory cloth (detail), linen embroidered with silk, Spain, 17th c **B** C
5 Wool hanging in Hungarian stitch, Elbeuf (detail), 1730s, 470 × 250cm VR̄ G

6 Swedish cushion cover, in wool and cotton (detail), Skåne, 1814 **B** D
7 Needlework sampler, Massachusetts, dated 1796, 44.6 × 55.2cm **B** F

Superbly embroidered silks were made for the aristocrats of France in the reign of Louis XIV. Workshops such as that of St Cyr produced superb work on canvas in a mixture of *gros point* and *petit point*. From the end of the 17th C French needlewomen practised tambour work—a chain stitch worked rapidly with a hook.

Domestic embroidery in colonial America, from the late 17th C, included crewelwork, practised with a greater economy of wool than in England. As in Europe, knotted-pile "Turkey work" was used for covering cushions, chairs and other furniture.

The 18th and 19th centuries. The 18th C saw a vogue for silks, velvets and damasks on furnishings, but embroidery remained popular for chairs, screens and card tables. Wool or silk on canvas gradually ousted wool on linen. Bargello and the "Hungarian" stitch, with flamelike designs in graduated colours, were much used techniques. (5) Also common were figurative designs in tent or cross stitch. *Chinoiseries* were popular, but from the early 18th C were overtaken by a new naturalism. Floral motifs abounded in the 1720s and 30s. Dresden work, employing both pulled stitches and white outline stitches on fine muslin or linen, was widely used as a substitute for lace.

American needlewomen in the 19th C were tireless makers of quilted bed coverlets, by either appliqué work or patchwork, sometimes using home-printed cottons. (3; p 105, no. 2)

In the machine age the trend in Western embroidery was towards smaller items, such as fire screens and sentimental pictures. Ayrshire work (whitework on muslin) was mostly used on baby clothes. More widely practised was *broderie anglaise*, a type of cotton whitework with cut holes worked round in buttonhole stitch. The best-known innovation of 19th-C German needlework was Berlin woolwork, which rapidly became an amateur vogue all over Europe. It was executed in coloured wools (often highlighted by beads), on canvas, following published designs on squared paper. Favourite themes were naturalistic flowers and domestic or biblical subjects. (2)

An appealing Italian embroidery type was "Assisi work", derived from a Renaissance style in which the ground was filled with cross-stitch and the pattern reserved in plain linen. Spanish embroidery has much in common with Italian, but with brighter colours, and the frequent appearance of Moorish influences. In Scandinavia whitework was especially popular, from the late 17th to the 19th C. Among the finer works of Scandinavian folk embroidery are the beautiful cushion covers from Skåne and other parts of Sweden. (6)

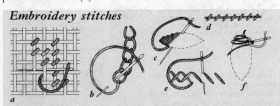

Embroidery stitches

a Tent stitch *b* Chain stitch *c* Satin stitch *d* Couching
e Cross stitch *f* Another type of couching

WOVEN SILKS

Throughout the Middle Ages and Renaissance the best European silks came from Italy and Spain. Genoa produced excellent heavy silks and velvets for furnishings until the late 18th C, and Venice continued to make fine brocades. But from the baroque period Lyons was the main centre for figured costume silks.

"Bizarre" silks, with complicated exotic designs originally inspired by imported silks from Macao, became fashionable throughout Europe in the period *c.*1695–1720. Initially they were made in Venice and Spain, and later at Spitalfields (London), Stockholm and elsewhere. Naturalistic floral patterns were introduced *c.*1730.

TOYS & DOLLS

Toys and dolls are normally subjected to a great deal of wear, and an error beginners often make is to assume that anything battered is necessarily old. However, there are enough 19th- and early 20th-C pieces in good condition to make this an attractive collecting area.

TOYS

A variety of toys was sold at fairs in 17th-C Europe: e.g. swords and drums, hobby horses, fiddles, dolls, jumping jacks and carved animals. Many such items were made in the forests of south Germany and distributed from Nuremberg. Elaborate toys of the early period were made only for the children of royalty or the aristocracy. To the luxury class belong the fine English, Dutch and German baby houses of the 18th C. Less costly toys of this era include tin, lead and printed cardboard soldiers, Noah's arks and rocking horses.

In the 19th C earlier styles and methods were often continued, making dating problematic. An important 19th-C development was the proliferation of scientific and optical sets. (4) Transport was another popular theme, as was the recreation of the grown-ups' world (toy tea sets, shops, etc.). (6, 9, 13)

Toys, 19th C

1 Late Victorian rocking horse, ht 114.3cm FC *D*
2 The "Opéra" toy theatre, published by Pellerin, Epinal, France, late 19th c FC *C*
3 Lithographed paper-covered doll's house, by the Bliss Mfg Co., USA, *c.*1890–1910, width 54.6cm ⓑ *D*

4 Zoëtrope, late 19th c, ht 59.5cm FC *C*
5 Wooden jumping jack FC *B*

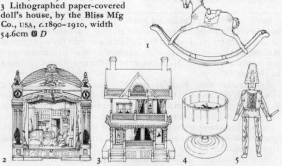

1

2   3   4   5

Metal toys. German-made tin and lead soldiers, known as "flats", became widely popular from the late 18th C onwards. But the German tin toys for which collectors now pay the most exorbitant prices are elaborate working models from the 1870–1914 period, by makers such as Bing, Märklin, Lehmann and Carette. (8, 13) Replicas were produced of trains, ships, cars, airships, factories and fire stations. Models for export, made in huge quantities, were given lettering, and sometimes flags, appropriate to their destination. Most tin toys were hand-enamelled before 1900, but by this time lithography was gradually making headway. Lehmann, founded in 1881, is known for its whimsical toys with highly colourful decoration. (11)

Metal toys, 19th and 20th C

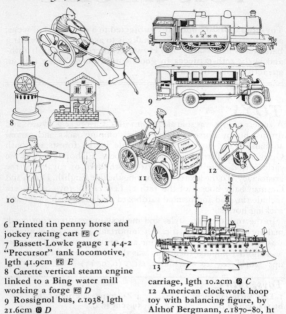

6 Printed tin penny horse and jockey racing cart [FC] *C*
7 Bassett-Lowke gauge 1 4-4-2 "Precursor" tank locomotive, lgth 41.9cm [FC] *E*
8 Carette vertical steam engine linked to a Bing water mill working a forge [FC] *D*
9 Rossignol bus, *c.*1938, lgth 21.6cm [B] *D*
10 American cast-iron bank, Creedmoor, 1877 [C] ⚲ *C*
11 Lehmann "Lolo" horseless carriage, lgth 10.2cm [B] *C*
12 American clockwork hoop toy with balancing figure, by Althof Bergmann, *c.*1870–80, ht 22.9cm [B] *E*
13 Märklin battleship, 1904, lgth 71.8cm [VR] *F*

Early locomotives included brass "floor-runners", clockwork trains tied to a point to give a rotary motion, and (mostly from the 1880s) steam trains. Trains were at first made with little attempt at realism, but before the turn of the century an obsessive attention to accuracy was apparent. Märklin marketed the first electric train sets in Europe in 1898.

Among the most popular tin toys made in France are the clockwork figures of Fernand Martin and the vehicles of Charles Rossignol. (9) Britain made few tin toys before the First World War. The field was dominated by Bassett-Lowke & Co., who after 1900 marked trains manufactured to their designs by Bing. Their first British-made trains appeared in 1910, ten years before the rival Hornby models hit the rails. (7)

By 1820 Connecticut had become the centre of a thriving tin toy industry, which soon spread to Philadelphia and New York. Hoop toys and wheeled bell toys were especially popular in the United States. (12) Ives, the most renowned of American makers, produced trains, dancing figures and a variety of other tinplate toys, as well as cast-iron floor-runner trains. Cast-iron money boxes, which often have ingenious mechanical movements, are a specialist area of American collecting. (10)

DOLLS

Cheap wooden dolls with articulated limbs were made extensively in Germany in the 18th and 19th C, especially in the Berchtesgaden and Grödnertal regions. Known as "Grödnertals" or "Dutch dolls", they are recognizable by their high waists, small heads and black-painted hair. (9) A more sophisticated type of doll had a head of papier mâché or "composition" on a jointed wooden or sewn fabric body. (1, 6) Sonneberg in Germany was a major centre for dolls of this kind. Sometimes the papier mâché heads were dipped into wax to form a clear complexion over the painted cheeks.

A superior method of wax doll making was perfected in London in the 19th C. Liquid wax was poured into moulds based on a sculpted original. A head and limbs created in this way were sewn to a fabric body, and human hair inserted. Some of the best English wax dolls were made from 1860 to 1900 by the Montanari and Pierotti families. (7)

Porcelain was not regularly in use before 1830. Heads were initially of glazed china with underglaze painted details, and later of "bisque" (biscuit) suited to detailed facial representation. (8) They were attached by sew holes to leather, wooden or fabric bodies. Fine porcelain heads were used in France on superbly dressed lady dolls (*Parisiennes*) made by the firms of Bru, Jumeau, Gaultier and others. (2) From *c*.1875 the emphasis changed to child-like dolls (*bébés*). Some china dolls were used for the famous Parisian automata, equipped with mechanisms for various movements. (5)

A particularly adventurous German producer was Kammer & Reinhardt (established 1886), who in 1909 introduced a new realistic type of bisque-headed baby doll—the first of a whole generation of lifelike German "character" dolls. (3) Simon & Halbig, Armand Marseille and Gebrüder Heubach were also among the leading German manufacturers.

Dolls

1 **American papier mâché doll**, with fabric body and leather arms, ht 58cm ⓑ *D*
2 **Bisque-headed fashion doll**, by Gaultier, Paris, *c*.1880, ht 40cm ⓑ *E*
3 **Character baby**, by Kestner, Germany, ht 57cm ⓑ *C*
4 **Bisque-headed feeding *bébé***, ht 27.9cm ⓑ *F*

5 **Jumeau mandoline-playing automaton**, *c*.1885, ht 51cm (with chair) ᴠ̃ʀ *F*
6 **Papier mâché-headed doll**, with wooden limbs, *c*.1850, ht 34.3cm ⓑ *D*
7 **Poured wax child doll**, ht 58.4cm ⓑ *D*
8 **Doll with glazed china head and limbs and sawdust-filled cloth body**, mid-19th c ꜰɢ *C*
9 **Large "Dutch doll"** ⓒ *A*

LOOKING GLASSES

The first experiments with metal-backed glass were inconclusive, but after the establishment of glasshouses at Murano, Venice, early in the 16th C, great advances were made in this field. Thereafter the Venetians enjoyed a long monopoly in the production of looking glasses. (The term "mirror" did not completely take over from "looking glass" until the 19th C.)

With Flanders, Germany was one of the first regions to set up manufactures on the Venetian model. Mannerism was a potent influence on European frames in the 16th C, succeeded in following centuries by baroque, rococo and neo-classicism. After the mid-17th C, when mirror making got under way in France, architects set a fashion for vast gilt-framed looking glasses that give the illusion of enlarging space. The best-known illustration of this idea was the Galerie des Glaces at Versailles, created by Charles Le Brun for Louis XIV. English and American taste was always much less grandiloquent.

Early English looking glasses were small, with proportionately large frames, usually of wood. The "cushion" type (from *c.*1675) had a squarish frame, sometimes with marquetry or incised lacquerwork. (1) Frames became lighter in the period 1690–1700, and often incorporated *verre églomisé* borders. Gilding, generally applied to carved gesso, was ubiquitous after 1750. Mirrors of the 1730s and later were often in an architectural style especially associated with William Kent: they were flanked by columns and

Looking glasses

3 **Architectural pier glass,** 1725–45 **B** **G**
4 **English *chinoiserie* looking glass,** *c.*1745 VR ᧱ *I*
5 **Venetian giltwood looking glass,** *c.*1700 **B** ᧱ *G*
6 **Oval gilt looking glass,** *c.*1780 **B** ᧱ *F*
7 **Cheval mirror,** *c.*1820 **FC** *E*
8 **American Sheraton-style toilet glass,** probably carved by Samuel MacIntyre, *c.*1800 VR ᧱ *H*

1 **Cushion looking glass,** with incised lacquer frame, *c.*1685, ht 12.7cm VR ᧱ *H*
2 **American girandole looking glass,** 1810–20 **B** ᧱ *G*

topped by a pediment. (3) The rococo led to a profusion of fussy scrolls and *chinoiseries*. (4) Neo-classicism, from the 1760s, promoted oval frames. (6) An important Regency type was the circular convex looking glass, often surmounted by an eagle. Because of patriotic associations, this style was also popular in America, where it was known as the "girandole". (2)

Pier glasses were made for the wall space between windows. Toilet mirrors, intended for a dressing table, were mounted on swivels between vertical supports with one or more drawers beneath. (8) Cheval mirrors are similar to toilet mirrors but lack the base cabinet. (7)

ART NOUVEAU

Art Nouveau was a progressive decorative style of the 1890s and early 1900s, divided into two main phases by the turn of the century. It originated in France, and was finally snuffed out by the First World War. The term "Art Nouveau" was taken from the name of a shop opened in Paris by Samuel Bing in 1895. In Austria the style was called *Sezessionstil*, in Germany *Jugendstil* ("youth style"), in Spain *Modernista*, while the Italians called it *Stile Liberty* after Liberty's, the English department store which so energetically promoted the new designs.

The nature of the style

Fluid, asymmetrical shapes derived from plants, water and other natural features later gave way to a more geometric feeling. This was encouraged by Japanese designs exhibited at international exhibitions in Paris and London. The emphasis of the style was on originality and craftsmanship.

The sinuous shapes of early, "curvilinear" Art Nouveau are perfectly exemplified in the *fin de siècle* decadence of book illustrations by Aubrey Beardsley and Charles Ricketts. In contrast, the post-1900 "rectilinear" phase, which moved towards the clinical purism of the Bauhaus, is summarized by the brilliant designs of Charles Rennie Mackintosh (1868–1928). He influenced the artists of the Wiener Werkstätte, who produced a Viennese version of Art Nouveau. In Britain the rectilinear style was associated with the Arts and Crafts Movement (whose aim was to restore lost standards of hand craftsmanship) and with the Celtic Revival (which looked back to the Celtic art of the Dark Ages).

FURNITURE

Samuel Bing's Galeries de l'Art Nouveau in the rue de Provence, and Julius Meier-Graefe's La Maison Moderne in the rue des Petits Champs, exhibited Art Nouveau to sophisticated Parisians of the 1890s. Bing sold the furniture of Georges de Feure, Edward Colonna and Eugène Gaillard; Meier-Graefe's shop-front was designed by the Belgian architect Henri van de Velde, who influenced Abel Landry, head of the Maison Moderne furniture workshops. Also working in the 1890s was Hector Guimard, whose furniture echoed his extravagant ironwork for the Métro station entrances. After *c.*1900 his carving became more subdued, and he made increasing use of pearwood. Rupert Carabin made furniture fantasies incorporating seductive carvings of nude women in poses of *fin de siècle* abandon.

Among the finest French Art Nouveau furniture was that made by the School of Nancy, dominated by Emile Gallé, who revived craftsmanship in marquetry. (3) The greatest cabinet-maker of the 1890s to benefit from Gallé's ideas was Louis Majorelle (1859–1926), who turned from rococo to a personal brand of Art Nouveau between the abstract and the naturalistic. (6)

In Britain, some proto-Art Nouveau pieces were made by the Century Guild (founded by A.H. Mackmurdo in 1882) and by C.F.A. Voysey. M.H. Baillie Scott, who collaborated with C.R.

Art Nouveau furniture

1 Bugatti corner seat, decorated with various woods and metals, *c.*1900 FG ♀ *F*

2 Oak chair, by C.R. Mackintosh, *c.*1900 Ⓑ ♀ *G*

3 Fruitwood marquetry pedestal table, signed by E. Gallé, *c.*1900, ht 114cm FG ♀ *F*

4 Oak cupboard, by Ernest Gimson, *c.*1910 Ⓑ *F*

5 Oak chair, by Gustav Stickley, *c.*1905 FG *E*

6 Mahogany wardrobe, with sculptured panels, by Louis Majorelle, *c.*1900–05, ht 240cm Ⓑ *I*

7 Oak chair by Charles Rohlfs, 1898 Ⓥ̸Ɽ *G*

Ashbee on a scheme for the Grand Duke of Hesse's Palace at Darmstadt in 1897, designed furniture for John White of Bedford, retailed at Liberty's. Ernest Gimson's pieces were elegantly clean-lined and often used delicate inlays as well as exploiting the natural grain of the wood. (4) The greatest master, however, was Charles Rennie Mackintosh, whose prodigal genius took flight in all kinds of experiments. His chairs have low, wide seats and very tall, thin backs. (2) Mackintosh was an important influence on commercial furnishings, and a china or book cabinet with leaded glass front in the Mackintosh style may be acquired readily, though not cheaply.

The assault of such artists on the shaping of public taste was felt in both Europe and North America. In Germany Richard Riemerschmid's designs were mid-way between the voluptuousness of Majorelle and the purity of Mackintosh. Belgians such as Henri van de Velde carried to extremes the concept of a totally designed environment, in which the furnishings related to the architecture. Progressive Italian furniture at this time was generally heavy and graceless (1), although a restrained Art Nouveau fluidity entered the work of Eugenio Quarti, and Pietro Zen's pieces were delicately rectilinear.

In the United States Gustav Stickley was drawn to the simplicity of Gimson's style. (5) In contrast, Charles Rohlfs created some pieces of fantastic over-elaboration. (7) On the West Coast, Charles Sumner Greene and his brother Henry interpreted Arts and Crafts ideals in their own distinctive way, while The Furniture Shop, founded in San Francisco in 1906, specialized in painted wood and brightly coloured inlays.

POTTERY AND PORCELAIN

A large proportion of the best ceramics of the late 19th and early 20th C bears little relation to Art Nouveau. The greatest French artist-craftsmen set up workshops not in the fashionable artistic centres of Paris or Nancy, where the style took root, but in villages scattered throughout the country. Of the leading potters, Ernest

Chaplet was based at Choisy-le-Roi, Auguste Delaherche at Armentières, Albert Dammouse at Sèvres, Jean Carriès at St-Amand-en-Puisaye in the Nièvre, and Adrien Dalpeyrat at Bourg-la-Reine. (6) Artists such as these drew inspiration from Japanese artefacts exhibited in Paris, as did so many exponents of Art Nouveau. But what impressed them in particular was the textures and colour effects of Japanese ceramics, not the spectacular graphics of the polychrome woodcuts.

There was more Art Nouveau feeling in the wares of the two big French porcelain factories than in those of the studio potters. Taxile Doat's designs for Sèvres and Georges de Feure's for Limoges are excellent examples. (4) Finer still are the designs by J. Juriaan Kok for the Rozenburg factory near The Hague—airy fantasies drawn with a beautiful fastidiousness on flame-like porcelain shapes. (5)

The bewildering variety of styles in Germany in this period ranged from the highly personal idioms of Hermann Mutz and other studio potters to the more commercial but still adventurous products of the Meissen and Berlin factories. In Italy, Doccia proved susceptible to a florid form of Art Nouveau. The most important Swedish manufacturers were Rörstrand and Gustavsberg, while in Denmark Thorvald Bindesbøll turned out vigorously wavy designs without a trace of otherworldliness. (1)

English potters such as Edwin Martin learnt the same lessons from Japanese ceramics as did their French contemporaries. (3) Art potteries founded in the 1860s and 70s expressed a new mood of individualism. Salt-glazed stoneware, produced notably by Doulton's, enjoyed a revival.

The most famous name in American art pottery of the late 19th-early 20th C is Rookwood (founded 1880), a factory noted above all for its rich green or brown glazes. (p 112, no. 1) Artus van Briggle, an ex-Rookwood man, set up his own pottery at Colorado Springs in 1899, employing Art Nouveau motifs. (2) The Grueby Faience Co., Boston, had meanwhile already challenged the supremacy of underglaze painting by experiments with matt glazes on simple forms. Other important American potteries of the time include the University City Pottery, Missouri (which lured Taxile Doat from Sèvres) and L.C. Tiffany's Corona Works, New York.

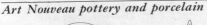

Art Nouveau pottery and porcelain

1 Earthenware dish, by Thorvald Bindesbøll, Valby, 1901 Ⓑ E

2 Vase, by Artus van Briggle, 1902 FC ♀ E

3 Snuff bottle, by Martin Bros, 1901, ht 6.3cm FC D

4 Porcelain gourd, decorated in *pâte sur pâte*, by Taxile Doat, c.1902 Ⓑ F

5 Rozenburg tea pot, by Juriaan Kok, 1903 Ⓑ G

6 Stoneware vase, by Auguste Delaherche, c.1890 FC D

GLASS

Of the many glassmakers who worked in the Art Nouveau style there are three who stand out as innovators: Gallé in France, Loetz in Austria, and Tiffany in the United States.

France. Emile Gallé (1846–1904), whose factory was at Nancy, was inspired by a vast range of sources: plant life, English cameo glass, Japanese art, Impressionism, and the literature of Baudelaire, Rimbaud and others. (5; p 107, no. 4) Among his most successful pieces were cased glass vessels, often in grey and amethyst. Pieces produced by his factory after his death were marked "Gallé" with a star beside the name. His most distinguished imitators were Auguste and Antonin Daum, also based on Nancy. Gabriel Argy-Rousseau, after the First World War, looked back to Art Nouveau as well as working in the new styles. (2)

Germany and Austria. The Loetz factory in Austria was founded in 1836. On the death of Johann Loetz in 1848 it was renamed by his widow the Glasfabrik Johann Loetz-Witwe. Loetz glass is most prized for its iridescence, introduced in the 1880s. (7)

Members of the Wiener Werkstätte did designs for a number of Austrian glassworks, including Loetz, Meyr's Neffe, Johann Oertel, Ludwig Moser & Söhne and J. & L. Lobmeyr.

Art Nouveau glass

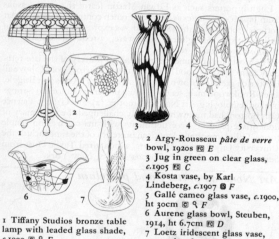

1 Tiffany Studios bronze table lamp with leaded glass shade, c.1900 © ♀ F

2 Argy-Rousseau *pâte de verre* bowl, 1920s FC E

3 Jug in green on clear glass, c.1905 FC C

4 Kosta vase, by Karl Lindeberg, c.1907 ⓑ F

5 Gallé cameo glass vase, c.1900, ht 30cm © ♀ F

6 Aurene glass bowl, Steuben, 1914, ht 6.7cm FC D

7 Loetz iridescent glass vase, c.1900, ht 26.3cm FC ♀ E

The major Art Nouveau glass designer in Germany was Karl Koepping, well known for tall pieces with curvilinear stems.

The United States. Louis Comfort Tiffany (1848–1933), son of the fashionable jeweller, was the giant among Art Nouveau glass designers in America. He founded his own company in 1878, and in 1880 patented a brand of iridescent coloured glass, "Favrile", which owed its satiny finish to a process involving vapourized metals. His early interest in stained glass windows was responsible for the distinctive Tiffany lampshade—a colourful glass mosaic often based on plant forms. (1)

Favrile glass was the inspiration of Steuben's "Aurene" glass, first produced in 1904. (6) Other manufacturers who followed the lead of Tiffany included the Quezal Art Glass and Decorating Co. of Brooklyn and Handel & Co. of Connecticut.

Scandinavia. Kosta and Reijmyre were the two most important glassworks in Sweden at the beginning of the 20th C. (4) They employed artists such as Gunnar G. Wennerberg and Alf Wallender, whose cased glass techniques owed much to the example of Gallé.

SILVER AND OTHER METALWORK

Silver. Probably the most distinguished of Art Nouveau silversmiths is Archibald Knox (1864–1933), whose work for Liberty's, particularly his pieces in their "Cymric" range (launched in 1899), reflected his passionate devotion to Celtic traditions. The commemorative spoons and buckles he designed for Edward VII's coronation in 1902 are available to collectors of relatively modest means.

Other British silver designers include Rex Silver, who worked in a style similar to Knox's, and C.R. Ashbee, who favoured honest-to-goodness hammered surfaces. Ashbee's Guild of Handicraft, which began working in silver and electroplate in 1889, explored the decorative uses of precious stones and enamelling. (3)

Continental silver is perhaps at its most purely Art Nouveau in the "whiplash-style" pieces of the French firm Cardeilhac. More important as decorative art were the creations of Josef Hoffmann, Koloman Moser and Dagobert Peche of the Wiener Werkstätte. Much of their work shows the influence of Ashbee and Mackintosh. Georg Jensen, at his workshop in Copenhagen, developed a sturdy, richly embellished idiom that earned him international repute.

Other metals. Liberty's "Tudric" range of pewter wares, with designs by Knox, was a seminal influence. (7, 8) For a succession of

---

Art Nouveau metalwork

1 Hand-hammered copper inkwell, Roycroft Copper Shop, c.1915 Ⓖ A
2 Silver vase, attributed to Rex Silver, 1901 ꜰꜱ D
3 Guild of Handicraft Ltd silver dish, with chrysoprase cabochon, by C.R. Ashbee, 1904 ꜰꜱ E
4 Pewter "peacock" jug, by Josef Olbrich, c.1901 Ⓑ F
5 German silvered metal mirror frame, WMF, c.1900, ht 37cm ꜰꜱ ꝙ E
6 Liberty's silver and enamel spoon ꜰꜱ C
7 Liberty's "Tudric" pewter clock, after 1904, ht 10cm ꜰꜱ D
8 "Tudric" pewter candlestick, by Archibald Knox, 1905 Ⓑ E

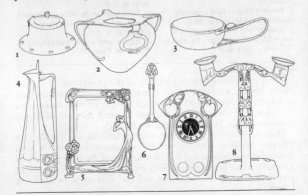

firms, Christopher Dresser designed electroplated pieces with a characteristic austerity of decoration, in a style that owed much to Japanese example.

Flamboyant metalwork was produced in Germany by P. Kayser Söhne of Krefeld (notable for pewterwares under the trade-name Kayser-Zinn) and Württembergische Metallwarenfabrik (WMF). (5) Small-scale decorative sculpture enjoyed a European vogue around the turn of the century, some of it representing the American dancer Loïe Fuller.

Metalwork thrived in the Arts and Crafts communities of the United States, where the Roycroft Copper Shop (East Aurora) and Dirk van Erp's Copper Shop (Oakland and San Francisco) produced unpretentious pieces that reached a wide market. (1)

JEWELLERY

René Lalique is linked in the popular mind with Art Deco glass (see p 176), but until *c.*1910 his main interest was jewellery. Extending the fashionable repertoire, he favoured semi-precious stones and non-precious materials such as carved horn. Above all, he was a skilful enameller. His motifs included characters of legend and the grotesque creatures of Symbolist art, often transmuted into semi-

Art Nouveau jewellery

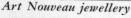

1 **Gold, enamel and pearl pendant,** by Georges Fouquet after a design by A. Mucha, *c.*1900 VR *I*
2 **French enamelled peacock feather buckle,** *c.*1900 FG *D*
3 **Enamelled brooch-pendant,** set with a moonstone, by Henry Wilson, *c.*1913 ◙ *F*

4 **Gold pendant set with opals, diamonds, emeralds and pearls,** by Philippe Wolfers, 1901 VR *I*
5 **Enamel dragonfly brooch,** set in silver-gilt FG ९ *C*
6 **Pendant in platinum, diamonds and engraved glass,** by René Lalique, *c.*1900, lgth 6cm ◙ ९ *F*
7 **Belt buckle in silver-coloured metal,** probably American, *c.*1900 G ९ *C*
8 **Agate and silver buckle,** by Vever of Paris FG *C*

abstract forms. (6)

Other prominent French jewellers of the period were Paul and Henri Vever, whose excellent enamelling was Lalique-inspired, and Lucien Gaillard, well known for his carved horn haircombs. (8) Georges Fouquet commissioned a small number of highly elaborate jewels from Alphonse Mucha. (1)

The only jeweller in Europe to rival Lalique was the Belgian Philippe Wolfers, who imbued his stylized natural forms with Symbolist associations. (4) British jewellery of the same period was generally more restrained; among its highlights are the work of Henry Wilson, J. Paul Cooper and the enamelled pendants of Liberty's. (3)

ART DECO

The term "Art Deco" is derived from the title of the exhibition which first introduced the style in Europe—the Paris "Exposition des Arts Décoratifs" of 1925. Most experts now accept 1920–40 as the convenient date limits of Art Deco, though a few of them use the term only for the decorative arts of 1920–30, and call those of 1930–40 "Modernist".

The nature of the style

In essence Art Deco was domesticated cubism. It brought into the home—into carpets, wallpapers and sideboards—as well as into cinema and hotel architecture and liner design, the fragmentation of forms favoured by the Cubists in France, the Futurists in Italy and the Vorticists in England. It was also promiscuously eclectic, snapping up influences from the Russian Ballet (which replaced the pastel shades of Art Nouveau with lurid mauves, oranges and lime greens), from ancient Egyptian art (following the opening of Tutankhamun's tomb in 1922) and from central American Indian art, including the stepped designs of Aztec temples.

There is a marked difference between 1920s and 1930s Deco. The keynote of the 20s was reaction against the First World War. It was the time of the Bright Young Things, of fast sports cars, cocktail cabinets and jazz bands. After the 1929 Crash there was less frivolity, more political awareness. The decorative arts changed to match the mood. Art Deco of the 20s is delicate and curvilinear, but in the 30s the lines straighten out, the clean-cut forms of the machine are often the model, pieces are bolder and more "hard-edge".

FURNITURE

France. The exquisitely crafted French furniture of the 1920s has a delicate feminine character. Much of it was an updated version of neo-classical Louis XVI, with a dash of the Orient (e.g. tassel handles for cabinet doors; lacquer, used most brilliantly by Jean Dunand). The outstanding master was Emile-Jacques Ruhlmann (1879–1933), who often worked in rich and rare woods from the French colonies, such as striated macassar ebony, and in ivory, which he used for key plates and other trimmings. (8)

Art Deco furniture was sold by big stores, as Art Nouveau had been by Liberty's. Maurice Dufrène (1876–1955) and Paul Follot (1877–1941), two of Ruhlmann's rivals designing very much in his manner, respectively took charge of the La Maîtrise ateliers for the Galeries Lafayette, and of the Atelier Pomone at Bon Marché. Other designers of this period whose work is now prized include Djo Bourgeois, Marcel Coard, André Groult, Paul Iribe, Léon Jallot, Jules Leleu, and Suë et Mare. (11, 12) Pierre Legrain did some very individual "Egyptian" designs in palm wood and parchment.

Pierre Chareau (1883–1950), Jean-Michel Frank, and Pierre Legrain with his glass and metal piano of 1929, led a reaction against the preciousness of early Art Deco, for which the natural market was couturiers and others in the fashion world. (1) The

Art Deco furniture

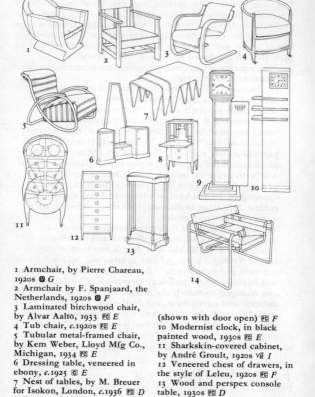

1 **Armchair, by Pierre Chareau, 1920s** Ⓑ *G*
2 **Armchair by F. Spanjaard, the Netherlands, 1920s** Ⓑ *F*
3 **Laminated birchwood chair, by Alvar Aalto, 1933** Ⓕ Ⓒ *E*
4 **Tub chair, c.1920s** Ⓕ Ⓒ *E*
5 **Tubular metal-framed chair, by Kem Weber, Lloyd Mfg Co., Michigan, 1934** Ⓕ Ⓒ *E*
6 **Dressing table, veneered in ebony, c.1925** Ⓒ *E*
7 **Nest of tables, by M. Breuer for Isokon, London, c.1936** Ⓕ Ⓒ *D*
8 **Bureau, based on a design by Ruhlmann, c.1935** Ⓖ *G*
9 **"Clocktail" cabinet, c.1930**
(shown with door open) Ⓕ Ⓒ *F*
10 **Modernist clock, in black painted wood, 1930s** Ⓕ Ⓒ *E*
11 **Sharkskin-covered cabinet, by André Groult, 1920s** Ⓥ Ⓡ *I*
12 **Veneered chest of drawers, in the style of Leleu, 1920s** Ⓕ Ⓒ *F*
13 **Wood and perspex console table, 1930s** Ⓕ Ⓒ *D*
14 **Armchair in tubular steel and leather, designed by Marcel Breuer, 1920s** Ⓕ Ⓒ ⚲ *F*

reaction had no major impact, however, and it was left to Germany and the United States to achieve a style that related to the new mechanized and "fragmented" world.

Germany. The Bauhaus designers Marcel Breuer and Mies van der Rohe made furniture so in keeping with the machine age that even today it looks ultra-modern. (14) The new prescription for furniture design was tubular steel, streamlining and scientific analysis of human posture.

The United States. America was already setting the pace in literature, music and other arts. New Orleans was the epicentre of jazz, to whose fragmented rhythms Europe now moved. Above all America led the way in architecture, with the skyscraper. Frank Lloyd Wright, like the leading Art Nouveau architects, designed furniture to go with his buildings. Donald Deskey's furniture for Radio City Music Hall, New York (1933), shows the later phase of Art Deco in its most mature form. Paul T. Frankl, an Austrian architect who settled in America in 1914, designed wooden bookcases in the form of skyscrapers.

Britain. In England machine-age Deco is well illustrated by the work of Eileen Gray (1879–1976), best known for her lacquered screens. Betty Joel favoured generous curves and patterned veneers. Jack Pritchard of Isokon made excellent steel-frame pieces.

Scandinavia. Kaare Klint in Denmark designed functional furniture for the firm of Rudolph Rasmussen from 1928, and was highly influential in Sweden. The Swede Carl Malmsten worked with inlays and expensive woods in a spirit akin to that of the 18th C. Bentwood was used inventively by Bruno Mathsson and, above all, Alvar Aalto. (3)

POTTERY AND PORCELAIN

Ceramics are a perfect example of the Jekyll and Hyde aspects of Art Deco. On the one hand are the subdued, often oriental-influenced French wares collected by rich connoisseurs—beautifully potted and subtly glazed pieces by studio potters such as Emile Decoeur, Emile Lenoble, Jean Mayodon and René Buthaud (1); on the other, the garish "pop" and unabashedly commercial products of Clarice Cliff and the Carlton Pottery. It is a choice between purist aesthetics and the spirit of the period.

Collectors who choose Decoeurs and Lenobles will generally be credited with superior taste to those who go for Cliffs and Carltons. But the posh French ceramics are too often tame and derivative. Some are almost indistinguishable from Chinese and Japanese wares—and the same goes for the (again marvellously potted) wares of the same period by the great Bernard Leach and William Staite Murray. Clarice Cliff and Carlton introduced a Disney-like style that was new in ceramics, and its shock-effect was deliberate: not for nothing did Cliff call her main pattern "Bizarre". (3, 5) These pieces are increasingly collected.

Art Deco pottery and porcelain

1 Earthenware vase, by Emile Lenoble c.1920, ht 28cm FC C
2 Saxbo stoneware vase FC C
3 Carlton Ware porcelain plate FC C
4 Wedgwood earthenware vase, by Keith Murray, c.1930, ht 19.8cm FC D

5 "Bizarre" cup, saucer and teapot, by Clarice Cliff, 1929 C C
6 Teaset by Midwinter, Staffordshire, c.1935 C B
7 Plaster head, with carmine hat and lips C A
8 Figure, by the Serapis Fayence factory, Vienna, 1925 B E

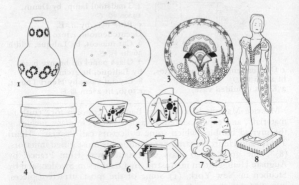

Eminently collectable too in the "low-brow" range are the domestic wares of Shelley Potteries, Doulton figures and the ceramic wall-heads (some in the image of Marlene Dietrich) made by Goldscheider (in Austria) and others. (7) The delightful animal models of Lemanceau, usually cream-glazed, fall half-way between the pretensions of the studio and the brash appeal of the deliberately commercial, as do the clean-lined wares designed by Keith Murray for Wedgwood. (4)

The purest expression of functionalism in Scandinavian ceramics is perhaps the stonewares made at the Saxbo workshops in Copenhagen from 1929. (2)

GLASS

The giant in this medium is René Lalique (1860–1945), best known for a misty opalescent blue glass. He also worked in clear glass, with moulded and etched designs. Main products include lamps, clocks, scent bottles and motor car mascots (including a cruel-beaked eagle which Nazi leaders favoured on the front of their black Mercedes cars in the 1930s). Though mass-produced and highly commercial, his work looks handmade. (6, 7)

The mushroom-shaped lamps of Antonin Daum have a purist Deco simplicity (4); and François-Emile Decorchemont adapted his earlier style to make stylized Deco fishes and classic vases which nobody could mistake for Art Nouveau. (5)

Art Deco glass

Sweden, 1934 FG *D*
3 Decanter, possibly French, 1930s, ht 21.5cm C *C*
4 Toadstool lamp, by Daum, 1920s FG *C*
5 Blue fish, by F.-E. Decorchemont, c.1930 B *F*
6 Car mascot, by Lalique, width 26cm FG *E*
7 Glass panel on bronze base, by Lalique, ht 43cm B *H*
8 Crystal vase, by Henri Thuret, c.1930, ht 27cm B *E*

1 Orrefors engraved vase, 1930s, ht 28cm FG *D*
2 Kosta moulded vase,

Maurice Marinot had the post-Bauhaus concern for "truth to material", and experimented with new effects in glass, including the myriad bubbles which some collectors call "caviar". Henri Thuret and Henri Navarre were among his most gifted imitators. (8) Some good Deco glass was made away from France: by Auguste Heiligenstein in Austria, by Orrefors in Sweden, and by Steuben in New York. (1) Some of the most attractive pieces, however, are anonymous.

SILVER

Jean Puiforcat (1897–1945) is one of the geniuses of Art Deco. (4) He was influenced by painters rather than by silversmiths, and decided that "hard-edge" silver was an ideal medium into which to translate cubism. Some influence perhaps came from Aztec art, from which he may have taken the idea of combining silver and rock-crystal.

Art Deco silver

1 Salt cellar for the *Normandie*, by Christofle, 1935 FC *D*
2 Teapot, by Jean Fouquet ⍟ *F*
3 Cocktail shaker, by Ken Weber, 1928, ht 24.4cm FC *D*
4 Vegetable dish with jade handle, by Puiforcat ⍟ *F*
5 Sweetmeat bowl, by Christofle, *c.*1910–20 FC *D*
6 Vase, by Georg Jensen, ht 10.2cm C ⍰ *C*
7 Austrian fluted casket with plastic handles, *c.*1920 FC *E*

Another important French silver producer was L'Orfèvrerie Christofle (founded 1839), which made some delightfully whimsical novelties, as well as the grand and quite unwhimsical silver for the *Normandie* liner. (1, 5) Tétard Frères carried the marriage of cubism and silver perhaps too far in tea wares which were perfect oblongs. Gérard Sandoz, better known for his jewellery, made silver *tête-à-tête* services and fancifully decorated cigarette cases.

Early 1920s silver by the Wiener Werkstätte (e.g. by Dagobert Peche), with finely fluted designs, just qualifies as Deco. So does the silver of the Dane Georg Jensen, which has an unmistakable Nordic cast, related to the British Celtic style. (6) In England Charles Boyton made Deco domestic wares, as did Gio Ponti in Italy. The American industrial designer Kem Weber (1889–1963) designed some magnificent stylized silver for the Friedman Silver Co., New York, in the late 1920s. (3)

JEWELLERY AND OTHER DECORATIVE OBJECTS

Jewellery. The best designers—whose machine-age geometric work is magnificent—were Raymond Templier, Jean Fouquet, Gérard Sandoz and Paul Brandt. (5) Stunning precious-stone jewellery by Cartier, Boucheron and Van Cleef & Arpels proved that the First World War had not killed off luxury. Below these is a vast range of cheap jewellery, some in plastics with the Egyptian "Cleopatra" style much in evidence.

Metalwork. For the aesthetic purists, bronzes by Gustav Miklos, hammered copper by Claudius Linossier and ironwork by Edgar

Art Deco jewellery and other artefacts

1 Celluloid hairbrush Ⓒ A
2 Bronze and ivory dancing girl on marble base, by Chiparus, 1920s ht 57cm Ⓒ ♀ F

3 Platinum and diamond bracelet Ⓕ Ⓖ G
4 Fan, 1920s Ⓒ A
5 Pendant in platinum, coral, jet and brilliants, by Jean Fouquet, 1920 Ⓡ I

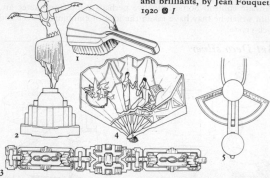

Brandt. For uninhibited *im*purists, sculptures by Demetre Chiparus and Frederick Preiss in extravagantly Deco poses rendered in a mad mix of materials. (2) The brilliantly coloured enamels of C. Fauré command high prices.

Rugs and carpets. There are many good anonymous examples, but Edouard Bénédictus made superb carpets in the earlier Deco style, while Gustav Miklos and Marion Dorn designed fine rugs in the later more hard-edged style.

Fans. Many top restaurants and hotel ballrooms gave away fans, with a pretty Deco design on one side and the establishment's name on the other. (4)

Plastics. In 1907 the first totally synthetic material was developed in America—phenolformaldehyde resin, commonly known as "Bakelite". Plastics are now beginning to be regarded as an art form, and there is a big range for the collector, from jewellery and hairbrush sets to inkstands and radio cabinets. (1)

Registration of design marks in Britain

The 1839 and 1842 Design Acts afforded copyright protection to designers of various classes of artefact. Patent-holders were allotted a diamond-shaped mark, which was applied to the item concerned. From 1842 to 1867 the year letter was put at the top of the diamond, but from 1868 to 1883 it appeared in the right-hand corner (see diagram).

KEY TO YEAR LETTERS

A 1845 (top) or 1871 (right)
B 1858 (top only)
C 1844 (top) or 1870 (right)
D 1852 (top) or 1878 (right)
E 1855 (top) or 1881 (right)
F 1847 (top) or 1873 (right)
G 1863 (top only)
H 1843 (top) or 1869 (right)
I 1846 (top) or 1872 (right)
J 1854 (top) or 1880 (right)
K 1857 (top) or 1883 (right)
L 1856 (top) or 1882 (right)
M 1859 (top only)
N 1864 (top only)
O 1862 (top only)
P 1851 (top) or 1877 (right)
Q 1866 (top only)
R 1861 (top only)

S 1849 (top) or 1875 (right)
T 1867 (top only)
U 1848 (top) or 1874 (right)
V 1850 (top) or 1876 (right)
W 1865 (top) or (1st to 6th Mar. only)
X 1842 (top) or 1868 (right)
Y 1853 (top) or 1879 (right)
Z 1860 (top only)

Class number (ceramics)

IV

16 — Day of month

6 Ⓡ d I

Year letter (1872)

Month letter

G

ANTIQUES FAIRS

Austria
  Vienna Art and Antiques Fair *Spring and Autumn*

Belgium
  Brussels: Belgian Antiques Fair *Spring*
  Ghent: Flemish Antiques Fair *April*

Britain
  Bath: West of England Antiques Fair *May*
  Guildford: Surrey Antiques Fair *October*
  Harrogate: Northern Antique Dealers Fair *September*
  London: Burlington House Fair *Spring*
    Chelsea Antiques Fairs *March and September*
    Fine Art and Antiques Fair, Olympia *June*
    Grosvenor House Antiques Fair (provisional title) *Summer*

Denmark
  Copenhagen: Danish Antique Dealers Fair *March*

France
  Grenoble Art and Antiques Fair *January*
  Paris: Biennale Internationale des Antiquaires
    September/October (even years)
  Toulouse Antique Dealers Fair *Autumn*

Germany
  Cologne or Dusseldorf: West German Fine Art and
    Antiques Fair *March*
  Hanover Art and Antiques Fair *Spring*
  Munich: German Art and Antiques Fair *October/November*

Ireland
  Dublin: Irish Antiques Fair *August*

Italy
  Florence International Antiques Biennale *October (odd years)*

The Netherlands
  Breda Antiques Fair *March/April*
  Delft Antique Dealers' Fair *October*
  Maastricht: "Antique Maestricht" *March*

Sweden
  Helsingborg Art and Antiques Fair *July/August*
  Stockholm International Antiques Fair *March/April*

Switzerland
  Basle: Swiss Art and Antiques Fair *March/April*
  Zurich Antiques Fair *Late Spring*

The United States
  Atlanta: High Museum Antiques Show *October/November*
  Boston: Ellis Memorial Antiques Show *October*
  Houston: Theta Charity Show *September*
  Kent Antiques Show, Connecticut *August*
  Miami: National Antiques Show *January*
  Milwaukee Antiques Show *September*
  Natchez Garden Club Antiques Show, Mississippi *April/May*
  New York: Fall Antiques Show, Hudson River at West 55th St
    Autumn
    Winter Antiques Show, Park Avenue at 67th St,
    January/February
  Philadelphia: University Hospital Antiques Show *April*

For further information on antiques fairs in Europe and the United
States, readers are advised to consult the *Antiques Trade Gazette*,
London (telephone 01-836 0323).

CERAMICS MARKS

Marks on ceramics may be applied underglaze or overglaze, or incised or impressed into the clay before firing. Commonly found fakes include the Meissen crossed swords, Sèvres interlaced L.S. and Chelsea anchor. Chinese reign marks are unreliable as an indication of date, as earlier ones were often copies as an act of homage to former masters. "Pseudo-Chinese" marks were frequently used by European factories. (Numbers in italics after an entry refer to relevant pages in the text.)

Porcelain

Berlin Gotzkowsky's factory, 1761–3; Royal Factory, from 1763 *41*

Bow *c.*1750; 1760–76; Mr Tebo's mark

Bristol 1773–81; *c.*1775 *34*

Buen Retiro 1760–1803, *44, 45*

Capodimonte 1743–59 *44*

Caughley 1722–99; after 1783 *33*

Chantilly 1726–40; 1740–1800 *38*

Chelsea 1745–9; 1745–9; anchor (raised 1749–53, red 1753–8, gold 1758–70) *30–32*

Chelsea-Derby 1770–84 *32*

Coalport (Coalbrookdale) *c.*1810–25; *c.*1861–75 *33–4*

Copenhagen 18th C, 1830–45 *42*

Derby 1784–1810; Bloor period, 1811–48 *32*

Doccia late 18th–early 19th C *44*

Frankenthal 1756–9; 1762–75 *41*

Fürstenberg 1753–70 *41*

Höchst 1758–65 *41*

Knowles, Taylor & Knowles (E. Liverpool, Ohio) Lotus Ware *46*

Longton Hall 1751–3 *32*

Marieberg 1766–9 *42*

K. P. F.

Meissen monogram of Augustus the Strong, 1723–36; from 1722; from 1724; pseudo-Chinese mark, 1721–31; after 1763; after 1774 *39–40*

.D.V.

Mennecy 1740–73 *38*

Minton *c.*1805–16; *c.*1850–70 *35*

NANTGARW.

Nantgarw 1813–20 *34*

Naples 1771–1834 *44*

New Hall *c.*1800 *34*

Nymphenburg
1755–65 *41*

Plymouth 1768–70
pseudo-Chinese mark *34*

Rockingham
1826–42 *34–5*

 Sᵗ C.
T

St Cloud
1693–1722; 1722–6 *37–8*

Sèvres 1754; 1778;
1793–1800;1852–70 *38–9*

COPELAND

Spode (Stoke-on Trent)
after 1829 *35*

Swansea 1814–30 *34*

Vienna from 1744 *41*

Vincennes see Sèvres

Worcester Dr Wall,
1751–83 (first three
marks); imitation Meissen
mark, 1768–72
32–3

Pottery

DOULTON
LAMBETH

Doulton
from *c.*1854

AK SE
❀ DVD
Dutch delft
Adrianus Kocks;
Samuel van Eenhoorn;
De Roos factory *41–2*

ETRUSCAN
Griffen, Smith & Hill
(Phoenixville, Penn.)
46

Herrebøe
(Norway) *43*

Leeds *28*

VP· VP
Marseilles
Veuve Perrin,
1748–93 *36–7*

Rookwood
(Cincinnati, Ohio) *46*

CC CC CC
V̄   V̄   V̄
     C   C
          E̅
Rörstrand after 1809 *42*

PH H
Strasbourg
Paul Hannong;
Joseph Hannong *37*

WEDGWOOD   WEDGWOOD
Wedgwood   & BENTLEY
Wedgwood
1759–69; 1769–80 *28*

Chinese reign marks

德 大
年 明
製 宣
Xuande (Hsüan Tê,
1426–35)

化 大
年 明
製 成
Chenghua
(Ch'êng Hua, 1465–87)

靖 大
年 明
製 嘉
Jiajing (Chîa Ching,
1522–66)

曆 大
年 明
製 萬
Wanli (Wan Li, 1573–1620)

熙 大
年 清
製 康
Kangxi (K'ang Hsi,
1662–1722)

正 大
年 清
製 雍
Yongzheng
(Yung Chêng; 1723–35)

隆 大
年 清
製 乾
Qianlong
(Ch'ien Lung, 1736–95)

SILVER MARKS

Only Britain has a consistent method of marking old silver. The Dutch system is fairly meticulous but has never been rigorously enforced. Marks used in other countries as a guarantee of quality and to indicate payment of tax seldom provide a convenient means of identification. Town marks, however, sometimes cast light on date as well as origin, owing to periodic design changes. The marks shown on these pages are a tiny selection from a vast range.

Town marks

Amsterdam 18th C

Cologne
late 17th C; mid-18th C

Geneva 18th C

Antwerp 1627–8

Copenhagen
from 1608

Genoa 17th–18th C

Augsburg
1723–35; 1787–9

Córdova 15th–16th C

Glasgow from 17th C
(rectangular since 1781)

Bergen (Norway)
18th–19th C

Cork (Eire)
both 17th–18th C

Hamburg
17th–18th C

Berlin late 18th C

Dordrecht 18th C

Leiden 17th C

Birmingham
from 1773

Dresden mid-18th C

Lisbon 17th–18th C

Brussels
both early 18th C

Dublin 17th–19th C

London 1478–1696
and 1736–1821
(uncrowned thereafter)

Chester (England)
1701–79; from 1780

Edinburgh
16th–17th C; from 1760

Moscow 1712; 1780

Christiana (Oslo)
1624–*c.*1820

Exeter (England)
1575–1698; 1701–19th C

Munich *c.*1700

Newcastle (England)
from 1672

St Petersburg
(Leningrad) 1776–1825

Turin 18th C

Nuremberg
1700–50; 19th C

Sheffield (England)
from 1773

Venice 17th–18th C

Paris 1684–7
(small items); 1764

Stockholm
1600–1700; 1700–1850

Vienna
1675–1737; 1737–84

Rome both late 17th C

Trondheim (Norway)

York (England)
1700–1857

Makers' marks

Hester Bateman
London after 1761

**François Thomas
Germain** Paris 18th C

**Jean-Baptiste-Claude
Odiot** Paris 18th–19th C

**Martin-Guillaume
Biennais**
Paris early 19th C

Jacob Hurd
Boston, Mass. first half
of 18th C

Paul Revere
Boston, Mass. 1735–1807

John Coney Boston,
Mass. after *c.* 1705

**Wenzel Jamnitzer
Nuremberg** 16th C

Paul Storr
London early 19th C

Adam van Vianen the
Netherlands 16th–17th C

Fineness and related marks

**Austro-Hungarian
Empire** 1806–24

Britain 1786–1820
(sovereign's head
duty mark, George III)

Italy 1873–1935
(purity of 900/1000)

England 1542–1822
(lion passant:
sterling purity);
1697–1864 (Britannia
with lion's head erased:
purity of 958/1000)

France 1798–1809
(purity of 950/1000);
1809–19 (guarantee
for small items)

The Netherlands
from 1814
(purity of 934/1000)

Sweden from 1752
(state control mark)

GLOSSARY

Numbers in italics after a definition refer to pages on which the term is clarified by an illustration.

Acanthus Decorative leaf motif.
Acorn clock Type of American shelf clock. *118*
Act of Parliament clock Wall clock of type used in inns after 1797 levy on timepieces in Britain. *115*
Air-twist stem Stem on drinking glasses etc. with spiral hollow core.
Albarello Drug pot of tin-glazed earthenware. *36*
Alentours Elaborate border on a tapestry. *158*
Andiron Metal stand used to support logs in a hearth.
Appliqué In needlework, the sewing of patches onto a piece of fabric to form a design. *160*
Apron-piece Ornamental bottompiece to a chair, cabinet etc.
Arita Japanese porcelain centre.
Armoire Large cupboard or wardrobe of monumental character. *16*
Armorial Coat of arms applied to silverware, ceramics etc.
Arts and Crafts Movement An attempt to revive interest in craftsmanship in the late 19th c.
Aumbry Food cupboard. *6*

Baluster Bulging vase-shaped form, commonly used on stems of drinking glasses etc. *51, 55*
Ball and claw Furniture foot, used on a cabriole leg. *14*
Bargello In needlework, a flamelike pattern worked in rows of upright stitches on canvas. Related to "Hungarian stitch". *161*
Baroque Grandly exuberant art style, originating in 17th-C Italy.
Basaltes Unglazed black stoneware perfected by Wedgwood.
Bergère Armchair with upholstered sides. *19*
Berlin woolwork Amateur embroidery on a canvas grid. *161*
Bianco sopra bianco Earthenware decoration, white on an off-white ground.
Biedermeier Solid, homely style popular in Germany and Austria, c.1820–50.
Bill Edged weapon on a long pole.
Biscuit Unglazed porcelain (or pottery).
Blackwork Embroidery in black thread, sometimes with gold.
Blanc de chine White porcelain, of type made at Dehua, China.
Bleeding bowl Shallow bowl with flat, pierced handle; also known as a "porringer" (USA) *141*
Block front Typically American treatment of front of a piece of furniture: a flattened recessed curve between flattened bulges. *24*
Blown-moulded glass Blown glass decorated or shaped by moulds.
Blue and white Style of underglaze ceramics decoration, originating in China.
Blue-dash charger Delftware dish with border of blue brushstrokes.
Blueing Decorative and rust-proofing heat treatment applied to metal parts of weapons.

Bobbin lace Alternative name for pillow lace.
Bocage Background of foliage to a porcelain figure.
Bombé Exaggeratedly curved. *18*
Bonbonnière Small box for sweetmeats.
Bone china Porcelain made by addition of bone ash.
Bonheur du jour Small writing table on tall legs.
Boulle Marquetry in tortoiseshell and brass. *98*
Bracket clock Portable clock, only occasionally found with a bracket. *115*
Break-arch dial Clock dial with semicircular arch. *115*
Breech-loader Gun with barrel that unscrews for loading.
Brocade Rich silken fabric with gold or silver threads.
Broderie anglaise Type of whitework embroidery with cut or punched open spaces finished by buttonhole stitch.
Brussels carpet Type of moquette carpet.
Bureau-bookcase Fall-front desk surmounted by an enclosed upper stage. *99*
Bureau plat Flat-topped writing-table. *13*
Burr walnut Intricately figured walnut veneer.
Buttonhole stitch Embroidery stitch used to finish raw edges.

Cabochon Domed, unfaceted gemstone.
Cabriole leg Furniture leg shaped like an elongated "S". *14*
Cachepôt Ornamental flowerpot.

Cameo Double-layered hardstone, gem or shell, carved in relief.

Cameo glass Relief carved in two or more layers of glass.

Canapé Sofa *13*

Cannetille Type of gold filigree work.

Canterbury Small music stand.

Carat Unit of purity in gold, weight in gemstones.

Carcanet Collar of jewels.

Carlton House table Writing-table with drawered top and superstructure.

Carriage clock Travelling clock with a handle.

Cartel clock Flamboyant wall clock.

Cartonnier Stationery-holder.

Carver Armchair with turned posts and spindles.

Cased glass See Overlay glass.

Cassapanca Wooden seat with chest underneath. *20*

Cassone Italian chest.

Caudle cup Alternative name for porringer. *121*

Celadons Chinese porcelain wares with greenish or bluish feldspathic glaze.

Chain stitch Common embroidery stitch. *162*

Champlevé Type of "inlaid" enamelling.

Chasing Hammered decoration on metal.

Châtelaine Clasp or brooch, worn at waist for suspension of small objects. *81*

Cheval glass Full-length mirror in a four-legged frame. *166*

Chiffonier Usually a small, low chest of drawers.

Chinoiserie European use of "Chinese" motifs, with pagodas etc.

Chintz Originally painted or stained cloths from India. Now refers to cotton cloth printed with floral designs.

Cire-perdue ("lost wax") Technique for casting bronze, using a wax model.

Cloisonné Type of enamelling, using "cells" with metal walls.

Coaster Tray or trolley for moving food or drink along a table.

Cock Arm holding flint in flintlock firearm. *72*

Commode Chest of drawers. *13*

Console table Side table permanently fixed against a wall. *13*

Couching Embroidery in which thread is laid on fabric and held down by stitching. *162*

Court cupboard Cupboard with lower stage open.

Creamware Creamy white earthenware.

Crewelwork Embroidery in worsteds on linen or woollen cloth.

Crisselling Cloudy defect in old glass.

Cristallo Early Venetian colourless glass.

Cross stitch Canvas embroidery stitch. *162*

Crystal Fine, colourless glass.

Cut-card work Applied decoration on silverware. *121*

Cut glass Glass geometrically cut on a lapidary's wheel.

Cutwork Embroidery technique in which part of fabric was cut away and holes filled with needlework.

Damascening Inlaying of iron or steel with gold or silver.

Damask Reversible figured monochrome fabric, in silk, wool, linen etc.

Delftware Tin-glazed earthenware from England or the Low Countries.

Deutsche Blumen Naturalistic floral decoration on ceramics.

Ding (ting) Chinese food vessel. *145*

Diptych Picture on two leaves, opening like a book.

Directoire style Current in France at end of 18th c.

Dish ring Circular stand for dishes. *125*

Drawn work A forerunner of lace, made from linen from which some threads are drawn out, the rest grouped and whipped over to form patterns.

Dresden "lace" Drawn work on muslin.

Dutch doll Wooden doll of an early kind.

Earthenware Baked clay.

Ebéniste French cabinet-maker.

Ebonized Stained black in imitation of ebony.

Ecuelle Shallow bowl and cover with two handles. *127*

Empire style Neo-classicism current in early 19th-c France, characterized by Egyptian motifs, drapes and glorification of Napoleon.

Enamel Form of glass which may be applied to metal by fusion under heat.

Enamel colours Pigments from metallic oxides, used for ceramics decoration.

Epergne Table centrepiece.

Escapement Regulating mechanism in a timepiece. *113*

Escritoire Writing cabinet.

Estoc Short sword. *75*

Etui Small case for scissors etc. *103*

Façon de Venise Glassware imitating Venetian styles.

Faience Tin-glazed earthenware, esp. from France.

Famille rose Style of Chinese porcelain, decoration named after prominent rose-pink.

Famille verte Chinese porcelain decoration, dominated by various greens.

Federal style American furniture style, c.1785–1830.

Feldspathic glaze Containing feldspar rock.

Figure Natural pattern in wood.

Fire-dog See Andiron.

Flambé glaze Rich red glaze with splashes of blue.

Flat-chasing Relief decoration on metal with punch and hammer.

Flintlock Type of gun mechanism developed from the snaphaunce. *72*

Frizzen In firearms, an L-shaped combined steel and pan-cover. *72*

Furniture Metal fittings on a firearm.

Fusee Conical pulley used in clocks. *113*

Gadrooning Fluted edging on furniture etc. *14*

Gate-leg table Round or oval, with hinged leaves on gate-like supports. *6*

Gesso Wood substitute, for carving and gilding.

Girandole American circular convex mirror surmounted by eagle. *166* Or type of banjo clock; or candle sconce.

Girandole earrings With three pendants hanging from central stone. *79*

Glaze Glassy coating applied to ceramics.

Grisaille Painting in tones of grey.

Gros point Type of Venetian needlepoint lace. *160* Also, type of cross-stitch embroidery on canvas.

Grödnertal Early wooden doll. *165*

Gu (ku) Chinese wine goblet. *145*

Guéridon Small table.

Gui (kuei) Chinese food bowl. *145*

Guilloche Border of interlaced bands

enclosing rosettes.

Gul Polygon motif on Turkoman rugs. *150*

Halberd Edged weapon with axe blade beneath spike.

Hanger Light, curved single-edged sword.

Hard-paste True porcelain, in the Chinese manner.

Hatchli Oriental rug with large cross design. *152*

Highboy American tall chest of drawers on a commode or lowboy. *22*

High-warp tapestry Woven on an upright loom.

Hollow ware Vessels made to hold liquids.

Hooked rug American rug with rag pile.

Hu Chinese wine storage vessel. *145*

Huguenots French Protestants who emigrated after Revocation of Edict of Nantes (1685).

Humpen German cylindrical drinking glass. *62*

Indianische Blumen Orientalized flower decoration on ceramics.

Inlay Decoration using pieces of wood etc. set into recesses.

Inro Japanese case for seals etc. *93*

Intaglio Design carved out from surface of gemstone or glass.

Intarsia Pictorial form of inlay.

Jade Hard stone, either jadeite or nephrite.

Japanning Western imitation of Oriental lacquer work.

Japonaiserie Western treatment of Japanese themes.

Jardinière Vessel for flowers.

Jasper Fine-grained stoneware, perfected by Wedgwood.

Jue (chüeh) Chinese ritual bronze vessel. *145*

Kakiemon Asymmetrical style of decoration on Japanese porcelain. *51*

Kelim Middle-Eastern tapestry-woven rug. *150*

Knop Decorative swelling on stem of a drinking glass etc. *55*

Knotted carpet Made by knotting short lengths of yarn to warp threads of a plain woven fabric.

Kovsh Russian one-handled vessel. *131*

Lacquer Decorative varnish, Oriental in origin.

Lacy glass Pressed glass with designs in relief.

Lambrequin Drape-like ornament.

Lantern clock English brass clock (17th–18th c).

Lappets Flaps on a head-dress.

Latticinio Clear glass embedded with white interlacing patterns. *106*

Longcase Correct term for grandfather clock. *115*

Lowboy American flat-topped dressing table, with drawers. *23*

Low-warp tapestry Woven on a horizontal loom.

Lustre Ceramic decoration, using films of metals.

Maiolica Tin-glazed earthenware made in Italy and Spain.

Majolica Victorian earthenware with thick, coloured glaze.

Mannerism Sophisticated experimental treatment of Renaissance styles (16th C).

Marquetry Decorative veneers applied to furniture carcase. *97*

Matchlock Early type of firearm with mechanical ignition. *72*

Medallion rug Persian carpet with large central motif.

Metal Substance of glass, either molten or hard.

Millefiori Clear glass with embedded rods bearing tiny floral designs. *61*

Mille fleurs Floral sprays forming design on early tapestries.

Miquelet Type of flintlock popular in Italy and Spain. *72*

Mihrab Arch motif on Islamic prayer rug.

Monteith Punch bowl with notched rim.

Moquette Fabric woven on principle of velvet.

Mudéjar Decorative style used by Moslems in Christian Spain.

Needlepoint lace Made by buttonhole stitches with a single thread and a needle.

Neo-classicism Style of later 18th C, inspired by classical antiquity.

Netsuke Japanese toggle for suspending objects from a sash. *93*

Niello Black alloy inlaid decoratively on silver.

Object of vertu Small, decorative luxury object.

O.G. American 19th-C style of clock case. *118*

Okimono Japanese ornamental object.

Opaline glass Translucent milky glass, popular in 19th-C France.

Ormolu Gilt bronze.

Opaque-twist stem Stem on a drinking glass etc. with white spiralling core. *55*

Orphrey Strip of ecclesiastical embroidery, often with gold thread.

Overlay glass Superimposed layers of different colours, with "windows" cut through to show the body.

Pair case watch With hinged inner and separate outer case.

Parcel-gilt Partially gilded.

Parian ware White, unglazed porcelain resembling marble.

Parquetry Geometrical marquetry. *97*

Parure Set of matching jewellery.

Patch box Small, hinged box for beauty spots. *87* Also: receptacle in rifle for patches etc.

Patchwork Sewing together of scraps of material to make a continuous fabric, esp. for quilts.

Pâte sur pâte Relief decoration of porcelain in coats of white slip.

Patina Mellowed surface resulting from age and use.

Pediment Gabled top on bookcases, clocks etc. *14*

Pembroke table Small table with short drop leaves. *10*

Petit point Canvas embroidered in tent stitch, esp. on cushion and chair covers.

Pier glass Tall mirror designed for space between two windows.

Pietra dura Semiprecious stones used for table tops etc. *98*

Pillow lace Made from threads wound on bobbins.

Piqué Tortoiseshell inlaid with gold or silver.

Plique à jour Form of enamelling like cloisonné but without metal backing.

Point d'Angleterre Form of Flemish pillow lace.

Point de neige Delicate Venetian needlepoint lace. Also called *point de rose*.

Pole screen Adjustable fire-screen mounted on a pole. *22*

Pommel Decorative counterweight on hilt of an edged weapon.

Porringer Small, twohandled bowl. *121* Also: American term for bleeding bowl. *141*

Posset pot Vessel for posset (spiced hot milk curdled with wine or ale).

Press cupboard With upper and lower stages, both closed by doors. *6*

Pressed glass Shaped while molten by mould and plunger.

Prunt Decorative blob applied to glass stem.

Punto in aria Earliest form of needlepoint lace.

Puzzle jug Vessel with perforated neck. *27*

Quaich Scottish drinking bowl. *125*

Quillon Cross-guard of sword or dagger.

Quilting Technique for making padded coverlets etc.

Raku Type of Japanese earthenware used for tea ceremony vessels.

Redware Simple type of American domestic pottery.

Régence In France, first phase of rococo style.

Regency English late neo-classical style, early 19th C.

Renaissance Rebirth of ancient Roman ideals, and of art and letters, after end of Middle Ages.

Repoussé Designs raised on metal by beating from behind.

Reserve In ceramics, a surface left plain to receive decoration.

Reticella Precursor of needlepoint lace.

Rifling Spiral grooves cut on interior surface of a gun barrel.

Rococo Lively, delicate 18th-C style, often asymmetrical with s-shaped curves.

Römer (Roemer) Rhenish style of drinking glass. *63*

Rose point Finer version of *gros point* lace.

Rose cutting Gem cutting method, in which stone has flat base and pointed top. *80*

Rummer Shortstemmed drinking glass. *56*

Rya rugs Knotted rugs from Scandinavia, esp. Finland.

Salt Salt-cellar.
Sampler Embroidered panel, made as reference source or test-piece. *161*
Satin stitch Embroidery stitch commonly used to fill uneven shapes. *162*
Satsuma ware Type of Japanese pottery. *51*
Scagliola Material used for imitating marble or *pietra dura*.
Schwarzlot Black enamel decoration on glass or ceramics.
Sconce Wall-light with candleholders.
Seaweed marquetry In foliate patterns that resemble seaweed.
Secrétaire Various types of writing desk.
Secretary American term for bureau-bookcase. *99*
Sévigné Bow-shaped brooch.
Sgraffito Decoration on pottery by cutting through slip to expose body underneath.
Silesian stem Shouldered stem on a drinking glass etc. *55*
Skeleton clock With exposed mechanism in a glass dome. *115*
Slag glass Glass made using slag from iron foundries etc.
Slipware Earthenware decorated with slip—a diluted clay mixture.
Smocking In embroidery, rows of stitching used to hold gathers of fabric.
Snaphaunce In firearms, a precursor of the flintlock. *72*
Soft-paste porcelain Imitation porcelain made from various clays and ground glass.
Splat Vertical central section of a chair back.
Steel In a flintlock or snaphaunce firearm, part that produces spark when struck by flint. *72*

Sterling Standard of purity in British silver.
Stoneware Hard, non-porous pottery.
Stretcher Horizontal member joining chair or table legs.
Stumpwork Needlework with part of ornament raised over padding.
Sulphide Glassware embedded with plaque of white porcelain.

Table cutting Method of cutting a gemstone to give flat horizontal facet on top. *80*
Tambour On desks, a sliding front made of wooden strips. *24*
Tambour work Quick method of chain-stitch embroidery, worked with a hook on a tambour frame.
Tappit hen Scottish pewter measure. *141*
Tazza Wine cup with shallow bowl. *67*
Tent stitch Diagonal parallel stitches across intersecting threads. *162*
Toby jug Earthenware jug shaped as a seated figure.
Tôle Painted tinware.
Touch Pewterer's trade mark.
Transfer printing Printing from engraved plates by paper transfers onto ceramics or enamels.
Treen Small objects made of wood.
Trembleuse Saucer with raised ring to hold cup.
Trivet Stand for placing utensils near a fire. *139*
Tschinke Type of Germanic sporting rifle. *74*
Turkey work Upholstery, cushions, etc. knotted in manner of Near Eastern rugs.
Turning Shaping of furniture legs etc. on a pole lathe.
Twist turning Spiral turning on "barleysugar" furniture legs. *14*

Tyg Beaker with many handles. *27*

Vargueño Spanish 17th-C cabinet. *21*
Veneer Thin layer of wood of the type glued to furniture carcases.
Verdure Tapestry dominated by natural greenery. *159*
Verge escapement Earliest type of clock escapement. *113*
Vernis Martin 18th-C French japanning on wood.
Verre églomisé Glass decorated on reverse in colour and gold and silver foils.
Verrière See Monteith.
Wagon spring clock Powered by flat-leaved springs.
Wainscot chair Panelled or planked chair (16th–17th C).
Warp Threads running lengthways in a woven fabric.
Weft Threads running across a woven fabric, usually forming the pattern.
Whatnot Worktable or stand with three or more shelves. *11*
Wheel engraving Decoration of glass and semi-precious stones with a lapidary's wheel.
Wheel lock Type of firearm mechanism. *72*
Whitework Embroidery using white thread on a white ground.
Windsor chair With spindled back. *24*
Worsted Twisted yarn spun out of long, combed wool; or closely woven fabric made from this.
Wrigglework Zig-zag decoration engraved in pewter or silver.
Wucaí (Wu-ts'ai) Chinese porcelain painted in five enamel colours.

Zwischengoldglas Glass decorated with gold inside a glass envelope.

INDEX

Page numbers in italics refer to colour illustrations

PHOTOGRAPHIC ACKNOWLEDGEMENTS

Christie Manson & Woods Ltd., Fine Art Auctioneers: 103bl.
Cooper-Bridgeman: 99c, 100c, 102b, 105cl, 107t, 107c, 110b, 111tl.
The Dyson Perrins Museum Trust: 108c.
Gulbenkian Museum of Oriental Art: 101t.
Michael Holford: 102tl, 102tr, 103tr, 108tl, 112tl.
Angelo Hornak: 97tl, 97c, 98c, 100t, 100b, 104t, 106t, 106c, 107bl, 109b, 110cr, 111tr, 112b.

The National Trust: 97tr, 98tr, 98b, 99b, 101cr, 104b, 105t, 105cr, 108tr, 109t, 110t, 111c.
Phillips, the International Fine Art Auctioneers: 98tl, 99tl, 103cr, 103br, 104cl, 104cr, 105b, 106tr.
Pilkington Glass Museum: 106b.
Sotheby Belgravia: 99tr, 112tr.
Sotheby Parke Bernet & Co: 97b, 101cl, 101b, 102c, 103tl, 108b, 110cl, 111lb.
Josiah Wedgwood & Sons: 109c.